Gender, Sexuality and Violence in Organizations

Gender, Sexuality and Violence in Organizations

The Unspoken Forces of Organization Violations

Jeff Hearn and Wendy Parkin

SAGE Publications

London • Thousand Oaks • New Delhi

© Jeff Hearn and Wendy Parkin 2001

First published 2001

Apart from any fair dealing for the purposes of research or private
study, or criticism or review, as permitted under the Copyright,
Designs and Patents Act, 1988, this publication may be
reproduced, stored or transmitted in any form, or by any means,
only with the prior permission in writing of the publishers, or in
the case of reprographic reproduction, in accordance with the
terms of licences issued by the Copyright Licensing Agency.
Inquiries concerning reproduction outside those terms should be
sent to the publishers.

 SAGE Publications Ltd
6 Bonhill Street
London EC2A 4PU

SAGE Publications Inc
2455 Teller Road
Thousand Oaks, California 91320

SAGE Publications India Pvt Ltd
32, M-Block Market
Greater Kailash - I
New Delhi 110 048

British Library Cataloguing in Publication data

A catalogue record for this book is available from
the British Library

ISBN 0 7619 5911 4
ISBN 0 7619 5912 2 (pbk)

Library of Congress control number 2001131803

Typeset by SIVA Math Setters, Chennai, India
Printed in Great Britain by Athenaeum Press

This book is dedicated to Sajid Khan (1974–99),
a gentle man and friend, and to Anna and Sebastian

Contents

Figures and Tables

Figures

Tables

Acknowledgements

We are very grateful for a number of collaborations that have contributed to the development of this book – in particular, those with David Collinson, Margaret Collinson, Lorraine Green, Jalna Hanmer, Elizabeth Harlow, Marjut Jyrkinen, Anne Kovalainen, Mary Maynard and David Morgan. We are also indebted to Sari Carpentier for her assistance with the review of Finnish and Swedish research and policy literature. We thank Donna Hughes, Denise Salin and Pernilla Gripenberg for sharing ideas and information, Joanne Deakin for work on an early literature search, and Celia Davies, Jean Neumann and anonymous reviewers of *Human Relations* for detailed comments on an early presentation of some of these ideas (Hearn, 1994). We also thank anonymous reviewers of the initial proposal for this book for their helpful suggestions. A number of seminar, conference and other presentations have been made on this material, and we are grateful to all who have commented on these occasions. Thanks are offered to participants at the Gender Research Seminar at UMIST, January 1992, for their very helpful comments on some tentative first thoughts on this area.

   The writing of the book was greatly assisted by generous research funds from the Donner Foundation of Åbo Akademi University (1997–8), the Academy of Finland (1997, 1998–9) and the University of Huddersfield Research Support Fund (1999). The second of these fundings was part of the research programme, 'Images of Women's Health: Social Construction of Gendered Health'. We thank all colleagues and students at the Universities of Bradford, Huddersfield, Manchester and Åbo Akademi who assisted in the development of this project. Particular thanks are offered to Elianne Riska, Solveig Bergman, Harriet Silius and all in the sociology doctoral research seminar at Åbo. The final stages of writing were completed whilst Jeff Hearn was Guest Professor at the Work Research Centre, University of Tampere, and the Swedish School of Economics and Business Administration, Helsinki, and additional thanks are extended to Emmi Lattu, Guje Sevón, Ingmar Björkman, Tuula Heiskanen, Päivi Korvajärvi and colleagues there. Anne Elton at the University of Huddersfield Library, and Teemu Tallberg and Hannele Varsa provided bibliographic assistance, for which we are very grateful.

   Special thanks are offered to Karen Phillips, Lauren McAllister and all at Sage. We thank Liisa Husu and Malcolm Parkin for everything.

We are grateful to the following for permission to reproduce figures and tables from:

Poyner, B. and Warne, C. (1986). *Violence to Staff: A Basis for Assessment and Prevention*. London: Tavistock Institute of Human Relations/Health and Safety Executive.

Salin, D. (1999). *Explaining Workplace Bullying: a Review of Enabling, Motivating, and Triggering Factors in the Work Environment.* Helsinki: Meddelanden Working Papers, Svenska handelshögskolan.

Standing, H. and Nicolini, D. (1997). *Review of Workplace-related Violence,* Contract Research Report 143/1997. London: HSE.

Timmerman, G. and Bajema, C. (1999). Sexual harassment in Northwest Europe. *The European Journal of Women's Studies,* 6, 419–39.

Introduction

The Unspoken within Organizations

Organizations persist through unspoken forces. Many of these forces are *matters* of gender, sexuality, violence and violation. There is, without doubt, a very wide range of ways in which organizations and organizational worlds exist in relation to gender, sexuality, violence and violation. Indeed what we call organization is often infused with gender, sexuality and violation – hence the concepts of organization gender, organization sexuality (Hearn and Parkin, 1987, 1995) and organization violation.

So what is the unspoken? And how are these silences, silencings, recognitions, disappearings and surfacings maintained? To speak (of) the unspoken is to make concrete silences that persist in and indeed comprise organizations. These silences include the very conceptualization of organization itself; the general understandings of how organizations are gendered; the specific structuring of organizations; and construction of gendered subjects in organizations (Harlow et al., 1995). Noise, din, silence and silencing, as part of the unspoken forces of organizational worlds, are thus gendered. Both literally and metaphorically, they are part of the gendered domination of organizations:

> … 'din' is literal and metaphoric, with the literal din of machinery being enhanced by the metaphoric din of ownership and supremacy through numbers and structures. Silence too is literal, though it is important to separate out silence through choice from being silenced through intimidation, threat, exclusion, marginalization and put-downs. Din and silence are not seen as exclusively opposite, for silence can be imposed through silent bullying and coercion, which is really din, and the din of oppressed groups whose grievances fail to be heard is actually silence. (Harlow et al., 1995: 96)

Silence may mean the absence of noise and be part of the plight of the oppressed but can also be part of domination, as in managerial silences to requests to be heard and demands for change.

Our emphasis on the reproduction of organization through silence stands in tension with those social constructionist approaches that have come to interpret discourse as talk, speech and text. Whereas Michel Foucault, whatever the gendered inadequacies of his texts (Hearn and Parkin, 1987: 169), was at pains to describe and explore the intricacies of discourse as power/knowledge and power/resistance, some subsequent writers have tended to reduce discourse to that which is spoken and hearable, written and readable. This book is about the speaking of those unspoken forces, the making of the invisible visible and the less known more fully known. We are interested in the reconstruction of the silent, unspoken, not necessarily easily observable, but fundamentally material reality of organizations. We do not take the view that silence means either consent or absence of ideas or idealism. There is no sense of 'spirit' in our concern with silence.

The exact ways in which this silent materialism operates are clearly rather different for different facets of social reality. Let us take the example of violence. The occurrence of violence, that is, the doings of violence, in the past or the present or as future threat, are material in their practice, their effects, their structurings and their 'accumulations' over time. Violence not only brings the direct effects of direct damage, it also brings less direct effects, simply through the memory of previous actual or possible violences. Once violence has been done, including being threatened, an innocence has been lost – so that mere reference to that violence (verbally, by a look, or a slight movement or some other cue or clue) may be enough to invoke and connote violence, and thus the modification of material behaviour. Violence, like violation more generally, exists also in its recognition. But the more recognized violences of harassment, bullying and physical violence are only part of the wider violations of organizations. These also include more structured oppressions and more mundane violations of everyday organizational worlds.

Furthermore, the social and technological changes that appear to be affecting what we may call the gender–sexuality–violation complex in work organizations are changing and in somewhat contradictory ways: they may produce workplaces that are ever more like fortresses; they may produce calming environments within them; and workers may be increasingly given the responsibility to monitor their own behaviour in the most minute ways. Perhaps violence and potential violence at workplaces are paradoxically creating both more docile workers and more active citizens.

These matters demand attention to a very diverse set of concerns, including cultural and historical recognitions; diverse discursive representations; methodological problems; social scientific explanations of phenomena; and political agendas to reduce and stop violation in and around organizations.

This book is organized in seven broad chapters. Eight sets of focus material on specific examples of 'violations in organizations' are included. The first two chapters provide a conceptual and historical background. Chapter 1 includes a critical introductory overview of current thinking around organizational worlds, gender, sexuality and violence, and their relations to each other. It explores the ways in which organizations are gendered, sexualed[1] and made arenas of violence and violation, and how these in turn relate to other social divisions. In Chapter 2 we outline the historical location of organizations in time, and the relevance of this for understanding organizations as gendered, sexualed, violent and violating. This emphasizes the context of the structural power of (certain) heterosexual men and their relationship with the dominant social, economic and political orders. We thus critically examine, first patriarchy, then capitalism, and third the nation-state, as sedimented historical frameworks for understanding gender relations within contemporary organizations. This is illustrated by two sets of historical focus material: on organizational heterosexualities in the nineteenth-century

Industrial Revolution, and state and other organizational responses to men's violence to women and children.

Chapters 3 and 4 address respectively the practical and the theoretical recognition of violation in organizations. In Chapter 3 we discuss the recent growth of practical concerns about and recognition of sexual harassment, bullying and physical violence within organizations. This draws on a range of sources, including journalistic ones, to demonstrate the tension between the unspokenness of the forces of gender, sexuality, harassment, bullying and violence and attempts to speak out about them. Harassment, bullying and physical violence have usually been categorized separately without reference to each other, and this itself contributes to resistance to their being heard. Sexual harassment is clearly perceived as gendered, but bullying and physical violence do not necessarily involve recognition of gendered dimensions. Four sets of focus material are provided here – on the police, business, the military and air travel. The links between gender, sexuality, harassment, bullying and violence are examined as part of the more general concept of organization violation. Organization violations are conceptualized as spanning structural oppressions and mundane everyday violations in organizations. This recognizes that all these categories are violations of the person. Organizations provide an important key to the maintenance, reproduction and silencing of such violations. Chapter 4 examines theorizing on violence and violation in organizations. Organization violations are examined at macro, meso and micro levels, in relation to patriarchal social relations, capitalist social relations and relatively local cultural, nationalist, ethnic and other exclusionary social relations, as introduced in Chapter 2.

Chapters 5 and 6 examine two contrasting forms of organization that cut across these macro, meso and micro levels: the closed organization in relative isolation, and the transformation of organizations in the globalizing world. Thus Chapter 5 focuses on the closed organization in comparative isolation, with given boundaries and the intensification of internal organizational processes. Extended focus material on children's homes and other institutions demonstrates how such institutionalized settings may facilitate the regular violations of the person combined with their silencing through the stigmatized status of resident. By contrast, Chapter 6 focuses on the transformation of boundaries, boundarylessness and pervasive, expanding organizational forms, which in turn demand new ways of understanding. This is illustrated by focus material on the global 'sex industry'. These two chapters are not simply a restatement of the established contrast between closed and open organizations or systems; it is a contrasting of difference, of two forms that are not opposites.

The final chapter addresses the implications of these matters for politics and policy, in social theory and knowledge formation; organizational, management and legal policy, including cyberpolicy; and the politics of risk and of oppression. We conclude with a discussion of the need for violation-free organizations and workplaces.

This book can be read in several ways. After the first chapter, there are several options. If your main interest is history, then proceed to the next chapter; if it is the contemporary processes of recognition of violations in organizations, then Chapter 3 might be a place to begin; if it is theory that interests you most, then Chapter 4 is suggested. Those concerned with total institutions and similar organizations or with globalization and ICTs might prefer Chapters 5 or 6 respectively. Or you can begin at the end with politics and policy and work backwards! We hope you find the book useful, whatever your concerns, and we welcome feedback (jeff.hearn@man.ac.uk, p.w.parkin@hud.ac.uk).

1

Gender, Sexuality, Violation and Organizational Worlds

How Did We Get Here?

Organizations are gendered; that much we know. When we started researching and writing together on organizations in the late 1970s our primary interest was on gender relations in organizations. We first began to assemble information on the gender division of labour, the gender division of authority and, to a lesser extent, sexuality in and around organizations. At the time we drew on almost whatever sources we could find (Hearn and Parkin, 1983, 1992). In familiarizing ourselves with what had and had not been studied, we gradually became aware of the inadequacies in much literature of the time. These can be characterized through a number of tendencies:

- to consider gender, if at all, in rather simple, dualist ways, most obviously in the use of sex/gender role models of gender relations that have since been subject to overwhelming critique;[1]
- to focus primarily, often exclusively, on the division of labour;
- to consider organizations out of the context of their societal relations, including the domestic relations of organizational members; and
- to neglect or ignore sexuality.

Since then, the field of gender relations, sexuality and organizations has expanded greatly, indeed so much so that now we have filing cabinets full of the stuff. In a rather strange way, the development of the field, the state of our filing cabinets and our own biographies have changed in parallel. Our recent lives have mirrored the fields we have chosen to study.[2] Thus the task now is not to establish the field of gender relations, sexuality and organizations. That is already done – even though the supposedly non-gendered, but in fact gendered, mainstream keeps remembering to forget the fact. Rather we see our current task as developing and clarifying the field, in terms of specific concepts and issues – in effect trying to move it on, one more time.

Why Organizations?

Organization, singular, refers to the acts and process of social organizing. Organizations, plural, are those *particular* social collectivities that result from those acts and processes. But organizations are not to be thought of as mere outcomes. Instead they themselves should be understood as social processes that are in a state of becoming something else. Thus organizations, and indeed actions within organizations, are always embodied in social contexts. This context-embeddedness means that it is necessary in conceptualizing, analysing and writing about organizations to bear in mind that attempts to characterize organizations are limited and provisional.

One complication is that organizations are both *social places* of organizing and *social structurings* of social relations, whose interrelations are historically dynamic. Another is that organizations are not collectivities formed simply by the individual, intentional action of their founders and members. Rather, organizations always occur in the context of pre-existing (organizational) social relations. The search for any *tabula rasa* is in vain. To paraphrase Marx: 'organizations make history but not in the conditions of their choosing.'[3]

The notion of 'the organization' is thus itself somewhat problematic. At its simplest, the notion of an organization conjures up the picture of a factory, an office, even a university – something that can be seen, something that appears to function within four walls. But of course such an idea of an organization is a fantasy. The picture of the visible organizations does not even come from the heyday of the Industrial Revolution; it stems if anywhere from the eighteenth century, with the relatively isolated industrial mill that could be *seen*. It was with the passing of this organizational form to the multiple-unit 'organization' that could not be fully seen that, rather paradoxically, the idea of the organization, and thus organization theory, became constituted and more popularly available. By the height of the nineteenth-century Industrial Revolution in Great Britain and many industrialized countries, the isolated organization was already to a considerable extent decomposing and anachronistic. It was indeed its decomposition that was at the same time accompanied by its diffusion and expansion. As organizations 'grew in size' and became more consolidated, and indeed more powerful concentrations of resources, they also became more diffuse and less concentrated at particular times and places. Part of the reason for this was the mode of expansion of some organizations. Their expansion was not just upwards and outwards on the same site (within four walls or expanding those four walls), but it was also through horizontal and vertical *connection* and *integration*, and above all through geographical and temporal expansion and diffusion. The organization was no longer a simple place – or indeed a simple time.

The notion of organization, and hence organizations, has thus become progressively more complex. It still refers to the individual organization, but it also encompasses the conglomeration of organizations, as in multi-organizations. In this sense, 'the state', like the transnational corporation, is itself an organization even though it comprises many different organizations within it. And so within each organization (within such multi-organizations) there are of course further smaller sub-units that might often reasonably be called organizations too. At its simplest, one might therefore distinguish: (i) large complex multi-organizations of many other organizations; (ii) intermediate individual organizations; and (iii) small organizational sub-units. There is additionally a fourth category: (iv) cyber or paper organizations that do not exist in a specific time–place reality.

Whereas previously most organizations could be relatively geographically and spatially isolated in a particular place, this is increasingly becoming problematic, as organizations become organized across time, space and even cyberspace and cybertime. This means that the rather rapid change in the relationship of time and space – the so-called space-time continuum – makes it increasingly necessary to question the equation of organization and *place*. Accordingly, this in turn makes the distinction between organizations as places and organizations as the structurings of social relations more important. Thus, the once relatively stable equation of organization and place, *the assumed placing of organizations in a specific place*, is now being disrupted, and is probably to be disrupted further in the future. This means that the single place-based organization becomes reconceptualized as just one temporary organizational form (of social relations), not the major or most persistent form.

Organizations are commonly seen and understood as places of discourse, of activity, of communication, even of noise, rapidity and speed. Yet what happens in organization often also involves silence, not just in the sense of quietness, but in the sense of that which is not spoken. Organizations are continually structured and practised through *the unspoken*. Accordingly, one might re-understand organizations as very much (subject to) *unspoken forces*. These forces include gender, sexuality, violence and violation.

Why Organizational Worlds?

The concept of organization is far from unproblematic. While it may be increasingly difficult to define an organization in a fixed, absolute way, people do live and work in organizational worlds. The use of the term 'worlds' facilitates engagement with the perceptual worlds of organizational members and outsiders, such as customers. If an organizational member or outsider finds something gendered or sexual (or sexualed or sexualized), or harassing, violent or violating in an organization, then it *is* – for their purposes and in their reality. The concept of 'worlds' also conveys the way in which organizations often carry a sense of (dis)continuity, culture, discourse(s), life-world and moreover hegemonic domination of the 'definition of the situation'. Thus part of organizational worlds is the world of recognition (or lack of recognition) – be it of gender inequalities, sexuality, violence or violation. This can be reinforced for some, especially those within total institutions, as the organization is the world of residence. Yet the notion of organizational worlds also speaks to the socio-spatial and globalizing tendencies of organizations and organizational life – a different and indeterminate organizational world of the global. For these reasons, and especially with contemporary and likely future economic, social, technological and spatial changes, we talk of organizational worlds rather than reifying organizations. The discrete, separate organization may become less meaningful, in some senses ceases to exist. Organizational worlds may be a more accurate description of late modern organizational life.

Why Gender?

Gender and gendered power relations are major defining features of most, perhaps all, organizations. What we call 'organizations' are not just embedded in gender but entreated, soaked in, pervaded and constituted by and through gender; and furthermore at the same time organizational realities themselves construct and sometimes subvert dominant gender relations and even gender itself. When gender is referred to it may be usual to think of 'men and women' and the 'relations between them'; this is certainly part of gender, but it is only a part. For one thing, gender is just as relevant in relations between women and between men. These are still very much gendered relations. This is somewhat similar to the way questions of race and racialization are often relevant in understanding what is happening in situations and organizations that appear to only involve white people. More generally, gender has now taken on a mass of other more complex meanings; and some discussion of this is now necessary. These differential meanings and understandings of gender are themselves both contested and central to the analysis of (gendered) organizations.

The debate about the meaning of gender has continued to develop rapidly. The distinction between sex and gender was recognized in the 1960s and 1970s by feminists and others attempting to develop a more critical account of women's and men's relations and positions in society. It was a way of making it clear that what was often thought of as natural and biological was in fact social, cultural, historical and indeed political.[4] Oakley (1972, 1985) set out this differentiation between 'sex' as biological sex differences and 'gender' as the social and cultural constructions of those differences. This kind of sex/gender approach has been very important in generating greater attention to studies of sex differences and their relative absence,[5] sex/gender roles, sex role socialization and masculinity–femininity scales. Much of this work in the 1960s, 1970s and even the 1980s, particularly within psychology and social psychology, was, however, itself placed within the context of relatively positivist understandings of gender. This applied especially to the development of maculinity–femininity scales, their empirical refinement and use to correlate with other measures of the person.[6]

There are many complications in conceptualizing gender and defining what gender is, particularly so within positivist paradigms. One difficulty is: it depends on who is asking the question, and why; and it depends on who is answering the question, and why. For example, feminists are likely to have very different concerns from most men when talking about masculinity. Another pervasive constraint is the persistence of dualisms and dichotomies, for example, female/male; woman/man; feminine/masculine; femininity/masculinity; girls/boys. While clearly these are important differentiations, there is a sense in which they only speak to part of the possibilities of what gender is or might be in different situations and societies. Indeed, no longer is it possible to reproduce the dichotomous separation of sex and gender that characterized sex role theory of the 1960s and 1970s. Indeed, the sex/gender approach to gender somewhat paradoxically takes us back to biology. It rests on the assumption that a woman is someone who is a socially constructed member of the 'female sex', and a man is likewise a socially constructed member of the 'male sex'. The notion of 'sex' used here is usually shorthand for a number of physiological features, particularly primary sex characteristics and secondary sex characteristics.[7]

However, all the various primary and secondary features are not always so easily described as simply 'female' or 'male', and indeed may be further complicated by a range of biological, cultural and bio-cultural factors and conditions. Thus both 'females' and 'males', and 'women' and 'men' are variable categories, including old/young, (in)fertile, presumed females/males. Other complications to any simple sex/gender model arise from the existence of considerable cross-cultural variations in usual somatypes between cultures, following from working practices, diet and hereditary patterns.[8] Even with these and other difficulties, the sex/gender model has undoubtedly prompted a mass of path-breaking work on gender, gender relations and gendered power relations. Within this general perspective, there are many different approaches – some drawing on the notion of behaviour and developing the notion of sex/gender role; some attending to attitudes, self-concept and gender identity; some focusing on social categories and structural relations, as in the concept of collective sex/gender class. In many of these approaches gender has been understood as a way of moving away from biology and of recognizing a relatively autonomous set of social and cultural relations. Females are not simply 'women', as males are not 'men'; none of these is a unified category; female/male and women/men are not all inclusive of people and furthermore this varies greatly in different societies.

Of special significance has been the elaboration of distinctly sociological and social structural approaches to gender. These include the articulation of structural concepts of gender relations in patriarchy, gender systems and dominant gender orders. Such analyses were a major point of theoretical and political attention in the 1970s. However, by the late 1970s, at about the same time as sex role approaches were themselves being criticized, there were growing critiques of the concept of patriarchy. Similar arguments have also been made with regard to the critique of categoricalism[9] in conceptualizing gender (Connell, 1985, 1987). These developments can also be seen as part of the general critique of positivist social science that has gathered pace since the 1960s.

The outcome of these simultaneous, if somewhat separate, critiques of, first, social psychological concepts of gender as sex role and, second, overly structuralist concepts of gender as determined within patriarchy, has been a movement to a more differentiated, more pluralized, yet still *power-laden*, approach to gender. This is encapsulated in the notion of gendered power relations. An example of such an approach is that on masculinities by Carrigan, Connell and Lee (1985). This investigated relations between men and between men and women, resistance, social and intrapsychic constructions; and hegemonic, complicit, subordinated forms of masculinities. This reformulation of gender fits closely with revisions of patriarchy (or patriarchies) as historical, multiple structures.[10] In recent years, there has been increasing attention to gendered practices, processes of gendering, masculinity/ies; gendered material/discursive practices; gendered discourses and discourses of gender; plural/multiple/composite masculinities and femininities; the interrelations of gendered unities and gendered differences

(Collinson and Hearn, 1994; Hearn and Collinson, 1994); and life stories and subjectivities.

Another difficulty, that is receiving increasing attention even in the last few years, lies in the very distinction between 'sex' and 'gender'. Perhaps the greatest challenge to a simple, dualist view of gender is represented by transsexualism and transgenderism, in its widely different social and cultural forms. This has itself prompted a significant expansion of transgender studies and studies of transgenderism in recent years.[11] The sex–gender distinction has itself been subject to critical interrogation and deconstruction in recent years. Bondi (1998) has recently clarified the following three major problems with the distinction:[12]

- First, there is no convincing evidence that gender itself carries a necessary liberatory potential; just because gender is socially constructed does not mean that it can be changed any more easily than sex.[13]
- Second, the sex–gender distinction is closely linked to other dichotomies, most obviously nature–culture and body–mind. If gender corresponds, it might be asked why a concept of gender is necessary; if gender involves the transcendence of mind over body, then the question remains why should this 'unsexed' mind correspond to gender if it is wholly disconnected from sex. It can thus be argued that the sex–gender distinction reinforces its own dichotomies and even repositions the male/masculinity as the norm.[14]
- Third, the sex–gender distinction implies that sex and biology are pre-social or free of the social; but biology is itself constituted in the social.[15]

An influential commentator in this respect has been Butler (1990) who has argued cogently that the sex/gender distinction is itself a social and cultural construction; it is not that gender is the cultural arrangement of sex difference, but that the sex/gender difference is a cultural arrangement, dominantly constructed in terms of the 'heterosexual matrix'. Thereby our attention is directed to the social and cultural construction of the sexed body. This kind of approach has been a major way of reformulating the sociology of the body.[16] On the other hand, there is a danger in such an approach that the physical, biological, material body may be lost in the search for social inscription and performativity. In the light of this, a more measured movement may be made towards recognizing *both* the socio-cultural formation of the gendered body and its physical, biological, material existence; thus there is not just one possible relation of the biological sex/gender and the social sex/gender, but rather many possible such relations and interrelations in different societal and social situations.

Thus gender is not one 'thing'; it is contested, very complex and differentiated. It is necessary now to provide an open-ended definition of gender. A very useful definition of gender has been produced by Joan Scott in the context of historical research into gender relations:

> My definition of gender relationships has two parts and several subsets. They are interrelated but must be analytically distinct. The core of the definition rests on an integral connection between two propositions: gender is a constitutive element of social relationships based on perceived differences between the sexes, and gender is a primary way of signifying relationships of power. Changes in the organization of social

relationships always correspond to changes in representations of power but the direction of change is not necessarily one way. As a constitutive element of social relationships based on perceived differences between the sexes, gender involves four interrelated elements: first, culturally available symbols that evoke multiple (and often contradictory) representations. Second, normative concepts that set forth interpretations of the meanings of symbols, that attempt to limit and contain their metaphoric possibilities. These concepts are expressed in religious, educational, scientific, legal and political doctrines and typically take the form of a fixed binary opposition, categorically and unequivocally asserting the meaning of male and female, masculine and feminine. In fact, these normative statements depend on the refusal or repression of alternative possibilities, and sometimes, overt contests about them take place (at what moments and under what circumstances ought to be a concern of historians). The point of new historical investigations is to disrupt the notion of fixity, to discover the nature of the debate or repression that leads to the appearance of timeless permanence in binary gender representation. This kind of analysis must include a notion of politics as well as reference to social institutions and organizations – the third aspect of gender relationships....

The fourth aspect of gender is subjective identity.... Historians need ... to examine the ways in which gendered identities are substantively constructed and relate their findings to a range of activities, social organizations and historically specific cultural representations. The best efforts in this area so far have been, not surprisingly, biographies. (1986: 1097–8)

Connell (1998) has suggested the following summary of conclusions from recent historical and contemporary empirical studies of masculinities: plurality of masculinities (and thus other gendered forms); hierarchy and hegemony; collective masculinities (and thus other gendered forms); bodies as arenas; active construction; contradiction; and dynamics. These points seem to us to apply equally well to the conceptualization of gender more generally. All of these aspects of gender relations are to be found in organizations, and organizational structures and processes. Organizations are indeed gendered in a number of distinct ways. The movement towards the recognition of such gendered organizations has been gradual rather than sudden; and the development of more gendered organization theory has to be placed in the context of some of the preoccupations of mainstream/malestream theory and theorizing.

Towards Gendered Organization Theory

The early modern development of organizational analysis is typically presented as agendered. Yet the analyses of, say, Classical Theory and Scientific Management were overwhelmingly by men, about men, for men. These prescriptions could also be interpreted as attempts by men managers to control growing numbers of women or migrant workers in particular commercial and state sectors in the early twentieth century. Classical Theory and related theories carry implicit, and sometimes explicit, conceptualizations of gender and sexuality (see Hearn and Parkin, 1987: 17–21). Within those theories and managerial practices are detailed statements on the way men are assumed to manage and be managed, the control of the body and sexuality, and many other relevant questions. On the other hand, even Frederick Taylor was well aware of the importance of morale, motivation and indeed the emotions. He thus proposed the appointment of the 'functional foreman' whose duties included attending to the morale of the workers he controlled (Taylor, 1947). In a different sense, Taylorist management can be understood as an intensely emotional process for men managers themselves. This hinges on the contradictory effects of excessive control, of both others and the self, and the ways in which those most committed to control experienced 'loss of control' and 'anxiety' through their lives.[17]

Similarly, while bureaucratic organizations and Weberian theories thereof are often seen as emphasizing rationality or instrumentality rather than emotions, in practice bureaucracies are often intensely emotional. Weber himself saw the social construction of affectivity in bureaucracies and elsewhere as central. This was made clearer by Merton (1952) in describing bureaucracies as organizations where 'timidity, defensiveness, harshness and resentment are part of the daily round' (Albrow, 1992: 319).

Much subsequent organization theory, and, *par excellence*, Human Relations Theory, can be read as attempts by men not just to reorganize social relationships in organizations, but to incorporate gendered and sexual relations into organizational analysis in an agendered and asexual way. Gender and sexuality continued to be made implicit, neutered within neutral language. This is both a theoretical issue and a practical managerial issue, as Human Relations Theory has been used to legitimate increased managerial surveillance and control of workers; and particularly women's emotional and even sexual lives.[18] These themes are clear in the work of Elton Mayo (1960) and his associates but they also appear later in the work of Talcott Parsons and Robert Bales (1955). Their structural functionalism provided a very clear gendering not only of women's and men's roles in the family, groups and other social systems, but moreover in the very separation of the instrumental and the socio-emotional. Parsonian theorizing can be understood as a male attempt to translate a normative set of gendered social relations to a theoretical analysis and thence to future normative prescriptions, through the incorporation of gender, sexuality and emotions into agendered, asexual conceptualizations.

In the UK, the Tavistock 'School' with its own particular version of 'human relations' has been very influential in the development of organizational analysis and the conceptualization of gender and sexuality. While the extent to which it is a specific and identifiable school at all may be contentious (Miller, 1992), the emphasis that it brought to the fore was primarily the extension of psychoanalytic insights from individual to group and organizational dynamics through the development of problem-focused consultancy and intervention. This approach is necessarily gendered and sexualed in many ways. Assumptions about gender and sexuality are a fundamental part of psychoanalytic theorising, not just a contingent addition. In some cases, sexuality was a direct concern; more usually, sexuality was a present yet relatively minor component of analysis. The Tavistock programme's work has addressed the unconscious preoccupations of members of groups and organizations, including unconscious sexual preoccupations. This was seen in Bion's (1948, 1949, 1950) analysis of pairing in groups manifesting underlying sexual dynamics; Jaques's (1955) and Menzies's (1960) studies of defences against paranoid and depressive anxiety; and Bowlby's (1953) attention to the interrelation of institutional dynamics, and personal and sexual well-being. In so doing, the Tavistock programme has contributed significantly to 'the government of subjectivity and social life' (Miller and Rose, 1988).

Importantly, Human Relations Theory, Parsonian structural functionalism and the Tavistock 'School' have all, albeit in different ways, contributed to the establishment of the system as the prime paradigm for the analysis of organizations. In one sense, the system reduces social divisions, including gender and sexuality, to systemic language; in another, systems thinking often reproduces gendered dualities between goal attainment and system maintenance. Systemic theorizing can thus be used to either obscure gender and sexuality or to justify and perpetuate the 'maintenance' roles of women in lower organizational positions. Even so, Human Relations and related traditions have shown glimmerings of the development of the field of gender, sexuality and organizations. Organizational analysis has often been centrally concerned with human relations rather than social structures. When links have been made between 'human relations', gender and sexuality, it has usually been in terms of interpersonal, emotional relationships rather than social structural relations of power and dominance.

Why Gendered Organizations?

Recent research and literature on the gendering of organizations has been strongly influenced by debates in and around feminism. During the 1970s and 1980s, the two most prolific feminist or feminist-influenced sets of literature on gender and organizations have come from Marxist and socialist feminism; and writing on 'women in management', especially from North America. As already noted, sexuality was not generally the central focus of interest of these studies. More recently, there have been increasing numbers of feminist and pro-feminist studies on gender, and on particular divisions of labour, in organizations, which in turn address sexuality to a greater or lesser extent.[19] Furthermore, in some radical and anarchist feminism the very idea of organization(s) is held to be dominated by men, and so subject to critical theory and practice.[20]

The fabric, texture and existence of organizations, both in their formation in the context of external social relations and in their internal structures, documentations and social texts, are gendered. Thus most organizations are doubly gendered, in the sense that the public domains and organizations within them are dominantly valued over the private domains, and that within organizations the structure and processes are themselves gendered. The internal workings of organizations are gendered in both the distribution of women and men, and the distribution of gendered practices. It is important to recognize the gendering of organizations even when they totally or almost totally consist of women or men.

While the number of different ways in which organizations can be gendered is immense, it may be helpful to build up a picture by focusing on a limited number of some typical differences:

1. The gendered division of labour, both formal and informal. Women and men may, through processes of inclusion and exclusion, specialize in particular

types of labour, so creating vertical and horizontal divisions within organizations.

2. Gendered divisions of authority, with men typically exerting more authority over both women and other men. These interactions of gendered divisions of labour and gendered divisions of authority produce, when consolidated in a formalized structure, gendered bureaucracy.[21]

3. Gendered processes between the centre and margins of organizations. These may be literally or metaphorically spatial in terms of the distribution of power and activity between the centre and the margins of organizations. The 'main aim' of organizations tends to be dominantly defined by men and men's interests (Cockburn, 1991). 'Front-line' activities are often staffed by women, while 'central' activities may be more often performed by men. The casualization, and hence implicit dispensability, of employment may also affect women workers more just as it may affect black workers and, in different ways, young and older workers.

4. The gendered relationship of organizational participants to their domestic and related responsibilities. Women typically continue to carry the double burden of childcare and other unpaid domestic work, and may carry a triple burden of care for other dependents, including parents, older people and people with disabilities.

5. Gendered processes in the operation of sexuality and violence within the organizations, including the occurrence of sexual harassment and the dominance of various forms of sexuality over others. Sexual processes interrelate with gendered violence in organizations.[22]

These five elements can be understood as part of a picture of how gendered organizations are constructed. In particular organizations these elements interact with each other in ways that may reinforce or contradict each other. Frequently these interactions are ambiguous, paradoxical and open to multiple interpretations. Thus, these gendered processes and their interrelationships should not be seen as monolithic. Indeed, of particular importance is the impact of atypical gendered positionings, either in terms of women or men occupying atypical positionings or in the use of atypical gendered practices. While atypical gendering may be a means of organizational change, not least in the transformation of the discourses of and on organizations, the positioning of 'women managers', 'women doctors', 'men secretaries', 'male nurses' and so on should not be seen as necessarily subversive. Indeed it is quite possible that the production of atypical gendering can reproduce dominant gendered patterns within organizations, albeit in more subtle ways (Oerton, 1996a).

This leads to two final issues in this section. First, there is the question of how gendered processes are reproduced in organizations. The elements and their interactions are above all occurrences in change, flux and becoming. Thus, although men's dominance is profound, it is neither monolithic nor unresisted. It has to be continually re-established, and in the process it can be challenged, subverted and destabilized. For these reasons, linguistic and discursive processes of differencing in organizations, for example, in definitions of what is and is not 'legitimate' or 'illegitimate', are crucial (Cockburn, 1990). Second, there is a need to be alive to the likely cross-cultural and historical inapplicability of particular gendered concepts, that may appear to be appropriate to the analysis of society and organizations here and now. These issues are explored further in later chapters.

Why Sexuality?

The recognition of sexuality as a central feature of organizations is relatively recent. While sexuality has been studied in organizational contexts from a wide range of disciplinary and theoretical positions, there have been a number of specific historical developments over the last thirty years or more that has led the increase of interest in organizations. Foremost amongst these is the development of Second Wave feminism, which highlighted gendered concerns with women's control over their own bodies and their sexuality and the specific naming of and opposition to sexual harassment. Women's control of their bodies, reproductive rights and sexuality lead to both a political and an academic agenda around sexuality in organizations. A second major stimulus to the examination of sexuality in organizations overlaps to some extent with the first. The modern lesbian and gay movements, that grew from the late 1960s, have been influential in a great many ways, though often at a deeper (post-)structural level than at the level of immediate action, remark or policy-making. While there have of course been surveys of and actions against lesbian and gay harassment and discrimination, the more profound impact has been in problematizing sexuality, especially heterosexuality, and, in recent years, 'homosexuality' too. Current perspectives on sexuality in organization are influenced by a wide variety of theoretical approaches, including poststructuralism, often following on the work of Michel Foucault; Marxism, feminism, especially radical feminism; psychoanalysis; and postmodernism.

A strong empirical focus on sexuality and organizations has developed in at least three main ways. First, the study of sexuality in organizations developed initially from journalistic and political interventions in and *naming* of sexual harassment in the mid-1970s. The first book analysing the problem was *Sexual Shakedown* produced by Lin Farley in 1978. This naming should not of course obscure the fact that sexual harassment was not new at all, merely that in the past it had often been taken for granted, was unnoticed, ignored or defined in other ways previously (see pp. 50–7). Since then studies and surveys of, action against and policies on sexual harassment have mushroomed. There followed general social analyses, detailed examinations of legal cases (MacKinnon, 1979) and broad social surveys (Gutek, 1985), all establishing the pervasiveness and frequency of sexual harassment by men. In 1987 the Ministry of Health and Social Affairs in Finland published a survey and bibliography, giving details of 341 publications and ten bibliographies on sexual harassment (Högbacka et al., 1987). The work of Kauppinen and Gruber, and Haavio-Mannila and colleagues has introduced a stronger comparative element to analysis, and connected sexual harassment to broad questions of gendered organizations and work (Kauppinen and Gruber, 1993a, 1993b; Haavio-Mannila, 1994, 1998).

Secondly, there has been a smaller development of empirical studies of heterosexual relationships and sexual liaisons in organizations.[23] Though some of the early examples of these studies cannot be said to have been particularly critical, they can, in a general sense, be understood in the context of the growing attempts to develop explicit social theorizing on heterosexuality (Wilkinson and Kitzinger, 1993), 'compulsory heterosexuality' (Rich, 1983), 'hierarchic heterosexuality' (Hearn, 1987) and 'hegemonic heterosexuality' (Frank, 1987).

Thirdly, another important strand of empirical studies developed in the 1980s on lesbians' and gay men's experiences in organizations, particularly, though not only, experiences of discrimination and violation.[24] As with sexual harassment surveys, these were often initially part of campaigns or other political interventions.[25] Recent studies have examined the wider experiences of lesbians and gay men throughout organizations, including business (Woods and Lucas, 1993; Signorile, 1994), the public sector (Skelton, 1999; Humphrey, 2000), the police (Burke, 1993), the military (Cammermeyer, 1995; Hall, 1995) and the community sector (Oerton, 1996a, 1996b).

These empirical studies have been accompanied by general reviews of the place of sexuality within organizations. The book *'Sex' at 'Work'* (Hearn and Parkin, 1987, 1995) outlined ways in which organizations construct sexuality, sexuality constructs organizations, and organizations and sexuality may occur simultaneously – hence the notion of 'organization sexuality'. In describing this simultaneous phenomenon, we noted how this may occur in terms of movement and proximity, feelings and emotions, ideology and consciousness, and language and imagery. This work also pointed centrally to the problem of the power of men and the pervasiveness of the 'male sexual narrative' (Dyer, 1985) in organizations. These themes have been explored in much greater detail in *The Sexuality of Organization* (Hearn et al., 1989) and other case studies (for example, Cockburn, 1991; Collinson, 1992). The *Sexuality of Organization* book was a diverse collection. However, in different ways, the contributors placed sexuality as an important element in the understanding of organizational process, and not just something that is added on to the analysis. For example, Deborah Sheppard (1989: 142) argued that 'The notion of organizational structure as an objective, empirical and genderless reality is itself a gendered notion', partly through the presence of sexuality and sexual(ized) process in organizations. The book explores through both theoretical reviews and empirical case studies the intimate overlap between sexuality and organizations/organizing. It emphasizes the pervasive dominance of heterosexuality in most organizations.

Cynthia Cockburn has also taken up these themes in a number of publications, including *Brothers* (1983), 'Equal Opportunities' Intervene (1990) and *In the Way of Women* (1991). Her work is wide ranging in considering the variety of ways that men maintain and reproduce power over women, particularly in paid work organizations. This variety extends to the place of sexual domination alongside and in relation to, say, labour market domination; the interrelation of different oppressions and social divisions; and indeed the variety of actions and interests of different groups of men, for example, by 'class', 'race' and indeed sexuality.

Rosemary Pringle makes her prime focus gender and sexuality, particularly in analysing bureaucracies and the boss–secretary relationships there (1988, 1989). She is insistent on the need to record the extent of gender and sexual power and domination in organizations, and she is also especially concerned to analyse the pervasiveness and complexity of power. In doing so, she draws critically on post-structuralist theory to chart the ways in which gender/sexual power relations operate in multiple directions and may be only understood more fully by resort to psycho-dynamic, unconscious and fantasy processes. One potential difficulty of this kind of development is that the analysis of complexities and power can be read, we would argue, falsely, as diluting power analysis.

These general and detailed empirical studies and surveys have emphasized the interconnection of sexuality and power in organizations, and the pervasiveness of the power of men, particularly heterosexual men (Cockburn, 1991; Collinson, 1992). They have also shown how sexual processes and organizational processes are intimately connected, in both the general structuring of organizations and in the detail of everyday interaction. '(Re-)eroticizations' of organizations have been expounded and critiqued (Brewis and Grey, 1994; Brewis and Linstead, 2000). Organizations, like discourses, are sexually encoded (cf. Grosz, 1987), both for organizational members in organizational cultures and organizational analysts of organizations (Calás and Smircich, 1991). Attempting to make sense of these issues brings us back to some of the basic questions of organizational analysis; in other ways, it raises quite novel questions.

In much of this broad literature on organizations, gender and sexuality, two sub-perspectives may be recognized, often in some kind of tension. However, this tension may be seen not as a problem but rather as dynamic and (re)productive. These two sub-perspectives may be characterized as, firstly, that which focuses on material oppressions, and, secondly, that which focuses on discursive construc-tions. These two are sometimes seen as in opposition, as in some debates between modernism and postmodernism, or they may be seen as converging. Material oppressions are being understood in increasingly complex, differentiated and multiple ways, just as the (re)production of discourse and discursive construc-tions is a material, organizational and technological accomplishment. Perhaps the main lesson of discursive perspectives is the need to look beyond and deconstruct the obvious, the dominant taken-for-granted, by which organizations are constructed and analysed. This entails the deconstruction of those perspectives that hold, or seek to hold, dominant control within organizations, often those of the modernist project(s) and paradigm(s). In so doing, emphasis is shifted to the sub-texts of organizations, such as sexuality and forms of sexual process. Discourses of and around organizations are themselves sexually encoded. Similarly, violence and certain forms of violent process constitute other subtexts of organizations; and discourses of and around organizations are violently-encoded, as, for example, in notions of threat.

By focusing on material oppressions, organizations are seen as sites and struc-tures of oppression. That is not to demonize organizations, nor is it to ignore the positive or facilitative or creative aspects of organizations. Oppression can be conceptualized as shorthand for a series of social processes, by and through which particular dominant groups and classes oppress others in various ways. It is difficult to reduce oppression to one single explanation. In speaking of the oppressed and oppression, we refer to the way certain constructions or categories of people may be relatively consistently treated in ways that denigrate or under-value or hurt or proscribe more favoured courses of action for them as individuals and/or collectivities. The variety of ways and areas in and through which men (may) oppress include biological reproduction; sexuality; caring and nurturing; and violences. These can be thought of as types of reproduction of social life; other forms include paid employment and cultural forms. The forms that oppres-sion may take range from direct violence and force to the indirect use of violence through hierarchy and the unfair allocation of resources, as in most organizations. For such patterns of oppression to continue, men oppress each other – in the making of 'men', especially when boys and young men engage in competition, violence, resistance and oppressing themselves. Thus in both sub-perspectives, organizations can be seen as structured, gendered/sexualed, sexually encoded (though not necessarily sexualized) and indeed violenced reproductions. Organi-zations may be analysed through cultural reproductive materialism that is simul-taneously discursive and material (Hearn, 1992b, 1993).

Another contentious element in the field is the very meaning of sexuality. Though few would restrict 'sexuality' to physical sexual contact or even sexual–social relations, some commentators tend to limit sexuality to social practices that relate to desire and its social construction while others hardly distinguish sexuality from gender.[26] Another dimension of difference that in some ways cuts across the first is whether sexuality is understood primarily in conscious even intentional terms, less conscious terms or even unconscious terms. For example, a hetero-sexual primary text may be underlain by a homosexual/ homosocial subtext. This in turn suggests different models of organizations and organizing – as action-based structures or sub-structures of unconscious processes.

Why Sexualed Organizations?

In the light of these debates, some authors have attempted to distinguish a sexual-ity paradigm and a gender paradigm in organizational analysis. We remain extremely doubtful about this possibility. While organizational analysis focusing on sexuality is often neglected and needs to be more fully developed, this is not to be understood in any way that is competitive with 'gender'. Whilst we have written at length on the neglect of sexuality in organizations, and have attempted to rectify this omission, we do *not* think that the establishment of any separate 'sexuality and organizations' field or 'sexuality paradigm', in competition with the analysis of gendered power relations, should follow. To be absolutely clear on this: we do not advocate a separate paradigm for sexuality and organizations. We would make similar arguments on any would-be paradigm of violence, violation and organizations.

A challenge is how to increase the focus on sexuality whilst not creating a separable object of analysis. We have previously discussed extensively the relationship of sexuality, gendered power relations and organizations.[27] Sexuality can be understood as both a foundation of gender (MacKinnon, 1982) and a focused aspect of gender relations. There is no necessary connection between studying sexuality and anti-modernism/postmodernism or studying gender and modernism. Sexuality is a fundamental material aspect of the reproduction of patriarchies and patriarchal relations. The social (re)production of sexuality is a major, but not of course the only, element in the formation of the gendered body. Likewise, sexuality constitutes one of the (many) effects of the body. The body is a material foundation, a social formation and a site of social effects of patriarchies and patriarchal relations.

Having said that, we do argue that it is necessary to understand organizations, or at least most organizations, as *sexualed*. This is for several reasons. First, sexual arrangements in the private domains provide the base infrastructure, principally through women's unpaid labour in families, for the public domain organizations. Second, in many organizations the concept of sexual work is a useful element in analysis. This addresses the relationship of work/labour to sexuality. Rather than seeing work as something that can then be sexualized, we argue that a much closer relationship between work and sexuality is possible. This entails the very definitions of sexuality and work. In some contexts sexuality in organizations, and indeed elsewhere, is a form of work. Organizations can be seen as arenas of sexual labour, just as they are of emotional labour and other forms of labour. Accordingly, an important concept in much of our own and others' work is that of sexual work and sexual labour.[28] These concepts are also developed elsewhere (for example, Hearn, 1987). For this we are indebted to Lucy Bland and her colleagues (1978) who had previously written on the selling of sexuality as part of labour power: 'sexuality is thus both officially incorporated (in the body) and literally marginalised' (Hearn and Parkin, 1987: 102).

Third, and linked closely to these debates is that more generally around the status of 'the economic', and specifically capitalism, in the construction of sexuality and sexual harassment. 'Organization sexuality'[29] is not a specific product of capitalist labour processes, though they are relevant, along with many other processes. Sexual harassment cannot be 'explained' by capitalist labour market processes. In *'Sex' at 'Work'* (Hearn and Parkin, 1987: 84–9), we discussed ways in which dominant patriarchal constructions of organizations could be said to construct sexuality. These included the extension of capitalist labour process theories in that direction. This was followed by a counter-argument that sexuality can be understood as constructing organizations: that organizations are constructed by sexuality. This was followed by a further chapter on 'organization sexuality' – the simultaneous operation of organizations and sexuality. Sexuality, sexual harassment and organization sexuality are thus analysed in a complex way that builds an argument step by step. The dominant framework for understanding all of this is patriarchal social relations: capitalist labour market processes are one instance of patriarchal relations, not the explanation of organization sexuality. Or to put this slightly differently, '(p)roductive relations, including capitalist ones, are after all also forms and matters of sexuality, procreation, nurture and violence' (Hearn, 1987: 101). Capitalism is one form of patriarchy.

Fourth, most organizations continue to exist with and through dominant heterosexual norms, ideology, ethics and practices. In our own and others' work on sexuality, gender and organizations, a central theme has been the question of heterosexuality and the movement of debate away from essentialized, naturalized views of sexuality (see Hearn et al., 1989). We have thus addressed heterosexuality and particularly men's heterosexuality as the dominant form of sexuality; and subjected compulsory heterosexuality to critique.[30] (Hetero)sexual harassment is seen as wide-ranging sexualized activities, including unwanted touch, joking and invasion of space, so problematizing heterosexuality and recognizing its manifestations as power in organizations.[31]

Fifth, there is the general interrelation of gender and sexuality, as intimately, indeed definitionally, connected with each other (Bondi, 1998: 186). Gender occurs *along with* sexuality, and vice versa. It is rather difficult to conceive of gender and sexuality without the other. As Sedgwick (1991: 31) notes, 'without a concept of gender there could be, quite simply, no concept of homo- or heterosexuality'. On the other hand, while sexuality and gender are clearly far from co-extensive and should not be conflated with each other, we cannot know in advance how they will be different nor their exact relation to each other (Sedgwick, 1991: 27).

Sixth, despite the links between sexuality and gender, it is possible to make clear empirical distinctions between the sexual and gender dynamics in organizations or parts of organizations, for example in terms of the presence or absence of organizational members with different sexualities. In Sarah Rutherford's (1999) study of an airline company, the presence of gay men in some of the organization's divisions appeared to have clear impacts on the reduction of a harassing culture there.

Thus to argue that organizations are sexualed is not to say that sexuality is predominant.

Why Violences? Why Violation?

Violence has not been a central concern of mainstream organization theory. The recognition of the importance of gender and sexuality in organizations has provided groundwork for analysing violence in organizations and organizations through the perspective of violence. In this, feminist theory and practice on gender, sexuality and violence, in and outside organizations, have been central. The link between gender, sexuality and violence is most obvious with the recognition of sexual harassment, sexual violence and sexual abuse in and by organizations. Sexual harassment studies demonstrate both the power of male heterosexuality and men's violence in organizations. The complexities of interrelations of sexuality, violence and organizations remain relatively underexplored.[32] Our focus on organizations through violence is not only because of the recognition of sexual harassment as a form of (sexual) violence but because feminist work more generally, particularly on sexuality, has increasingly acknowledged the underlying importance of men's violence. The overlap between sexual harassment and 'normal' heterosexual relations has been highlighted (Thomas and Kitzinger, 1994).

Forms of sexuality, especially men's heterosexuality, not usually constructed as sexual harassment or sexual violence, may be understood in terms of their relationship to or reconstruction as sexual violence (Dworkin, 1979; MacKinnon, 1983). Hierarchy and dominance, in organizations as elsewhere, have been explored as subject to eroticization, for many men at least.[33] Domination by men is clearly and characteristically associated with violence. Homicide and most other violence is primarily perpetrated by men. While men's collective, institutional and interpersonal domination of violence is immense, it is important to also recognize women's and indeed children's violence. An emphasis on violence as a fundamental part of the gendered analysis of society is part of feminist theory and practice. Opposition to men's violence is a major personal and political focus within feminism. For men to respond positively to feminism, to be profeminist, necessitates direct attention to men's power and violence. Men's violence is a major element in the perpetuation of that power and a necessary object of analysis and intervention in feminist and profeminist theory and practice.

Violence is an especially complex and contested term. This is clear from an historical analysis of the changing recognition of what counts as (forms of) violence (see pp. 65–70). The use of the term 'violence' also usually implies recognition that a problem exists: that something is seen as unacceptable or threatening, and that the actions and practices labelled as 'violent' have at least some characteristics in common with others similarly labelled. In this sense, it is a concept with shifting moral referents. Violence in and around work organizations is an area of analysis that is especially complex and contested. Indeed contestations over the definitions (in particular what is included and excluded) are especially intense in the case of violence, and are central in the social construction, social experience and social reproduction of violence in and around organizations. Debates and dilemmas around the definition of violence include those on: intention to harm; extent of physical contact; harmful effects and damage; differential perceptions, for example of violator and violated; and interpersonal and structural violence.

Definitions of violence can thus vary greatly. Let us consider three possibilities. First, violence is often equated with *physical violence*, or certain kinds of violence that are seen as 'serious' (see Hearn, 1998). This can apply in everyday definitions, especially of those being violent, and in official definitions. In criminal law this generally means the 'unjustified' use of physical force. The 1995 British Crime Survey defined 'work-related violence' as: 'Incidents of violence (wounding, common assault, robbery, and snatch theft) occurring while the victim was working. Incidents while travelling to and from work are excluded. Incidents not arising directly from the work are included. Incidents perpetrated by relatives or partners (domestic) are excluded.' This definition thus excludes harassment and bullying.

A second alternative, which is particularly relevant in organizational contexts, is to expand 'violence' to also include harassment and bullying. This view brings together debates on different forms of violence that are usually kept separate. Violence then includes sexual, racial and other harassments (unwanted, persistent physical or verbal behaviour of a sexual/racial nature);[34] and bullying (exposure repeatedly and over time to negative actions from one or more persons such that victims have difficulties defending themselves, as well as physical violence. Bullying includes, for example, isolation (people refusing to listen to you, people refusing to talk to you), slander (gossip behind your back, spreading false and groundless information), negative glances and gestures, laughing, sneering (Björkqvist et al., 1994; Vartia, 1995).

A third way is to adopt a broad, socially contextualized understanding of violence as violation. Accordingly, we define violence as those structures, actions, events and experiences that violate or cause violation or are considered as violating. They are usually, but not necessarily, performed by a violator or violators upon the violated. Violence can thus be seen as much more than physical violence, harassment and bullying. It can also include intimidation, interrogation, surveillance, persecution, subjugation, discrimination and exclusion that lead to experiences of violation. This is close to what Judith Bessant (1998) calls 'opaque violence'. As she comments, 'In relationships where significant long-term power disparities exist, then inequality can easily slip into violence. This occurs regularly in workplaces as well as many other institutions' (p. 9). This raises the question of how violence and violation relate to broad questions of oppression, inequality and (gender and other forms of) equity.[35] Violations, including oppressions and discriminations, are likely to have negative effects on physical and mental health and well-being.[36]

Violence and violation are thus *social* phenomena. Violation usually, though not always, includes some kind of *force or potential force*: force *by* the violator; forced violation *of* the violated. Violence as violation includes structured oppression, harassment, bullying and violences, and mundane, everyday violations within organizational worlds. Dominant forms of violence as violation in organizations are by men to women, children or other men. They range across verbal, emotional, psychological, cognitive, representational and visual attacks, threats and degradation; enactment of psychological harm; physical assaults; use of weapons and other objects; destruction of property; rape; and murder. These distinctions may in practice break down, as in the understanding of all forms of violence from men to women as sexual violence (Kelly, 1987). There are also several standpoints from which to define violence as violation: the violator; the violated; those of other social actors involved in dealing with violence, for example lawmakers or enforcers; and those of analysts, who may or may not be involved in such intervention. In some situations the position, observation and sometimes relatively passive participation of audiences is especially important (Gabriel, 1998). These perspectives are, however, not always distinct; someone may occupy all locations simultaneously. All are mediated through representations and perceptions, usually differently for violators and violated, men and women. Violence involves violation; but violation is a broader, more useful concept for our purposes. This focus on violation has important methodological significance. Just as sexuality is not a fixed thing or even simply a set of acts, but a process of desiring, so similarly, a focus on violation refers to a process of damaging. These processes involve the desiring or damaging event and responses to desire/damage, and are, moreover, embodied, material and discursive.

Why Violenced Organizations? Why Violations in Organizations?

Violence and violation figure in relation to organizations in many ways. The developing focus on organizations through sexual/gendered violence and violation comes from a number of directions – from harassment studies; from feminist work on men's violence as a major element of men's social power; from work on violence by organizations, on bullying and physical violence in organizations and on organizational responses to violence, usually men's violence. Organizations can be seen as sites or structures of violence and violation, and be understood as constellations of violent/violating, potentially or threatened violent/violating actions, behaviours, intentions and experiences.

Violence and violation can be more or less institutionalized in particular organizations, and even in whole societies, such as the Third Reich. Violation may also include the creation of the conditions of violence, whether social structurally or when someone's presence is violating. Violation can be dramatic or subtle, occasional or continuous, chronic and endemic (as in slave workplaces), generally invisible and 'unnecessary' (as inequalities are *so* entrenched), normalized and naturalized (as in the acceptance of sexual harassment as part of some jobs), an indication of changing power relations (perhaps through challenging previous power relations) or a reassertion of power by dominant groups (as in men's responses to women's power). Violence and violations in and around organizations can be ways of reinforcing relations of domination and subordination; of developing resistance; of refining gradations of status and power; and facilitating alliances, coalitions, inclusions, exclusions and scapegoating (cf. Gabriel, 1998). Violences and violations can in turn be ways of maintaining subtexts and multiple oppressions in particular organizations, in organization and in society more generally. However, it should also be emphasized that violence and violations are not simply means for or structurings of *other* forms of power, domination and oppression. They are forms of power, domination and oppression in themselves that structure organizations. While such a perspective can mean that violence as violation may blur into power relations (Hearn, 1992a, 1998), a key distinction is that power relations are not necessarily violating. The very existence of organizations can also be violating.

From Gender to Sexuality to Violation? Towards the Gender–Sexuality–Violation Complex

The critical edge of organizational analysis has appeared to move from *agendered* approaches, to those implicitly *incorporating* gender and sexuality, to those recognizing *social divisions* (of which gender is one example), onto the *more explicit recognition* of first gender and gender relations, then sexuality, and now violence and violation. Such a 'progression' is not a narrowing of focus in organizational analysis but a series of theoretical repositionings. Assumptions that agendered approaches are broader than gendered approaches, and gender relations are broader than sexuality or violence, carry with them hierarchical assumptions on reality that place concepts before experience. The account presented may appear to chart some movement from gender to sexuality to violence and violation, a kind of reverse modernism, in which progressively more fundamental 'forces' are noted, recognized, made conscious, interpreted and critiqued. It may appear as linear, yet it is not. Our work has, in some senses, shifted in these directions, but of course gender, sexuality, violence and violation have always been present. It is consciousness of such social processes that may change in the analysis and transformation of organizations.

It is inaccurate to portray 'gender' or 'sexuality' as strictly separate from each other. 'Gender' is formed in relation to 'sexuality'; it is neither determinate nor derivative of sexuality. Gender occurs *along with* sexuality, and vice versa; it is difficult to conceive of gender and sexuality without the other, even if in some instances the cultural context of sexuality or gender seems absent. Thus it might be more appropriate to talk of the gender–sexuality relation than 'gender and sexuality' or 'gender, sexuality and violence'. We could continue this logic, creating further complexes around gender–sexuality–race, gender–sexuality–class, or amalgamations of four or more conceptual divisions. However, while all the permutations of gender, sexuality, race, class, age, disability (amongst other social divisions) are important, there is a special significance in certain associations, at least in certain social contexts. Why is this? With the difficulty of conceiving gender without (a)sexuality and sexuality without (a)gender, these two notions generally depend for their existence upon the other through the reference to the socially sexed body. On the other hand, most other social divisions, while probably interconnected with gender and sexuality, may not always depend upon gender and sexuality for their cultural existence. While gender and sexuality can be deployed in ways similar to the use of such social divisions as class and race, we need to be aware of how the relation of gender and sexuality is qualitatively different to that of, say, gender and class, or gender and race (Bondi, 1998: 186). In this kind of society at least, violence is clearly very closely intertwined with gender and sexuality.

This means not looking at *separate* questions such as 'gender' or 'sexuality' (Savage and Witz, 1992) or 'gender and violence', but understanding relations of oppressions in the social processes of organizations. What organizations are and what is taken to happen in most work organizations is *fundamentally constituted* in the interrelations of gender, sexuality, violation and other oppressions, divisions and differences. Organizations and what happens in them are fundamentally social, formed through various social relations, of which gender, sexuality and violation are the prime focuses here. We thus address the interconnections of gender, sexuality, violation, and organizations – what might be called 'the gender–sexuality–violation complex'. There is an urgent need to examine gendered/sexualed violations in and around organizations. This is more than a listing of 'events'; rather charting interconnections is part of the process of theorizing and developing theory. Generally, violence and violation are very closely linked with, but not totally determined by, structural power differences. While our focus is on gender and sexuality, it is important not to privilege sexuality and gender over other divisions and oppressions, such as race and racism. Though gender and sexuality seem persistently significant in the explanation of violation, particular violations are mediated through other social divisions, such as age and class. The incredible variety of cultural formations and structuring of practices called organizations can itself often be violating to some; the very (re)production of organization(s) can be a form of violence and violation.

2

Histories

Locating Organizations in Social Time

> In 1864, three years after women had been appointed as clerks in the US
> Treasury Department, a special congressional committee, instituted to investi-
> gate 'certain charges against the Treasury Department', reported on the sexual
> harassment and propositioning of women clerks by some men supervisors
>
> (Aron, 1987)

> In 1872 the British Post Office experimented in employing male and female staff
> and putting them in the same room. Management considered the experiment a
> success, in 'raising the tone' and 'decency' of the male staff.
>
> (Delgado, 1979)

> In 1892 at a weaving mill in Nelson, Lancashire, the 'immoral proposals' and
> 'indecent language' of an overlooker, Houghton Greenwood, were the subject of
> a committee of inquiry of local clergy, in which his and other men supervisors'
> actions were condemned and the responsibilities of the employers were stressed.
>
> (Fowler, 1985)

What was happening here? How are we to understand these and similar historical events? How are these historical events relevant today? What do they tell us
about the processes of gender, sexuality and violence in organizations? We introduce these examples, and return to them later in the chapter, to show how history
is very much a matter of the present and current organizational concerns are historically constituted. There are many events in contemporary organizations, that
both echo and appear to stand apart from these from the nineteenth century, some
of which we discuss in later chapters.

Organizations exist in histories. Gender, sexuality, violence and violation are, like
organizations, social and cultural ways of arranging bodies in social time and social
space. They are all consistently structured and intensely variable. Organizations
exist and are located within their own histories and geographies, and those of the
societies within which they are located. Locating gendered, sexualed and violenced
organizations necessitates attention to organizational contexts; gendered and other
social divisions; gendered societies and cultures; and gendered histories and
geographies.

It is quite impossible to write 'a' history of gender, sexuality, violation and organizations here in one chapter. Instead we give some examples of how histories are important in the analysis and change of gender, sexuality, violation and organizations, as a guide to how such perspectives may be relevant for your own analytical and political concerns. We first outline a general framework of dominant historical connections between gender, sexuality, violation and organizations. We then introduce three key historical concepts and approaches: the gender order (such as patriarchy), the economic (such as capitalism) and the political (such as the nation-state). These are *sedimented* concepts, so that each provides the basis for and underlies the next; they do not supersede each other. The next section considers the societal concepts of gender order and patriarchies. This is followed by examination of the relationship of macro-economic organizational change in the pre-modern, early modern and capitalist periods. This provides the framework for a more specific discussion of gendered/sexualed/violenced organizations within 'economic patriarchies'. Special attention is given to the first of several focus studies: on the construction of organizational heterosexualities in the Industrial Revolution. The final section on the nation, the state, warfare and welfare includes a second focus study on state and welfare organizational responses to men's violence to women and children.

Dominant Historical Constructions and Connections

Time and histories are relevant to the understanding of gender, sexuality, violation and organizations in several fundamental ways. These include:

- as providing a context of organizations;
- in showing organizations as historical consolidations of gender, sexuality and violation;
- in conceptualizing organizations as consolidations of social relations over time, even of time;
- in highlighting the historical continuities and discontinuities around gender, sexuality and violation that are evident in organizations.

To address these issues necessitates an historical reconceptualization of organizations, in terms of the social relations of gender, sexuality and violation. Gender, sexuality and violation in and of organizations and the organization(s) of gender, sexuality and violation are historical phenomena. The relations between them are not fixed or even determinate: there is not one set of formulae that stipulates how, for example, gender produces sexuality which produces violence, or that violence and sexuality produce gender. These are all social, cultural phenomena, not the building bricks of positivist models. The relations between them are socially and culturally variable. Organizations have their own stories, their own particular 'life stories'. One way of understanding organizations is through telling that story, as if it is a life history. This may also be a way of developing an understanding of time-based locations of both yourself and organizations which you know.

Along with the changes in the social and cultural nature of gender, sexuality and violation, there are some remarkably persistent historical patterns in their interrelations, societally and organizationally:

- dominant gender relations and dominant gender orders more generally have frequently involved the structural power of men, or certain men, over women and children;
- dominant sexual relations and dominant sexual orders have frequently involved the structural power of heterosexuality and heterosexual people, especially (certain) heterosexual men, over non-heterosexuality, non-heterosexuals and women's sexualities;
- dominant relations and practices of violation have frequently involved men's use of violence towards women, children, other men and themselves.

In these enduring ways at least there have been substantial connections between *dominant* forms of gender relations, sexual relations, relations of violation and organizations. Indeed dominant constructions and patterns in each social arena have reinforced each other, particularly in terms of:

- how gender is constructed;
- what 'men', 'women', 'boys' and 'girls' are, and what are the major social forms they take;
- men's powers against and in relation to women's powers;
- how sexuality is constructed and the social forms it takes;
- heterosexual powers against and in relation to lesbian, gay, bisexual and non-heterosexual powers;
- how violation is constructed and the social forms it takes;
- men's violences against and in relation to women, children and each other;
- how organizations are constructed and the social forms they take;
- men's organizational powers, heterosexual organizational powers and organizational violations against and in relation to those who are organizationally subordinated.

While these various elements can all reinforce each other, these relations should not be understood in any functionalist way. They may often be mutually reinforcing but this can still mean that there are many possible alternative practices and structures of gendered, sexualed and violenced power in organizations. These variations intermesh with and reproduce dominant gender relations in organizations (usually men gaining social value over women), organization sexuality (usually heterosexuals over non-heterosexuals) and indeed often, though not always, violation. Furthermore within even dominant forms of organizational structures, both continuing dominance and resistance are reproduced, changed or subverted by individual and collective agency.

These variable social relations of gender, sexuality and violence are likely to reinforce and reproduce other practical and structural variations in organizations.

These variations can be observed in:

- organizational power, hierarchy, position, authority;
- pay and other material rewards;
- employment tenure and temporal form of employment contract or other relation (for example, 'permanent', 'temporary', 'casual', 'full-time', 'part-time');
- occupational distributions and other divisions of labour, and their valorization;
- relation of labour to the 'non-organizational' and the domestic;
- professional and other formal statuses;
- informal valorizations;
- the extent to which 'unemployment' and 'being unemployed' are recorded;
- socio-spatial location, including location in boundary/non-boundary positions in organizations and location in more central 'core' or less marginal positions.

Sedimented social 'logics' that might link these elements more closely together include:

- The dominant gender/sexual order of a society is reproduced within and by organizations, and this general dominant order involves the reproduction of processes of subordination, including violation, within and by organizations. This kind of account fits with the concept of gender regime or patriarchy, in which gender, sexuality and gendered/sexual violence are themselves causal elements. This approach is exemplified by theories of patriarchy.
- The dominant economic order, such as capitalism or feudalism, constructs both dominant gender patterns and dominant organizational forms and structures. This account gives causal power to the economic, with the other elements – gender, sexuality, violation and organizations – constructed by that relation to varying extents. Connections between these elements arise as secondary to or dependent on determining economic forces. This is exemplified by Marxism and Marxist feminism.
- The dominant political and organizational structures, and particularly state and bureaucratic organizations, *themselves* construct gender, sexuality and violation. This account portrays organizations as more autonomous, 'rational' and (paradoxically gender-) neutral arenas, and is as such compatible with much mainstream modernist organization theory, including the Weberian rationalization thesis and convergence theory. In practice, organizations are gendered/sexualed and sites of other exclusions through, for example, racialization and ethnicization.

In each case, there are several kinds of connections with organizations and organizational analysis: in the specific form of social relations within organizations (for example, capitalist relations); in the form and structure of organization themselves (for example, capitalist organizations); and in the wider context of the society within which organizations are located (for example, capitalist society). Each of these general approaches or 'logics' gives priority to one major element in too simple a way. Along with all metanarratives, they omit many other things. A more adequate approach draws on all these 'logics', recognizing that *gendered/sexualed/violenced* social forms, structures and processes occur

TABLE 2.1 *The gender order, the economic and the political*

Main perspective	The gender order	The economic	The political
Major example	Patriarchy	Capitalism	Modern nation-state
Historical timescale of main example	Long/ancient	Medium	Relatively recent/ modern
Dominant gender relations	Patriarchal gender relations (dominance of men)	Patriarchal capitalist gender relations (dominance of men and capital)	Patriarchal capitalist state gender relations (dominance of men, capital and the state)
Dominant sexual relations	Patriarchal heterosexuality	Patriarchal capitalist (hetero)sexuality	Patriarchal capitalist state (hetero)sexuality
Dominant relations of violence and violation	Men's patriarchal violence and violation	Gendered/sexual violence and violation in the capitalist process and its expansion	Consolidation, expansion and control of gendered/ sexual violence and violation

through the mediations of both general *socio-economic* and specific *organizational* forms, structures and processes, and that in turn the *socio-economic* and the *organizational* occur through *gendered/sexualed/violenced* social forms. Particular social divisions exist in and through other social divisions.

Let us now look at these three 'logics', in order to build up a more complex picture of the relevance of time and histories. The first, centred on patriarchy, provides the longest time perspective; patriarchy precedes capitalism. The second, capitalism, operates *within* the historical context of patriarchy. The third, the nation-state, operates *within* the context of capitalism and patriarchy, and is the most recent historical phenomenon. These initial three perspectives constitute a simple framework with which to discuss some broad historical approaches to gendered organizations. Each encompasses the next, and provides a sedimented context for that which follows. All these historical contexts have profound implications for the gendering of immediate organizational contexts (Table 2.1).

This kind of broad scheme is clearly only a starting point of analysis: it directs attention to the variable forms of social and historical context that may guide analysis. It might also suggest a shift from more global perspectives, to societal economic perspectives, to more local, political, national and organizational concerns. This is of course only a small part of the story. In particular, there are intense counter-trends towards globalization – economic, political, cultural – which are examined in Chapter 6.

Patriarchy and Gender Orders

Conceptualizations and Critiques

Placing organizations within a societal context can be done more or less abstractly. One can try and produce gendered histories of the cultural context of particular organizations; one can begin from the organization in question and look at the broader patterns within which the organization is placed; or one can try and conceptualize the whole of the society (in gendered terms) and then try to place the organization within that societal context. In such views the dominant gender/sexual order is reproduced within and by organizations, and this involves the reproduction of processes of gendered/sexualed/violenced subordination within and by organizations. The most developed body of theory that approaches the question in the last way is 'patriarchy' theory. Even so, there have been surprisingly few attempts to relate general societal theories of patriarchy to organizational analysis.[1] At the very least, it can be argued that within this theoretical framework of 'patriarchy', organizations are likely to be both set within patriarchal societal relations and often be characterized by patriarchal relations in themselves. As these are important matters for an historical perspective on organizations, we now consider some of the major approaches to patriarchy.

While 'patriarchy' literally refers to the rule of the father(s), the concept has been developed most fully in recent years in relation to the rule of men or adult men. Such forms of 'rule' by men are not fixed social relations. It is perhaps more useful to think in terms of 'relations of ruling' (Smith, 1990) rather than absolute rule. Such relations of ruling are both material and ideological (Dobash and Dobash, 1979), including their operation within organizations. The historical significance of patriarchy lies in its persistence: patriarchy pre-dates capitalism. There are many ways of conceptualizing patriarchy and its predominant bases. These include: as pre-capitalist property relations (Marx and Engels, 1970); as pre-modern political/authority relations (Elshtain, 1981); as material/economic mode of production (Delphy, 1977, 1984); as domination of sexuality (MacKinnon, 1982); as domination of biological reproduction (Firestone, 1970); as domination of reproduction more generally.[2] In each case, one would expect organizations to be set within these societal relations and be characterized by social relations that reproduce them. Despite the political and analytical importance of the concept of patriarchy within feminist theory and practice, by the late 1970s there were increasing uncertainties around and criticisms of the concept.[3] A considerable number of problem areas were highlighted. These included whether the concept of patriarchy:

- was presented in a universal or too universalist way, whereby it returned analysis towards biology;
- necessarily focuses on single cause rather than the multiplicity of ways gender is defined;
- tends to reinforce dualist analyses, most obviously of capitalism and patriarchy;
- depends upon the idea of a gender class, and how viable is such an idea (this is challenged by seeing gender as practice rather than as more fixed categories);
- underemphasizes or even undermines women's action and resistance to transform the situation;
- is ethnocentric, as noted especially by black feminists.

The concept has thus been criticized for being both over-generalized and over-particular. In the late 1970s the concept was subject to various feminist and feministic autocritiques, almost from all sides (as opposed to hostile anti-feminist critiques which were and are rarely far away).[4] Since the early 1980s the concept of patriarchy has continued to be re-theorized in feminist and profeminist debates – in three major and related ways. First, patriarchy has been analysed more specifically as a set of diverse sites/arenas/structures/processes. Walby (1986, 1990) has identified six major patriarchal structures or structures of patriarchy: capitalist work, the family, the state, violence, sexuality, culture. These are similar to the set of structures of patriarchy elaborated by Hearn (1987): reproduction of labour power, procreation, regeneration/degeneration, violence, sexuality, ideology. Itzin (1995) has set out a materialist analysis of family, labour market, organizations, education/socialization, representation and gender-based violence, as a framework for locating gender, sexuality and violence in organizations.

Second, patriarchy has been historicized and periodized, especially in terms of historical shifts from private patriarchy to public patriarchy (Hearn, 1992b). Contrasts can be drawn between private/kinship/familial patriarchy and public/capitalist patriarchy. These focus on various key historical changes in the period from the mid-eighteenth century to the 1960s, including the spread of wage labour (Ursel, 1986), monopoly capitalism (Brown, 1981), the growth of the post-war state (Hernes, 1987) and the growth of the welfare state (Borchorst and Siim, 1987).[5] Malcolm Waters (1989) has developed such historicized frameworks in his analysis of 'masculine gender systems', by putting together two dimensions: the primacy of the domestic or the public/extended over the other; and the degree of differentiation of the domestic and the public. This yields four rather than two possibilities. Where there is a high differentiation of the public and the domestic, Waters uses the term viriarchy (rule of adult males) in preference to patriarchy. The four forms are thus:

- direct domestic patriarchy (patriarchy 'proper');
- extended public patriarchy (feudalism);
- direct domestic viriarchy (early capitalism);
- extended public viriarchy (late capitalism).

This last case is the most distant from 'patriarchy proper' and closest to the social conditions of much of the contemporary industrialized world. The concept of extended viriarchy also overlaps with those of capitalist patriarchy, reorganized patriarchy or state patriarchy or welfare in a welfare society (Holter, 1984). Comparison may also be drawn with fratriarchy (Reed, 1975). John Remy (1990) argues that there is need for a further concept of androcracy, combining patriarchy (characterized by hierarchical relations of men, especially older men over women, children and some other men) and fratriarchy (emphasizing more autonomous lateral relations between men, especially younger men).

Third, some feminists and profeminists have adopted other similar but more open-ended conceptual frameworks (Walby, 1997). Margaret Stacey has suggested the notion of the 'male dominated gender order' (Stacey, 1986).

R.W. Connell has written of the 'gender order' and 'gender regimes' (Connell, 1987). Yvonne Hirdman (1988, 1990)[6] has proposed the 'gender system', in which hierarchy and difference are two fundamental ways in which gender is socially organized, and within which more historically specific 'gender contracts' are negotiated between women and men, sometimes forcibly. Her notion of gender contracts operating within the gender system does not refer to a temporary settlement between capital and labour, but one between men and women – often married, heterosexual men/fathers/husbands and married, heterosexual women/mothers/wives. Walby (1997) has addressed the substantive form of 'gender transformations' within the context of dominant gender regimes. One implication of this increasingly complexity is that we may now be more accurate to speak of 'patriarchies' in the plural (Hearn, 1992b). This is not only a question of the appreciation of different historical forms of patriarchy; it also follows from the relation of several realms or arenas of patriarchy, and the existence of overlapping mini-patriarchies throughout society.

Patriarchies and Organizations
With all these historically more recent forms of 'patriarchy' – public, reorganized, late capitalist, fratriarchal, extended viriarchical – organizations become much more important in society. In such societies it is certain men's power in organizations and the associated organizational relations that are characteristic, constitutive and defining of them. The place of organizations within public patriarchies is a key issue. Locating specific organizations within such forms of patriarchy, viriarchy or fratriarchy is important for several reasons. Organizations are fundamentally both structured social relations and interpersonal social relationships, both of which are fundamentally structured within public patriarchies. Attention to patriarchy and patriarchal relations addresses the societal context and the dominant forms of social relations within which specific organizations exist. It also raises the question of whether a specific organization reinforces or contradicts those social relations; in more substantive terms, it suggests the need to locate organizations in relation to the forms and structures of patriarchy. This includes assessing to what extent they produce, affirm or contest patriarchal social relations; and how they stand within, outside or on the margins of particular patriarchal institutions, such as the state. Furthermore, the recognition of the multiple form of patriarchies in turn suggests the need to recognize the various and multiple place of organizations within multiple patriarchies.

While there are clearly several difficulties with the concept of patriarchy, we do not see them as overriding the need for a broad social concept that addresses the persistent, though changing, historical societal dominance of men. There may indeed be a developing convergence between differentiated notions of patriarchies, and apparently more flexible notions of gender system, gender order and gender transformations. Whatever term is used, it is necessary to recognize the multi-dimensional nature of power relations around gender/sexuality/violation. For example, Rantalaiho (1997) emphasizes the importance of recognizing hierarchy *and* difference as two fundamental ways in which gender is socially organized (Hirdman, 1990), and the need to also recognize the persistence of 'compulsory heterosexuality' as a key feature. She notes the multi-level nature of the gender system, in terms of: social structures; cultural meanings; personal identities; social interactions; bodies and desires.[7] Similar differentiations may be made in relation to the concept of patriarchy, or more accurately patriarchies.

Economy

Slavery, Feudalism, Capitalism

Feminism has reformulated what is understood by economics and economies. Feminist economics is now certainly established, if still grossly underrecognized by the mainstream (Nelson, 1996).[8] It is likely that feminist economics will become a more powerful force in the future. The economic 'logic' of the historical construction of gendered/sexualed/violenced organizations cannot be denied. Such organizations need to be located within economic patriarchies. Most obviously, the economies of many 'civilizations' have been built on gendered violence, usually by certain men to women, children and other men. This is especially clear in *slave* societies – whether the Asiatic mode of production, the ancient forms of hydraulic economies of Mesopotamia, the Classical societies of the Mediterranean, pre-European slavery in Africa, the use of indentured labour in the North American plantations, European-organized slavery from Africa to Europe and the 'New World', or contemporary slavery. In most cases this has involved men as organizers of these slave trades. In such societies organizations are pervaded and underwritten by violence, usually men's violence.

What is particularly important is the way in which the element of slavery can co-exist with sophisticated notions of citizenship for non-slaves. This applied in the Classical worlds of both Greece and Rome, where adult male (non-slave) citizens were commonly distinguished from adult women, children and slaves. The presence of slavery, and the embedded violence that entails in the dominant institutions and organizations of such societies, does not mean that relatively peaceful social relations cannot be maintained amongst at least some of the more fortunate non-slaves. It might be useful at this point to make a distinction between societies where slavery is part of the formal fabric of society (for example, in the public institutions of the state following the conquest of peoples by armies) and societies where slavery operates but more covertly, sometimes in opposition to the state or other formal public machinery, as is still the case in many parts of the world. While few contemporary countries officially support or condone slavery, there is the continuation of socio-economic conditions in which people are not able to leave the places where they happen to live and work if they want to. In some cases children are born into or sold into such conditions: they are effectively born or made slaves.

In some cases slave trading is itself overtly sexualized, as in the selling of young women explicitly for sexual purposes; in other cases, sexualization appears to be less direct, as, for example, in the association of sexual degradation and the degradation of other forms of labour. Clearly slave systems provide many opportunities, both structurally and to particular individuals, for the extension of the ownership of particular kinds of (apparently non-sexualized) labour to the ownership of the body and sexuality. The ideology of slavery may be presented in terms of the ownership of labour but in practice it is almost always also the ownership of the body, and thus sexuality. Thus slavery is almost always sexualized, and capable of becoming sexualized. While slavery has usually been conducted primarily by men, it would be a mistake to see women as only the victims of slavery. Women have participated in the conduct of slavery, though usually much less prominently, and have benefited as members of owning classes, and occasionally as rulers, from the surplus values slavery creates.

It is similarly possible to rethink other 'economic' systems in gendered terms. Indeed it is likely that no ungendered economic system has yet been invented. Feudalism may in one sense be a way of organizing the land, labour and law at a time of limited technological development, but it also operates in its many forms with gendered patterns of land tenure, ownership, occupancy and usage. So while it is quite possible for there to be ladies, as well as lords, of the manor, in (gendered) practice this is much less likely to be the case. Similarly, there were certainly powerful women leaders in feudal times, most obviously through marriage, family relationship, religious position (for example, heads of women's orders) or local community standing. But in gendered terms feudalism can be understood as an extension of patriarchal principles of authority, ownership, duty and obligation from the family beyond and throughout the society, to local communities, religious organizations and ultimately monarchies, larger or smaller in regime, and thence 'god'.

(Patriarchal) fatherhood has historically been an institution of power.[9] Extensions of patriarchal family relations of authority and obligation to organizations and society beyond suggest a closer look at that family form is necessary for understanding the subsequent development of organizational forms. For many centuries early modern relations of the family and the incipient state were sanctioned by local religious institutions along with local forms of feudal or post-feudal governance. Marriage, families, motherhood and fatherhood were framed within biologistic discourses, with taken-for-granted definitions of the head of the household, more or less explicitly reinforced and affirmed by legal, quasi-legal, religious or communal practices. However, it is important to acknowledge the great variability in patriarchal social and family forms that existed prior to the early state interventions of the eighteenth and nineteenth centuries in Europe.[10] The patriarchal family cannot simply be equated with bourgeois or petit bourgeois forms, even if they remain the clearest statements of patriarchal legal ownership of wives, children and relatives as property (Stone, 1977; Elshtain, 1981).

The absolutism of the individual patriarch provided one model of profoundly gendered social relations for society that may even include a confluence of familial, communal, religious, monarchical, state and organizational powers. In effect the patriarchal family becomes a model for organizations, the monarchy, the state and the economy, with the reproduction of gendered hierarchical authorities over members within organizations. Many organizations may thus be characterized as historically and dominantly patriarchal, and at best paternalist.

The shift from feudalism to early forms of capitalism, such as mercantile capitalism, can be understood in many ways. Patriarchal powers, along with their considerable variation at the level of the family, provide one important basis for the movement from feudalism. The organization and sometime expansion of local family production often took place on these same direct patriarchal principles. This demanded a material surplus of goods. The accumulation of surpluses itself arose for a variety of reasons – from the increasing power and impact of baronial, monarchical and other elite classes; urban social organization through guilds and other social concentrations and associations; religious establishments as centres of capital accumulation, industrialization and in turn early capitalism; the acceleration of large-scale organization of land and land use through enclosures and clearances; the extension of trade on unequal terms; the exploitation of more distant parts of the world and the creation of reserves of raw materials through conquest, colonialism and imperialism.

R.W. Connell's (1993) article, 'The big picture', provides an exemplary political sociology of cultural and historical patterns through the lens of gender (see also Connell, 1998). While focusing primarily on the historical construction of men and masculinities, his analysis necessarily addresses broad patterns of gender relations more generally. He emphasizes both the historical domination of, initially, certain European and, later, North American economic and political powers, and the historical variation and specificity of local pre-colonial relations, sexuality and violence. This is not to say that the quite different gendered patterns, in, say, early Confucian, neo-Confucian China and pre-colonial Papua New Guinea (Connell, 1993: 604–5), did not also include domination by men; rather the modes of those dominations were different from the subsequent Euro/American colonial forms.

With this in mind, Connell (1993) then details four major decisive changes in European life in the period 1450–1650. These were:

- '... the disruption of medieval Catholicism by the spread of Renaissance culture and by the Protestant Reformation ...' (p. 607). This is the terrain of Weber and the analysis of the Protestant (and certain kind of masculine) ethic.
- 'The creation of the first overseas empires by the Atlantic seaboard states (Portugal and Spain, then Holland, England and France) was a gendered enterprise from the start, an outgrowth of the segregated men's occupations of soldiering and sea trading' (p. 607).
- 'The growth of cities fuelled by commercial capitalism – Antwerp, London, Amsterdam – created a mass milieu for everyday life that was more anonymous, and more coherently regulated, than the countryside' (p. 607).
- 'The onset of large-scale European civil war – the sixteenth–seventeenth-century wars of religion, merging into the dynastic wars of the seventeenth–eighteenth centuries – disrupted established gender orders profoundly' (p. 608). This in turn linked with and led to what were the first radical assertions of gender equality, the consolidation of strong state structures and the increased centrality of warfare.

While for the last hundred years or more the concept of men as 'world leaders' has evolved, men have long led the world in exploration, adventuring, conquest, appropriation, expropriation, colonialism, imperialism, pioneering, pillaging, raping, crusading, collective destruction and wars and warfare. The histories of nation-building, empire-building and militarism are largely histories of men, or rather certain kinds of men (see pp. 39–43). Furthermore, these gendered processes of family, economy and organization have expanded through the exertion of huge amounts of colonialist and imperialist violence, very largely by men. Such gendered insights have rarely been fully incorporated into histories, even most gendered histories, of capitalism. These violences by men within these historical processes of patriarchy, imperialism and capitalism clearly affect women and men quite differently. Not only do women suffer the violation of men's violence, but men experience each other's violence, whether through the military, in 'economic expansion' or in their upbringing as boys. In such ways both boys and girls may be subject to violence. In bringing up some boys to perform and reproduce violence of economic and military imperialism, they are also prepared for male heterosexual able-bodied narratives, for example, through the control of certain emotions, violent sports, rough play, and so on.

The gendered history of capitalism and capitalist organizations is extremely complex. It involves historical changes in the very forms of social relations, often contradictory social relations, throughout societies. For example, the relation of patriarchal families and the development of factory capitalism is particularly complex and contradictory. On the one hand, the patriarchal family provided a social and economic base for the development of early capitalist economic enterprises; as such, pre-capitalist social forms provided the social infrastructure for later, capitalist social forms. These family forms, though pre-capitalist, have assisted capitalist development through the provision of huge quantities of unpaid labour, as analysed in the domestic labour debate of the 1970s. They have also been of major historical significance in the production and reproduction of gendered divisions of labour, in particular gender segregations and exclusions, in organizations. However, capitalist development and capitalist organizations can be seen as antagonistic to patriarchal family forms. This is summed up in the dictum that capital and capitalists do not care one bit about the sex/gender of workers, as long as they continue to produce surplus value. In this sense capitalism is an historical force which more or less progressively overrides the socio-political significance of the patriarchal family and even gender more generally. The classic patriarchal family can thus be said to be subject to erosion. Such historical 'overcoming' of gender fits with the notion that (working-class) women as members of the proletariat are to be liberated through, first, wage labour and, second, the overthrowing of wage labour. This perspective can slip easily into the assumption that women are peripheral to the ('true') class system (Sydie, 1987: 104). Within both these broad approaches there is a danger that the family may become the unit of analysis into which 'women' disappear (Sydie, 1987: 103).

A rather comparable set of contradictions can be identified in the intersection of sexuality and capitalism. On the one hand, capitalism develops through the perpetuation of gendered hierarchies of heterosexuality, in the family, in capitalist organizations, in the consumer marketplace and in civil society. On the other, capitalism and urbanization together have been major forces undermining heterosexual hegemony (D'Emilio, 1983; D'Emilio and Freedman, 1988). This has occurred in the creation of the social conditions for greater sexual specialization possible within cities and under capitalism; in the creation of the 'pink economy' in cities; and the possibility (perhaps more theoretically than empirically) that capital and capitalists do not care about the sexuality of workers as long as they produce surplus value.

These contradictory relations of gender, sexuality, family and economic class fed directly into the gendered division of labour under capitalism. The specific form of this industrial expansion, of course, changed substantially with the movements from mercantile to factory and industrial capitalism, and from the supersession of primary (mining, fishing, farming, hunting and forestry) industry by manufacturing industry. This secondary industry was intensely gendered and gender segregated throughout its development. In Great Britain in 1871 over 36 per cent of employed women worked in textiles, clothing and footwear industries, as against less than 12 per cent of employed men. Meanwhile, mining and quarrying (6.5 per cent of men:0.3 per cent of women), metals (5.2:0.3), construction (8.9:0.03), and transport and communications (7.3:0.4) were all predominantly employers of men rather than women. By far the largest category of employment for women (46 as against 3.9) was 'miscellaneous services', meaning particularly 'domestic service'.

The gendering of nineteenth-century patriarchal capitalism was not only a question of shifts in the gender division of labour, important though they clearly are. They also extended to the social processes that led to and underlay industrialization, and to the detailed conduct of the labour process itself. The movement of population into urban areas was rapid, and in some cases in the nineteeenth century, especially in Scotland and Ireland, was from effectively feudal conditions of land tenure. Eviction was sometimes brutal and violent, leading to transportation and settlement in the cities. For example, in 1851 all, up to 2,000, of the crofters of the Scottish island of Barra were forcibly evicted, with families broken up and all possessions confiscated, to serve the interests of the owners (Johnson, 1909: 2–4). Meanwhile, capitalist development, particularly in the nineteenth century, produced very great forces for the intensification of the exploitation and oppression of women and children, as well as men, in the labour process of mining and the manufacturing factory system. This was a clearly and openly violent system of economic relations in many cases, not least through the use of violent discipline in the factory. The factory system of the late eighteenth and nineteenth centuries produced appalling working conditions and social conditions more generally, structured by age and gender.

While the degradation of women, children and men, often in aged and gendered workgroups, was horrific, this was not an utterly remorseless process. Indeed the slow process of 'reform' was a bitter testimony to the persistence of these degrading conditions. By the 1830s there were some limited reforms in Great Britain: from 1833 in theory two hours of education was provided for every child in the cotton, wool, worsted and flax industries. The 1842 Mines and Collieries Act excluded women and children from the mines. The 1844 Factories Act sought to regulate women in factories for the first time, but an ambiguity in the wording of the law meant that the case for its enforcement was lost in court in 1850. By then there was still no effective Ten Hours Act and nine-year-old children still worked in the factories. In that year working time was limited to twelve hours; reduced to ten hours in 1874. In 1891 the minimum age for work in factories was set at eleven.

Late nineteenth- and early twentieth-century development can be characterized as the shift from factory capitalism to monopoly capitalism. There are many aspects to this transformation, and all are gendered in significant ways. They include:

- the growth of the scale of production;
- the development of more advanced technologies and mass production;
- the increasing commodification of more spheres and activities;
- the increasing separation of ownership and control;
- the increasing division of labour and diversification of skills and functions;
- the falling rate of profit;
- the internationalization of capital and the growth of imperialism as the general mode of exploitation;
- the growth of the organization of labour, especially through trade unions;
- the extension of limited liability and corporate financial arrangements;
- the extension of vertical and horizontal integration in the economy;
- the increased interlocking of capital and labour. (Hearn, 1992b: 96–7)

An especially important aspect of these gendered changes was the decline of domestic service as a major employer of women and the rise, in Britain and many countries of the North, from the 1870s of the organizational service sector, in the form of office, administrative, typing and clerical work, as well as related tasks such as telephonists (Hearn, 1992b: 150–60). Again, this work sector was intensely gendered, and arguably sexualed too. The ongoing formation and re-formation of gendered divisions of labour in organizations, both as managerially defined in the job and as actually done in everyday practice, is one of the central features of patriarchal capitalist development. As discussed in general terms in relation to the family, there are powerful forces within patriarchal capitalism towards both the reduction and the reinforcement of gendered divisions in work, jobs, employment and unemployment. On the one hand, capital might be expected to move towards equalizing reward according the operation of 'the market'; on the other, capital benefits from market segregation and the maintenance of some (gendered) workers' wages at even lower levels than necessary to produce surplus value.

In some work, organizations and sectors, these gendered processes have been enhanced by the selling of gendered/sexual work/labour and labour-power (Bland et al., 1978; Hearn and Parkin, 1987). While this clearly applies in sex work (Delacoste and Alexander, 1988), there is a very important sense in which this is only the surface of a much larger set of organizations and organizational labour processes. Secretaries, receptionists, television 'hostesses', air cabin staff, salespersons in boutiques are predominantly women, and may often, though not always, involve the selling of sexuality as part of labour-power (Bland et al., 1978; Pringle, 1988). These sexualizing and sexualed organizational processes apply to a considerable range of other work, including publicity 'girls', models, aerobics instructors, keep-fit coaches, sports and body workers, and some face-to-face selling. More recently, they have been documented in the hotel, catering and tourism industries (Adkins, 1995). While most of these kinds of work fall within the service sector, 'customer care' more generally may involve an implicit selling of sexual labour-power.

Recent service industry expansion has been further complicated by the growth of the quarternary information industry in computing, data processing, telephone selling, telecommunications and some forms of education, training and other service and tertiary activities. This opens up the possibility of forms of work that appear to separate sexuality from the labour process; this may be exemplified in telephone-call centres, where the appearance of the operative is completely unavailable to the public-in-contact, making possible all manner of bizarre and 'private' ways of being, dressing and behaving out of the sight of callers. On the other hand, sexuality may 'reappear': in the social relations between workers and managers in the work environment; in the relation between paid work life, home life and leisure; and in the transformation of all manner of personal and social qualities into the voice of the telephone worker. Not only may the voice convey trustworthiness, informativeness and helpfulness (or their absence), but sexuality too.[11]

The key general point is that the idea of the agendered, asexual, aviolenced worker is a fiction; workers and organizational members do not exist in social abstraction; they are gendered, sexualed and violenced, partly by their position and presence, and indeed absence, within gendered, sexualed, violenced organizations.[12] The complexity of these processes of gendered change is illustrated by the transformations of sexuality, particularly heterosexuality, in capitalist organizations in the Industrial Revolution in Britain and the USA, that we briefly introduced at the beginning of the chapter. From the eighteenth century intensification of industrialization was accompanied by increasing concerns with (hetero)sexuality and how to organize it in organizations.

Focus #1: Patriarchal Capitalist Organizational Heterosexualities in the Industrial Revolution

In 1772 the head accounts clerk was sacked by Josiah Wedgewood on the grounds of embezzlement, extravagance and sexual misdemeanours (McKendrick et al., 1983: 61). Considerable debate followed in the early nineteenth century, particularly amongst men, about the dangers of sexuality, especially in relation to women's presence in factories and other relatively large-scale industrial workplaces.

By the 1840s and 1850s the mixing of women and men in workplaces was subject to challenge. Sylvia Walby (1986: 115–16) has characterized the patriarchal nature of dominant discourse, and especially 'the male bourgeoisie's hypocritical stance on female sexuality', at this time:

> Publicly, these men adhered to the condemnation of non-marital sexuality, particularly for women. In so far as conditions in paid work were held to encourage female sexual activity then they were especially condemned. The factories were believed to encourage sexual contact between the female operatives and the male operatives and masters. The wages enabled women to buy drink and consequent drunkenness was also held to encourage 'immorality'. ... The conditions in the mines particularly horrified the Commissioners who investigated them in 1840–2.

The Parliamentary Papers of 1842 (Vol. XV: 24) noted:

> In great numbers of the coal-pits of this district the men work in a state of perfect nakedness and are in this state assisted in their labour by females of all ages, from girls of six years old to women of twenty-one, these females themselves being quite naked from the waist down.[13]

Walby continues:

> The presence of men and women together working in near darkness was held to be an invitation for all sorts of immoral practices. The commission was obsessed with the sexual conduct of the colliery women ... . Behaviours such as drunkenness, immodesty and profanity were also held to indicate the likelihood of promiscuity. The Commissioners focused on this aspect of women's work underground to the neglect of other aspects such as physical suffering. There are continual references to the state of undress that the male and female workers are to be found in. (1986: 115–16)

These kinds of debates, though dealing with very different kinds of workplaces, have some interesting parallels with men's concerns later in the century with the entrance of women into office work in both the capitalist and state sectors. A fascinating account of these processes is provided by Cindy Sondik Aron (1987) in her detailed documentary study of federal government offices in the United States from 1860 to 1900. In 1864, only three years after women had been appointed as clerks in the Treasury Department, a special congressional committee was instituted to investigate 'certain charges against the Treasury Department'. This reported that some men supervisors had sexually harassed and propositioned women clerks. This fed into contemporary fears that it was such employment that corrupted women. This sentiment was expressed in the book, *The Sights and Sounds of the National Capital*, published in 1869 by John Ellis:'The acceptance of a Government Clerkship by a woman is her first step on the road to ruin.'

According to Aron (1987: 169):

> These working women posed an enormous challenge to the Victorian middle class because they threatened to invalidate the standards by which middle-class society judged a woman's character ... . Where male and female spheres remained distinct, society [men?] could easily distinguish the 'good' from the 'bad'. Respectable ladies exercised great care, especially when outside their homes, churches, or schoolrooms, to follow rules of decorum that guaranteed their reputation as virtuous women. But those women who left their sphere, flouted the rules, and placed themselves in compromising situations ... .

This can be compared with the situation that was developing in the Post Office in Great Britain about the same time:

> [I]n 1872 the Post Office experimented in employing male and female staff and putting them in the same room. 'It was considered to be a hazardous experiment' wrote a senior official at the time, 'but we have never had reason to regret having tried it ... it raises the tone of the male staff by confining them during many hours of the day to a decency of conversation and demeanour which is not always to be found where men alone are employed.' (Delgado, 1979: 39)

Such delicate concerns existed alongside the possibility of developing a public discourse in favour of such 'decency' in both offices and factories.

As a last example, we consider a case from 1891–2. This was from an industrial setting again – this time a weaving mill in Nelson, Lancashire. It concerned the public responses – from workers, owners and community religious leaders, from Nelson and beyond – to the sexually violent actions of an overlooker, one Houghton Greenwood. The report of the committee of inquiry of local churchmen concluded:

> As rumours of a very odious character respecting Houghton Greenwood are in circulation it is necessary and only just to him to state that no charge of actual adultery has been made against him, and that there was nothing in the evidence to show that such a charge could have been made. The offences complained of by the Weavers' Committee were not of so serious a character; they accused him exclusively of language and conduct tending to immorality. After most carefully and thoughtfully weighing up all the evidence brought before us on both sides, during an investigation extending over four days we are reluctantly compelled to come to the conclusion that Houghton Greenwood has been guilty, first of making immoral proposals to a married woman, and secondly, of using indecent language to other females ... . It was with the deepest regret that we learned during the inquiry that the offences of which we have been compelled to adjudge Houghton Greenwood guilty, are not uncommon among men who have the oversight of the female operatives in other mills, and as ministers of religion, we most earnestly appeal to the employers of labour to practically recognise their duty in this matter and to seriously consider how essential it is to the happiness and well being of those under their charge as well as to their own credit to make the moral conduct of their workpeople a subject of nearer concern and of greater importance. We also wish to state that in our opinion the action of the Weavers Union in endeavouring to guard the morals of the workpeople is highly commendable ... .[14]

While it is unclear from the records available exactly what subsequently happened to Greenwood, the events show possible responses to harassment at the time.[15]

What can be deduced about gendered/sexualed/violenced organizations from this focus material? First, to state the obvious, concerns with sexuality in organizations are not new; they have been part and parcel of the modern collectivizing processes of work, employment and organization. Second, these organizational changes were characteristically ambiguous: both formal and desexualizing, and informal and sexualizing; both heterosexual and homosocial; both involving routine sexual harassment and recognizing such behaviour as illegitimate. Third, recognition of sexual harassment and intervention against it may often go hand in hand in the same public discourse. Fourth, some interesting comparisons can be made with commentaries on women in the office and management in the twentieth century. Calás and Smircich (1993: 75–6) have discussed how in 1935 the presence of women in offices as secretaries was analysed by *Fortune* magazine in terms of 'the relation of sex' and the imitation of marriage: 'women occupy the office because the male employer wants them there'; 'women of the office have won their place not by competition with men but by the exercise of qualities with which no competition was possible ...' (see Pringle, 1988). By the 1970s the 'women in management' literature (Bradford et al., 1975) discussed how women's sexuality may disrupt men's established homosocial patterns in management (cf. Roper, 1996).

The State and the Nation-State

Nation, State and Organizations

This section examines the relation of nation, state and organizations; it is concluded by focus material on British state and welfare organizational responses to men's violence to women and children. The state and the nation-state provide an important, and probably increasingly important, historical context for the understanding of organizations. Mainstream or malestream (O'Brien, 1981) debates on the state have frequently ignored gender relations, let alone sexuality and gendered/sexual violence, and have instead through their own practices reproduced patriarchal social relations (Burstyn, 1983). Indeed until the development of feminist scholarship,[16] debates on the state usually meant debates by men on men. State theory has been dominated by two major, usually agendered, traditions – liberal and Marxist.[17] To bring gender, sexuality and gendered/sexual violence to these questions more fully certainly does not mean expanding these agendered traditions; nor does it mean increasing the presence of men in theorizing; it does, however, mean theorizing men more critically and more explicitly. Men need to be analysed, like women, as gendered 'actors', in both theory and practice. This also means increasing women's presence within analysis, as theorists, actors and subjects of analysis, and explicitly gendering the relationship of women, men, state and citizenship. One part of this is to analyse the major forms of organizational relations to the (patriarchal) state – within (which part of) the state, on the periphery of the state, funded by the state, and so on.

The nation-state has been characteristically patriarchal; it has been intimately and dominantly associated with the construction of (some) men as citizens and (some) women sometimes as citizens. For example, one might consider men's relations to state formation, governmental centralization and expansion, the 'national economy', the national military–industrial complex, state–capital alliances, political participation and political enfranchisement of both women and men. The nation-state has been (represented as) a powerful centre of men's actions. Political development of the nation has often been men's preserve, or at least profoundly dominated by men until relatively recently. This is to be seen in the 'award' of suffrage by men to women, in men's domination of the law, military, the police, the civil service, the state machinery, parliaments and autocracies, and so on (Hearn, 1992b). The state, through the operation of civil law, family law, property law, population registration and numerous social and other policy regulations and procedures has, especially over the last two hundred years and now increasingly so, devised, sanctioned, constructed, constrained and determined what gendered citizens are. Men's actual, potential or absent citizenship has been developed and is maintained in relation to women. Above all there has persisted the pervasive assumption, influence and power of the enfranchised, autonomous, adult, heterosexual, married, fathering, family-heading, individual, male subject – a 'collective individual' both within and outside the state.

Historically, men have often acted in their collective interests as husbands, fathers, workers and managers, and occasionally acted against those interests, placing women's interests more highly. Histories of the state can be re-read not just in terms of the extension of agendered citizenship but as accounts in which men and women have different locations, positions and interests, as citizens, politicians, workers, managers, professionals, fathers/mothers, welfare recipients, and so on (Hernes, 1988a, 1988b; Borchorst, 1990, 1994). State development thus links with dominant assumptions on the social position and responsibilities of women and men as mothers, fathers, wives, husbands, housewives and 'bread-winners'. Women's and men's relations to citizenship, state and nation are thus far from uniform; in particular we might explicitly highlight men as controllers of the state, as the dominant group in the reproduction of political regimes, as adult male citizens, as fathers and as those (immigrant, black, young, homeless, and so on) excluded as citizens. Generally gendered conceptualizations of state and welfare are usually saying something about women and men in three main ways – in families (particularly the heterosexual family), in paid work and in the state (particularly as managers and decision-makers about welfare). Less usual, even in these gendered models, are commentaries on men or women managing the institutions of capital or outside the heterosexual family (for example, lesbian, gay or bisexual). This is even though many, perhaps most, states may be characterized as heterosexual and heterosexist.

The growth of the modern state is also fundamental to the construction of men's and women's relations to the nation – or more specifically the complex relations of country (space), state (political, legal and administrative authority) and nation (culture and ideology) (Yuval-Davis, 1997). The growth of the modern European nation-state can be seen as a move from indirect to direct rule. With indirect rule, a combination of urban militias, private armies of regional lords and rulers and feudal levies operated. Charles Tilly (1992: 179)[18] points out:

> (f)or several centuries before about 1750, the most effectively armed European states were those that could rent the most mercenary troops. Mercenaries – drawn especially from militarized and land-poor peasant regions such as Ireland, Scotland, Switzerland, Hesse, and Croatia – reached their European heyday in the sixteenth and seventeenth centuries, then began to lose ground in the eighteenth century, and had become insignificant with the Napoleonic wars.

During the seventeenth and eighteenth centuries, 'national' 'rulers turned away from the episodic use of militias and mercenary forces for warfare, trying instead to staff standing armies from their own populations [i.e. men] and to force the civilians in their own populations [i.e. women and men] to pay for the armies routinely and well' (Tilly, 1992: 178).

Increasingly, the implicit strategy of national rulers appeared to be the granting of national rights of proto-citizenship to a minimum set of people, that is, certain men, in a way that would guarantee the delivery of military resources to the state, as well as collaborating with the relatively privileged in exploiting and repressing almost all women and most men (see Tilly, 1992: 181). In one sense this model only expanded by degree with the *male* bourgeois revolutions of the mid-nineteenth century; but in another way there were important qualitative shifts during the early nineteenth century with the development of more intensive negotiations, involving legislatures, ministers and monarchs, over military expenditures. In the post-Napoleonic period the male European bourgeoisie were still sharply differentiated from workers but they were also engaged in contributing to a more general historical process whereby civil rights could be enlarged. Male suffrage was gradually extended during the nineteenth century, though it was not until 1867 that substantial numbers of male British workers were able to vote in national elections (Hearn, 1992b: 128ff.).

By the late nineteenth century, the state and its male managers were less preoccupied with the earlier problem of military expenditures and were turning their attention to much broader agendas, in response to the growing male citizenry. In the Bismarckian case, the newly formed male German state pre-empted the emerging negotiations between male workers, male capitalists and the male state itself, by installing a remarkable social contract from the top down. In Great Britain and elsewhere economic, social and welfare reform through the state was accompanied by slow organizational modernizations of both proto-national police forces and the military itself (Hearn, 1992b: 133–6). What are usually called rights of national citizenship can be located within a set of complex class, gendered and racialized histories, in which gendered violence has had a special place. It is upon this foundation that the state and the award of national rights of citizenship have been developed and extended. Men's, and in a different way women's, relation to the state, and to an extent country and nation, has been strongly mediated by the performance and control of violence, the construction of, obedience to and breaking of the law, the commitment to defend the country, and in turn to the institution of compulsory conscription. Gendered citizens' relation to the state, citizenship, rights and welfare can be connected to debates around the nation, national crises and particularly war, and the collective willingness or ability to enlarge the state and develop the welfare state. Wars and the ends of wars have been important times for social change and indeed political mobilization, with, for example, the granting of women's suffrage after the First World War in many countries and the introduction of welfare reforms after the Second World War. The welfare state and the warfare state have frequently grown together.

In a variety of ways the modern state has become a major controller of violence and potential violence, and a major producer of violence, injury, fear, torture and death. The scale of man-made (*sic*) death, often organized quite specifically by states, parastates and counter-states, is difficult to appreciate. Men have dominated these individual and collective actions, though of course women's and indeed children's place in such violence should not be ignored. The extreme case might appear to be the destructive machinery of the state under the Nazi regime of the Third Reich, with millions killed at Auschwitz-Birkenau and other concentration camps. However, there are many other examples of mass persecutions and destruction of people by states in recent history, in the Soviet Union, China, South East Asia and Central Africa, as well as relatively smaller scale genocides and sexual violences in Sri Lanka, the former Yugoslavia and elsewhere (Sluka, 2000). Writing in 1972, Gil Elliot calculated that in the twentieth century alone up to that point there had been 110 million man-made deaths, including 62 million by various forms of privation (death camps, slave labour, forced marches, imprisonment), 46 million from guns and bombs, and 2 million from chemicals (Elliot, 1972).[19] Suppiramaniam Nanthikesan (1999: 46) has noted how: 'recent conflicts around the globe show a trend of worsening situations in the form of deaths and injury for civilians during the conflict ....'[20] In 1998, 103 million people were affected by complex human emergencies ...[21] and at risk of death from starvation and disease'. A particular challenge is to bring together the analysis of these different kinds of violence, such as military violence, civilian devastation, rape and violence to women in the home.

The construction of men in and around the state, country and nation has often been very closely allied to the development of state violence and militarism, and the reproduction of men's violence. David Morgan (1994) has examined the interconnections between militarism and dominant (and occasionally counter-) forms of masculinities. He stresses the ways in which both the 'boundedness' and the 'pervasiveness' of the military/militarism seem to be strongly linked to its coding as masculine. While connections between militarism and masculinism have been remarkably persistent historically, new associations may be developing in 'post-militarist' societies.

In addition, these historical interrelations of masculinities, militarism and violence should not obscure the significance of women's military activity in particular times and places. In discussing the legendary Amazons of the kingdom of Dahomey, Ann Oakley (1972: 145) notes that: 'In 1845 it was estimated that, out of an army [of the king] of twelve thousand, five thousand were women ... armed with blunderbusses, muskets, and knives with eighteen inch blades ...' Women's involvement in more recent nation-formation, for example, in revolutionary struggles against colonial, imperialist and other powers, has also often been formidable, only for it to be undermined with the movement to 'peacetime' (Knauss, 1987). 'In the 1941 Yugoslav Liberation war ... around 100,000 women carried arms as active fighters, 25,000 were killed in action, 40,000 were wounded, and 3,000 became disabled, pensionable veterans' (Oakley, 1972: 145). In the Algerian Liberation war over 10,000 women took part in the struggle, of whom a fifth suffered imprisonment or death.

At the same time, the state is involved in another set of relations to violence and men's violence, namely that of (usually limited) control. An arena of special importance in charting these changing relations of gender, sexuality, violation and organizations are state and other organizational responses to men's violence to women and children. The historical context is especially important in understanding how such violence has been accepted, condoned, normalized and ignored, by both individuals and institutions. It has often been seen as a 'private matter', especially with men's violence to wives and other known women. Recent, increasing recognition of the problem by state agencies has arisen partly from the actions of the Women's Movement and partly from pressure via the UN and other international bodies, which gives such opposition to violence more mainstream political legitimacy.

Focus #2: UK State and Welfare Organizational Responses to Men's Violence to Women and Children

Modern British state intervention in the family can be dated from at least the mid-eighteenth century with the 1753 Hardwicke Act depriving betrothal of legal status, and closing legal, if not practical, access to clandestine marriage. State intervention in the family was initially dispersed and minimalist. Religion, medicine, science, law and welfare reform have all been important in stipulating 'correct' forms of the patriarchal family (as in the Marriage Act of 1836 and five subsequent Matrimonial Causes Acts up to 1895). State interventions have increased in both biological fatherhood (especially the recording of paternity and population censuses) and social fatherhood (especially the assignment of authority as 'head of the family', ownership of children and financial responsibilities). The state has become involved in an increasing range of ways in the construction of the family. Relatively rapid change in the accumulation of state powers occurred in the 1830s. The 1833 Factory Act began the regulation of child labour and as such was one of the first state interventions against fathers' authority; and the Education Act of the same year began government grants for education. From 1839 the rights of fathers over legitimate children was no longer seen as absolute, even though women and children remained the property of the husband/father until 1857.

At the same time, the state was also becoming more active in the construction of the family through limited intervention against men's violence in the family, though often only in a negative sense (Hearn, 1992b, 1996b). In 1853 the British Parliament passed the Act for the Better Prevention and Punishment of Aggravated Assaults upon Women and Children, but this '. . . did very little to deter husbands from abusing their wives and children' (Steiner-Scott, 1997: 127). The basic Act of Parliament that defines violence to the person is the Offences Against the Person Act, 1861, covering common assault, assault occasioning actual bodily harm, unlawful wounding and grievous bodily harm. However, this Act could not be said to operate in relation to men's violence to known women until subsequent reforms in the nineteenth and twentieth centuries. The extension of the criminal law into the field of wilful child neglect began with the Poor Law Amendment Act of 1868.

Significantly, the 1878 reform of the legal treatment of men's violence to women within marriage followed shortly after the Cruelty to Animals Act of 1876. Previously, the 'rule of thumb' had operated in the courts, whereby husbands were not permitted to use a stick broader than a thumb. The 1878 Matrimonial Causes Act allowed women to use cruelty as grounds for divorce. Magistrates were given powers to grant swift, cheap separation orders to women who could prove a specific incident of physical assault.

State law began to claim, if only in word, some jurisdiction over men's/ husbands'/fathers' violence, and so make distinctions, if only implicitly, between violence and sexuality in marriage, and violence and authority in childrearing. Controlling husbands' and fathers' violence is a fundamental aspect of constructing men's power more generally. Indeed, men's perceptions of violence to women are themselves affected by the definitions and constructions produced and reproduced in agencies.

At an 1882 meeting of the Liverpool Society of the Prevention of Cruelty to Animals, the suggestion was made to form a parallel society for the prevention of cruelty to children, which was instituted in 1883. In 1889 a further Poor Law Amendment Act gave poor law guardians powers over children in their control on all matters except religious upbringing. Also in 1889 the National Society for the Prevention of Cruelty to and Protection of Children was established, and in the same year the Protection of Children Act was passed – in effect the first 'Children's Charter'. This made it a misdemeanour to wilfully ill-treat, neglect or abandon a boy under 14 or a girl under 16 in a manner that was likely to cause unnecessary suffering or injury to health (Eekelaar, 1978: 68). The NSPCC grew rapidly with local branches managed by local committees and by 1909 250 inspectors operating nationwide as a buffer between committees and clientele, with 'drunkenness, accompanying dirt and squalor, accounting for a large share of the neglect' (Ferguson, 1990). State intervention in child welfare was codified in the 1908 Children Act, with the appointment of infant life protection workers and formal delegation of state powers to the NSPCC, as part of the wider Liberal Government social reforms from 1906.

Men's violence to women was an important focus of attention in both First Wave feminism (see Cobbe, 1878, 1894; Pankhurst, 1913) and Second Wave feminism (see, for example, The Bristol Women's Studies Group, 1979; Coote and Campbell, 1982). A number of British legal reforms around marriage were introduced towards the end of the nineteenth century. These included the Married Women's Property Act 1870, giving wives the right to keep their own earnings; the Married Women's Property Act 1882, introducing women's rights to keep property they owned in marriage or acquired later; the Maintenance of Wives Act 1886, empowering local magistrates to grant and enforce maintenance orders of no more than two pounds per week; and the Summary Jurisdiction (Married Women) Act 1895, easing women's protection from the court following persistent, rather than a specific, physical cruelty. In 1891, husbands lost their 'rights' to forcibly imprison their wife in the matrimonial home to obtain their 'conjugal rights' (R v Jackson, Court of Appeal, 1891), and the Custody of Children Act introduced the concept of 'unfit parenthood', usually in effect meaning motherhood.

Despite these reforms and moves towards formal equalization of women's and men's property rights in marriage, by the end of the nineteenth century in practice little had shifted men's authority relations over women and children in marriage. Husbands' and fathers' day-to-day domination and authority was routinely reinforced by the state, for example in the police avoidance of intervention in 'marital disputes'. Women's position was also generally weak in divorce proceedings and the award and receipt of maintenance (Brophy and Smart, 1982: 210). While the picture was mixed, late nineteenth-century reforms clarified the criminal law and shifted the family into the purview of the modern state. Second Wave feminism led to the reappraisal of legal responses to violence. However, even in 1967 when the first Matrimonial Homes Act was passed, 'matrimonial violence was a non-subject' (Freeman, 1987: 38). The Act was designed to preserve the rights of occupation of the non-owning and non-tenant spouse rather than to respond to violence. Following the establishment of the Women's Aid Federation in 1974 and the Parliamentary Select Committee on Violence in Marriage (Report from the Select Committee, 1975), the Domestic Violence and Matrimonial Proceedings Act was passed in 1976, giving additional powers of injunction, including for the unmarried, and of arrest. Subsequent reforms, such as the Matrimonial Homes Act 1983 strengthening the power of the ouster order, still, however, failed to produce a fundamental reform of state intervention in favour of women's freedom from violence (Binney et al., 1981; Atkins and Hoggett, 1984).

In recent years, there have been uneven attempts to reform British state policy and its implementation – in police forces with the enactment of 'domestic violence' pro-arrest policies; the policy of treating violence equally seriously regardless of its location or the relationship of the parties; and the creation of special units. Other state agencies, notably the Probation Service and the Crown Prosecution Service, have also given recent attention to this problem. The state, and particularly state agencies controlled by men, has made a series of concessions in response to men's violence to women, and particularly the action of Women's Aid. The state has sponsored particular social forms within the private domain. Increasingly, and rather gradually, the private powers of individual men have been brought into the purview, and sometimes the control, of the state. While legal and other state constructions of violence have generally played down its significance and limited its definition, at the same time awareness and recognition of the problem in law, policy statements and to an extent in implementation has gradually increased.

This material tells us several things about organizations and their responses to violence. First, it illustrates the historical contingency of definitions of, constructions of and responses to violence; and how these in turn impact on those of individuals leading their own lives. Second, the unevenness and variability of responses are apparent. Third, organizations are themselves not unified or monolithic; they harbour their own struggles and tensions, not least between policy formulation, implementation and agency practice. Fourth, these historical shifts point to the often intricate ways in which the material occurrence, experience and indeed pain of violence is interconnected with the discursive constructions of violence, not least by state agencies. These can literally be matters of life and death.

The Past in the Present

These observations on time and histories are of course not purely about the historical past; they are of continuing importance in contextualizing organizations in the present. Importantly, recent historical change has involved a combination of contradictory socio-political processes around gender, sexuality and violation in organizations: both greater awareness of gendered inequalities and the reinforcement of gendered patterns; of both sexualization and desexualization, so that organizations are becoming both more sexualized and less sexualized; and of both more explicit attempts to counter violence and the production of new and sometimes more subtle forms of violence and abuse in organizations.

These contradictory processes are especially profound when considered on the transnational and global scale.

While we have throughout this chapter approached location and context through history, there are many ways in which such historical location and context persist in the social construction of individuals in organizations. Historical location affects how individuals exist in and are formed in organizations. This raises issues around identity and subjectivity, such as: is the individual recognizable as a unified subject, or is it more accurate to speak of a deconstructed subject? Such questions are especially important when one tries to locate oneself within an organization where one works or one has a close knowledge of in some other way. One can ask what is your own historical context? What is the relation of the observer to the organization? Who are you when you are trying to locate yourself – as a member, an observer, an analyst, a researcher, a student, a worker, a newcomer, a client, a member of the public, and so on? How does this affect what you know, and can know and not know?

Finally, historical location and context is integral to understanding the changing recognition of violence and violation, both generally in society and specifically in organizations. It is thus to this historical process of recognition that we now turn.

3

Recognition

From Sexual Harassment, Bullying and Physical Violence to Organization Violations

The Recognition of Violation[1]

While gender and sexuality have been relatively neglected in mainstream organization studies, violence and violation have been even further marginalized there. It is in this context that the remainder of this book focuses on the relationships of violence, violation and organizations, and an analytical perspective on organizations through the lens of violence and violation. This chapter continues the historical trajectory of the previous, in focusing on contemporary organizational processes of recognition, and hence the importance of everyday and media sources.

Sexual harassment, bullying and physical violence do not 'just happen'. They are formed within complex organizational processes of recognition and response, and form part of the wider politics of and struggles for recognition that have become central in contemporary political movements.[2] The recognition of harassment, bullying and violence occurs within definite, yet changing, historical social relations. Whereas many struggles for recognition have been characterized by the formation of collective groupings of those in similar social situations, with the recognition of violence and violation, this has been more difficult. This is not only because of the relative isolation of many victims and survivors of violation in organizations, the damaging effects of violation and even the sense of shame and self-blame that can accompany it, but also because of the complex ways in which violence and violation contradict dominant ideological constructions of most organizations. Apart from those organizations and organizational members, usually men, who live by violence and who take their violence completely for granted, for most organizations and organizational members there is a degree of ambivalence, embarrassment, shame and seeking for justification in doing and disclosing violence (Johnson, 1986). Thus ambiguity can pervade violence: its doing, accounting for, reduction and stopping.

Processes of recognition of violence and violation are diverse; they involve the actions of members, managers, clients, journalists, activists, professionals, agencies and researchers. These organizational processes also encompass the forms of their own reproduction, and practices of naming and managing, such as policy documentation, grievance procedures and implementation. The processes by which violence and violation becomes recognized, named, problematized and managed within specific organizations remain under-researched. This involves different social processes in contrasting workplaces where issues of violence have or could come to the fore. Violences may be seen as problematic, may be contested or may be apparent (to observers or other outsiders) but not problematized within organizations.

Organizational differences include how violence is defined, named and dealt with by procedures, external interventions or other means, and contrasts between policies and everyday practices. While documentary evidence is important, the perceptions and experiences of individuals also need emphasis. Organizational members are likely to differentially experience the nature, extent and effects of violence; the relationship of the violator and the violated; organizational policies, reporting and support systems. Multiple definitions and understandings of violence are endemic. Perceptions and descriptions of acts as 'violence' and their problematization, whether by organizations or members, often imply theorizing causation, whether in individual or social forces. Everyday understandings of violence are linked to worldviews and models of human behaviour. Problematizations of violence, including accounts of causation, often include proposals for dealing with it and attempts to contain or reduce it.

Though there is a growing recognition of violence in and around contemporary organizations, it cannot be concluded that there is more violence in any absolute sense. In organizations, as elsewhere, the doing of violence affects the construction of violence, the recognition of violence and what counts as violence in the first place. The more that violence is done, the greater the intensity of violence and the more that violence is likely to be taken for granted. As more violence is done, the threshold of what counts as violence rises. As violence is subject to social disapproval, raising the threshold of what violence 'is' discounts at least some violence from consideration and dispute. In this sense, with more violence, less awareness of violence is likely: violence becomes normalized. With greater awareness of violence, the more that violence is likely to be identified. Doing violence may be followed by its recognition, complaint, contestation over the complaint, including *further dynamics of violation*.

An important issue in the moving threshold of violence is the extent to which it is conscious. Doing violence may objectify the receiver of violence, and in a different sense desensitize the doer of violence. For violence to continue the doer may become less conscious of himself and his bodily force, which may become naturalized and increasingly, with greater, more repeated violence, taken for granted. Consciousness of violence can change with telling of organizational stories about violence, usually around specific events. In such scenarios, specific violences, or accounts thereof, can become critical incidents with the development of organizational consciousness of violence. There is, however, the paradox that re-telling organizational stories of violence may lead to distancing from violence. In some contexts re-telling may involve taking on others' accounts and recounting them. In certain contexts professionalizations of accounts of violence are important, especially for those routinely dealing with violence. Processes of re-telling critical incidents are even more important when the violence is defined as 'serious'. Such series of events and experiences before, during and after violence form the recognition of violences.

The Separation of Sexual Harassment, Bullying and Physical Violence

Sexual harassment, bullying and physical violence in organizations have generally been seen as separate issues rather than functions of each other or overlapping forms of violation. There are often problems in clearly separating harassment, bullying and physical violence, with physical violence often being a feature of both harassment and bullying. Although there are problems with making firm distinctions between sexual harassment, bullying and physical violence, we will initially focus on each as we recognize these are usually separate foci of research and organizational policies. Also research and policies are at different stages with most recent research on bullying and physical violence in organizations comprising empirical surveys. There have been few conceptual or theoretical studies of the relationship between them, linking them to wider issues of power in organizations.

Sexual harassment, bullying and physical violence in organizations can all be seen as part of the unspoken processes of intimidation and violation that are slowly emerging into public awareness. Although not always linked with gender and sexuality, there are clear connections with the wider gendering and sexualing of organizations. Bullying cannot be divorced from the structures and hierarchies of power of the organization, particularly structures of management which are in turn gendered and sexualed. The analysis of sexual harassment, bullying and physical violence in organizations needs to locate them in the context of managerial practices and organizational power. This involves the examination of organizational responses and the outcomes of these processes in terms of both the manifestation of violence and the impact of procedures used to manage it. Managerial responses are particularly important since they may help to reduce it but can also exacerbate its impact.

The state of the art, or what is considered as such, is rather different in the three areas of sexual harassment, bullying and physical violence. Reading some texts on each area, one gets little sense of the insights provided in the others. This partly stems from the different constructions of the victims/survivors of sexual harassment, bullying and physical violence. Different 'constituencies' or 'communities' (or lack thereof) of victims/survivors are constructed for 'sexual harassment', 'bullying' and 'physical violence' in organizations. In none of these cases has there been a clear social movement of those with similar experiences. Comparison can be made with relatively isolated proto-movements, such as those based on age or disability groupings.[3]

While sexual harassment, bullying and violence are generally compartmentalized and categorized separately, our approach here is to first explore each in turn before examining similarities and differences and see them all as violations.

Focus material on sexual harassment in the police and business, bullying in the military, and violence in air travel is examined. This illustrates the ongoing prevalence and harm of each, particularly the difficulties of 'speaking' them and keeping them 'spoken' in the face of organizational pressures to silence them or see them as 'normal' aspects of workplace 'culture'. This material shows the interconnections of harassment, bullying and violence, and their relations to the power of gender and sexuality in organizations, particularly within management.

The Recognition of Harassment and Sexual Harassment

The recognition of harassment and sexual harassment is a contradictory process: the continuing lack of its recognition and its growing recognition are in constant tension. Interestingly, sexual harassment is the only one of the three realms of experience (with bullying and physical violence) that is explicitly gendered and sexualed. It includes both physical and non-physical violations. It was also the realm most widely recognized earliest in organizations. From the mid-1970s sexual harassment was recognized and analysed in journalistic, campaign, research and policy literature. Research included surveys, qualitative studies, legal investigations and studies of imaginary cases. Sexual harassment has been linked to broad gendered organizational analysis, and recently comparative analysis has increased.

An important part of recognition concerns language, as in the use of the language of 'sex' and 'conquest' in business and other organizational discourse. Heterosexuality is often embedded within metaphorical and literal gendered language and action within gendered organizations. In business organizations there is talk of *penetrating* markets (Hearn and Parkin, 1987; Collinson and Hearn, 1996); in military organizations recruits are encouraged to be more 'masculine' or derided by superiors as 'poofs' or 'women' (Addelston and Stiratt, 1996), both terms refering to 'weak', passive feminine sexuality and presence. The language of male control merges with the language of men's domination within organizations. The question of language becomes clearer when one notes the different conceptualizations of the problem of harrassment in different languages. For example, in Sweden and Finland there has been concern with the problem of sexual harassment from the late 1970s and early 1980s, and this has led to rather different emphases from the UK and North American debate.[4]

As more cases have come to public awareness through tribunals and courts, it could be argued that this constitutes growing recognition and greater opportunity to gain redress. Increasing numbers of harassment cases feature in the media, with some women winning substantial compensation for damage to health and loss of jobs. There is also increasing recognition of the high personal health cost in the process of bringing a claim before courts or tribunals. Those cases that are brought to law are the tip of a very large iceberg. For every such case there are countless women suffering from harassment, not daring to speak out or speaking out and suffering further. So why add further focus material in this chapter? This is for four reasons: to demonstrate the ongoing nature of the problem in spite of action against it; to consider the form and impact of media reports of it; to explore links between sexual harassment and bullying; and to make explicit the violation of harassment.

It is difficult to identify a comprehensive list of behaviours that could unequivocally be termed sexual harassment. However, it is possible to describe the sorts of behaviour usually seen as harassment. A typical list would include: 'physical conduct such as touching, pinching, physical actions which intimidate or embarrass (leering, whistling, suggestive gestures), physical sexual advances and assault; verbal conduct, such as statements which are experienced as insults, jokes of a derogatory nature, threatening or obscene language, verbal sexual advances; offensive materials which are seen to degrade or offend such as pornographic pictures, badges or graffiti' (Collier, 1995: 4). The main issue in definition is how the behaviour is *perceived and received* by the individual; it is harassment if it is felt to be so by the recipient. Rubenstein defines it as 'unwanted conduct of a sexual nature or conduct based on sex which is offensive to the recipient' (1992: 2). The European Commission's Code of Practice (1991) similarly notes that 'it is for each individual to determine what behaviour is acceptable to them and what they regard as offensive. It is the unwanted nature of the conduct which distinguishes sexual harassment from friendly behaviour which is welcome and mutual' (Collier, 1995: 3). Sexual harassment has wide-ranging consequences, ranging from women feeling ashamed and humiliated, to loss of confidence, becoming physically or mentally ill, loss of work through illness and leaving jobs.

There is now a proliferation of discourses on sexual harassment – organizational, managerial, policy, trade union, feminist, quantitative, and so on. High levels of harassment have been reported in many surveys worldwide. It has also been argued that all women experience sexual harassment (Wise and Stanley, 1987). Despite this, the dominant discourse is still probably that of the isolated harasser harassing the isolated victim. The experience is dominantly constructed as an intermittent behavioural harassing act rather than a process over time. The harassed person, usually a woman, is not generally constructed as identifying as a victim/survivor of harassment, as is with some other forms of sexual violence. There is still a stigma, sometimes couched in the spoken or unspoken question: 'Did she encourage him?' These constructions inhibit the formation of explicit collectivities of survivors. Thus, sexual harassment is often seen as a problem of the individual(s) concerned rather than a problem of workplaces. Since the late 1970s and early 1980s analyses of sexual harassment have sometimes placed it within a broad framework of gendered power relations. MacKinnon (1979: 1) defines sexual harassment in terms of its link to the power of men's heterosexuality: 'sexual harassment ... refers to the unwanted imposition of sexual requirements in the context of a relationship of unequal power. Central to the concept is the use of power derived from one social sphere to lever benefits or impose deprivations in another ... when one is sexual, the other material, the cumulative sanction is particularly potent.' Sedley and Benn (1982) emphasize that 'sexual harassment is to do with men exercising power over women in the workplace. This is a reflection of our male dominated society.' These general features are to be seen no more clearly than in sexual harassment in the police.

Focus #3: Sexual Harassment in the Police

Many recent examples of sexual harassment have been reported in work environments, such as the police, that have long been male preserves. Sexual harassment in the police has attracted a great deal of public attention in many parts of the world.[5] This has taken the form of research surveys, high-profile media investigations and individual scandals, as illustrated by the following three examples of media reports of sexual harassment in British police forces.

In 1996 a judge halted the trial of a police officer accused of indecent assault on the grounds that it should not have come to court but instead the officer should have been given a 'sound ticking off' (Bellos, 1996). The police officer had grabbed a colleague's breasts. The female officer involved said that bawdy police banter was common and did not particularly upset her but his actions in grabbing her breasts went a step further. The judge also commented that the actions of the police officer stemmed from the sort of behaviour 'that people are liable to indulge in when there is a lot of tension around'. He added that he thought that no serious purpose was being served by airing what goes on in busy police stations and it could do the police more harm than good.

This illustrates the powerlessness of those challenging from within and the difficulties of speaking out. It parallels the way in which women rape victims are treated. It also suggests some solidarity between the male judge and the police officers involved in excusing and finding acceptable explanations for men's violence.

A woman police training officer became a 'broken woman' after falling foul of a culture of ingrained racism and sexism in the force. After she spoke out about it she was hounded to the brink of nervous collapse. In addition to explicit sexual taunts and challenges she was passed over for promotion in favour of men with less experience than she had. After a successful tribunal appeal she was reinstated but when she returned to the job her life was made intolerable and she was invalided out of the force (Lacey, 1999).

Another woman police training officer with 26 years in the force said she had been refused promotion for being a woman and had experienced inappropriate racist and sexist language so many times it would be difficult to put a number to it. She said there was an understanding among her 600 women colleagues that it was not done to complain about any of the 4,600 male officers and an acceptance that this is the way it is (Wainwright, 1996).

These extracts fit a more general picture. In researching how the police deal with complaints of sexual assaults, Gregory and Lees (1999) identified a powerful male, racist culture. They investigated whether sexual harassment and bullying were more prevalent or more severe in environments that are atypical for women.[6] The need to 'fit' into men's cultures can mean that the process of proving oneself entails being seen as being able to 'take it': 'It was ... very much a case of equality for women on men's terms; those women who could emulate male working patterns had the best chance of surviving as police officers' (p. 27).

While such strong male cultures persist 'women officers are confronted by an impossible dilemma: they either become defeminized or deprofessionalized. If they perform their work competently, they are no longer seen as women; if they adopt subordinate roles and collude with male definitions of male and female roles they cannot fulfil their potential as police officers' (p. 28). A similar study of the Royal Ulster Constabulary, cited by Gregory and Lees, concluded that policewomen either became 'one of the boys' or they became victims, 'suffering in silence' (p. 28). 'Those who accepted the female role as defined for them by the occupational culture merely succeeded in attracting even more sexual horseplay from the men' (p. 28). It is necessary to consider the impact of atypical gendered positionings, jobs and practices. Women in atypical gendered jobs such as police are likely to be subject to more bullying and harassment through the excuse of adjustment to masculine norms.

Gregory and Lees (1999) cite Anderson et al.'s (1993) study of 1,800 policewomen in which nearly all had experienced some form of sexual harassment. Thirty per cent had experienced unwanted touching or pinching by fellow officers in the previous six months and 6 per cent had suffered serious sexual assault by a male colleague. These are not the actions of a small minority but are, like racism, endemic in police culture. Gregory and Lees highlight the strength and persistence of sexist, homophobic culture; the rise in bullying particularly around racist and sexist banter; the vast number of women suffering in silence and their fear of repercussions if they complain; the bullying of those who do and any who support them; the understanding of sexual harassment as part of the continuum of male violence against women.

Focus #4: Sexual Harassment in Business

Sexual harassment in business has attracted less public attention, but is no less harmful.

The world's biggest law firm in California was ordered to pay over seven million dollars to a woman secretary who had only worked there for two months. The firm was penalized because other partners knew of the behaviour of one of the top billers who would grab the secretary's breasts and drop sweets into her blouse pocket. He was ordered to pay a personal amount as well as the firm being ordered to pay because they had known and not acted (Dyer, 1994).

A USA report on the broker industry indicated that 17 former women employees of one company had been awarded substantial damages for grotesque abuses of power by senior executives fuelled by cocaine. Not one of the employees was still working for the company when they took the decision to register an official complaint. Those who did complain, even hesitantly, were ignored or dismissed. In addition and what made the situation impossible was that the people they were supposed to complain to were guilty of the behaviour being complained about. There was an area of the office which formed a thoroughfare through which the women passed several times a day. This area was called the pit and consisted of male brokers who sat, lurked, terrorized and preyed on the women by subjecting them to a daily torrent and virtual hailstorm of sexual harassment loudly broadcast by voice and the firm's microphone. As well as calling the women grossly insulting names there were repeated requests for 'blow jobs'. This was only a small part of the daily abuse with blatant preferment for those who granted sexual favours (Coles, 1998).

In a London oil-broking market office the men categorized all women who entered the office, including women traders, according to their perceived sexual availability. They gave names to each category, with the most derogatory for older women or those deemed 'lesbians' for stating women's rights. 'Babes' who were assessed as sexually available were used for social occasions but not perceived as being for promotion. The women seen as 'one of the boys' were those who could compete within the environment and were most likely to be successful (Brooks-Gordon, 1995).

What is clear is the ongoing problem of the power of heterosexual men, operating in structures of power and dominance, in continuing to maintain cultures of harassment.[7] Women within many organizations are sexually commodified by men, who may present themselves as non-sexual beings whilst using conquest sexual imagery and metaphor, conducting relationships at work and sexually harassing women in the workplace (Hearn and Parkin, 1987, 1995). Gutek (1989) writes of how men use their sexuality more than women and in more diverse and exploitative ways but how paradoxically male sexuality is made invisible whilst female sexuality is put under the spotlight. In these ways sexual harassment is inextricably linked with gender.

The focus material shows the difficulty of separating harassment from bullying and violation. It illustrates the difficulties of voicing complaints when women endure harassment and the fear of careers being destroyed if they speak out. Many victims suffer in silence and often complaints are not taken seriously if the behaviour is perceived as a joke on the man's behalf (Sims et al., 1993). Epstein (1994) cites many instances of men touching women or talking to women in a way they perceived as demeaning and infantilizing but because the behaviour was not self-perceived as sexual these women had little recourse to official complaints procedures. In many organizations equal opportunities policies exist so it might be expected that anti-harassment policies would operate with management implementing them and taking complaints seriously. Many subjected to harassment find management actively complicit or ignoring what happens. Franks (1999) suggests that workplaces are changing so fast and with increased insecurity that there are strong pressures not to challenge but to cling on to what one has got.[8] Even when organizations recruit by equal opportunities this may not extend to work practice, so reproducing harassment.[9]

Racial and Related Forms of Harassment

'Sexual' harassment may not always be directly sexual. Harassment can of course be experienced by women on grounds other than those that are sexual. Also harassment can be experienced by men who are not perceived as fitting in, such as gay men, newcomers, black and ethnic minority men, outsiders, young men, older men, men with disabilities, 'foreigners'. Thus is it necessary to name age harassment, disability harassment, and so on. In this context some suggest the term 'personal harassment'. Some research into sexual harassment also addresses racial harassment. Racial harassment, like sexual harassment, is endemic in some organizations, as illustrated by the London Metropolitan Police handling of the Stephen Lawrence case (McPherson, 1999). In the UK two out of every five black and Asian police officers have made some form of complaint about racism in the force (Blackstock and Rees, 1998). Reports of racism in many settings reaffirm this. For example, a recent report (Travis, 1998) highlighted problems of racism in the Home Office with managers accused of engaging in bullying, racist banter and victimization of black staff as well as decisions about promotion and recruitment clouded by prejudice. A study into graduate employment showed that white graduates are almost twice as likely to be offered jobs in top British companies as their black and Asian counterparts (Milne, 1998). Similarly, black and Asian cricketers have tended to play outside the established league structures because of resistance and animosity from white players and officials (George, 1998).

Another dimension to racism is exemplified by a white man who won an employment tribunal for racial discrimination after standing by his black friends at work. The three men worked in a cable-laying team sent to a predominantly white town. They were sacked for being 'scruffy' even though more smartly dressed than other teams. The white man was taken to one side and told he could continue in work as there was no problem with him. In view of this racism, he quit the company and took it to tribunal (Wainwright, 1999). As with men in patriarchy, white people are inevitably part of a system of oppression but can be part of the problem or the solution.

Changing Recognitions of Harassment

Contemporary recognitions and understandings of sexual, racial and other harassments are also becoming more complex through internationalism. They are becoming more subject to international debate, as in EU policy, and, in a different way, worldwide media coverage of several (in)famous US sagas, notably those of Clarence Thomas – Anita Hill (Morrison, 1992) and Bill Clinton – Monica Lewinsky (*Symposium* ... , 1999).

A recent comparative review is that on research throughout the European Union (European Commission, 1999; Timmerman and Bajema, 1999) (see Table 3.1). One of the striking things about this review is the great variation in the results of the various European researches. This could be for a number of reasons: variation in the breadth of the definition of sexual harassment used (Fitzgerald and Shullman, 1993) in terms of form of behaviour, length of timespan, focus on personal or other experiences, as well as variations by national and cultural context and occupations and sectors studied.

In earlier local and national studies there have been some interesting 'inversions' with higher figures of harassment to women produced in women's non-traditional sectors than traditional sectors (Leeds TUCRIC, 1983; Gutek and Morasch, 1982). One might speculate on the greater cultural acceptance of sexual harassment in some national cultural contexts that might partially explain lower figures than where there is less harassment. Comparative studies of the variable relationship of sexual harassment and sexual cultures in workplaces are an important research field (see pp. 11).

TABLE 3.1   *Incidence of sexual harassment by country and by sex in north-west Europe (Timmerman and Bajema, 1999)*

Country	Sexual harassment of women (per cent)	Sexual harassment of men (per cent)
Austria	81 (national study)	
	73 (local government)	
	33 (several branches)	
	17 (training on the job)	
Belgium	29 (secretaries)	
Denmark	11 (national study)	
Finland	34 (11 occupational groups)	26 (11 occupational groups)
	27 (national study sexual life)	30 (national study sexual life)
	11 (university staff)[a]	11 (university staff)[a]
	17 (Finnish parliament)	
	9 (SAK, several unions)	3 (SAK, several unions)
	17 (union)	
Germany	72 (national survey)	
	80 (local government)	
	30 (private sector)	
	50 at least (local government)	
Ireland	25 (civil service)	1 (civil service)
	45 (Electricity Supply Board)	
	14 (retail sector)	5 (retail sector)
Luxembourg	78 objective criteria (national study)	
	13 subjective criteria (national study)	
Netherlands	32 (national study)	
	58 (several case studies)	
	54 (local government)	27 (local government)
	56 at least (police)	
	25 (secretaries)	
	13 (industrial office workers)	
Norway	90 (women´s magazine)	
	8 (several occupations)	
	8 (labour union)	
Sweden	17 (national study)	
	2 (national study, 22% health care)	1 (national study)
	53 (ambulance personnel)	14 (ambulance personnel)
	30 (university hospital)	
	15 (university)	4 (university)
	23 (wood industry)	4 (wood industry)
	27 (metro)	
	9 (social insurance office)	4 (social insurance office)
UK	54 (national study)	about 9 (national study)
	47 (temp. agency)	14 (temp. agency)
	89 (health service)	51 (health service)
	90 (police, 1992)	

[a] This is an overall rate of both women and men.

Sexual harassment is also being recognized, especially in academic debate, as closely linked to what is taken to be 'normal male heterosexuality' (Thomas and Kitzinger, 1994), yet also more connected with other social divisions, such as age and racialization. Debates are also becoming subtler and recognizing the subtlety of some harassment. An important area of policy and practice development here has been on the relation of sexual harassment and 'consensual (sexual) relations'. This has been especially important in some universities and other educational institutions, where, for example, younger (often women) students and older (often men) staff may be or have been in sexual or social-sexual relationships. These may be defined as 'consensual' (by one or both parties) at one stage but 'harassing' or 'non-consensual' at another stage (by one or both parties, most likely the less powerful). What may be defined by both parties at one stage as 'consensual' may be understood in the context of organizational power relations as abuse of power. There are, however, some fine lines here. The 25-year-old teacher and the 20-year-old student who 'fall in love with each other' do seem to be a different case from the 35-year-old teacher who every year (or Friday night) seeks out and 'falls in love' with a different 20-year-old student. Either way there are clear issues of professional conduct involved just as there are in many other workplaces where there are situations of trust, such as therapy, counselling, medical and health-related work. For these reasons some organizations and professional associations adopt guidelines and policies that discourage, advise staff to make formal declaration of and even prohibit such 'consensual relations'. Those in close personal relationships, including family relatives, may also be advised against or even prohibited from working in the same department.[10] Outright prohibition by organizations, unless it is part of the basic professional code, as with doctors, is a complex legal field not least because of human rights questions.

The Recognition of Bullying

While bullying has been recognized for a long time as a problem in schools, especially boys' schools, bullying has become more widely recognized as an important issue in adult workplaces in the 1980s (Tattum and Lane, 1988). We introduce definitions of bullying, before outlining some ways in which it has become a more public issue in organizations as increasing numbers of cases are being reported. As with sexual harassment, those going to tribunal are few compared with the numbers staying quiet for fear of job loss. The information outlined is from various sources, including media reports, campaigns, trade union action and research. This mirrors earlier work when such sources were used to contribute to 'voicing' the power of sexuality in workplaces.[11]

Definitions

Definitions range from a couple of sentences on a fact sheet (IPD, 1998) to six pages in a book with detailed listing of bullying behaviours (Field, 1996: 41–6). Quine (1999) suggests that 'most definitions of workplace bullying share three elements that are influenced by case law definitions in the related areas of racial and sexual harassment. First, bullying is defined in terms of its effect on the recipient not the intention of the bully; thus it is subject to variations in personal perception. Second, there must be a negative effect on the victim. Third, the bullying behaviour must be persistent' (p. 229). Randall (1997) includes sexual harassment within his analysis of bullying. Bully OnLine (1999) lists the following behaviours, and suggests that bullying is for control and subjugation, not performance enhancement:

- consistent criticism, fault-finding, nit-picking, undermining;
- being overruled, marginalized, isolated, excluded;
- threatened, shouted at, humiliated, belittled, patronized;
- singled out, treated differently from everybody else;
- set unrealistic changing goals and deadlines;
- overburdened with work, or denied all work;
- responsibility increased but authority removed;
- plagiarism, stealing your work and the credit for it;
- excessive monitoring, coercing staff to make false complaints;
- denial of annual, sickness or compassionate leave;
- twisting, distorting, misrepresenting all you say and do;
- unjustified verbal/written warnings or disciplinary action;
- being forced into resignation or early/ill-health retirement.

The key is 'unwanted behaviour which the recipient finds intimidating, upsetting, embarrassing, humiliating or offensive'. The intention of the perpetrator is not paramount but whether the behaviour is experienced as bullying, is unacceptable by normal standards and is disadvantageous (IPD, 1998). Persistent behaviours can range from physical violence through to a person being ignored and the psychological abuse of power. The effects of bullying include stress, psychiatric problems and lower self-confidence. Extreme cases have led to suicide. Bully OnLine (1999) suggests that bullying causes psychiatric injury and results in demotivation, resentment, disenchantment, alienation, inefficiency, dysfunction, low morale and high staff turnover. It suggests two types of bullying: corporate bullying where the employer feels free to abuse the workforce without fear of being called to account; and serial bullying which is described as a compulsive, addictive behaviour where one person picks on another, usually a subordinate and bullies them senseless.

Modes of Recognition

Concerns about bullying and its recognition have arisen in several different contexts such as media reports; personal experience and campaigns, trade union concerns; legal aspects and tribunals; and studies on incidence. Bullying, as with sexual harassment, has often been taken for granted, ignored or defined in other ways such as 'initiation' or 'horseplay'. A recurring theme, as with sexual harassment, is the denial and complicity of management and the difficulty of complaining when management is directly involved. Bullying, in contrast to sexual harassment, has been recognized more recently and is generally not constructed as gendered/sexualed. There is a limited but growing range of discourses around bullying, and, as with sexual harassment, individualistic constructions are dominant. Concern with bullying has been taken up in many countries. In Sweden and Finland initially the focus of concern with 'mobbning'[12] started in schools, and was subsequently recognized in other organizations. The notion of 'mobbning' has probably taken more of a central place within the debates on violence in organizations in Sweden than has 'bullying' in the UK. While media debate has continued around bullying in schools, some of the most high-profile and indeed intense media reports on bullying have been from the military.

Focus #5: Harassment and Bullying in the Military

A woman member of the Territorial Army was unable to work after suffering from depression after a three-year stint when she suffered an ongoing campaign of bullying and harassment including being raped by an officer. The woman had been unable to work after leaving the army. She alleged that from joining, it was made clear that she was not welcome in an overwhelmingly male group. In psychiatric evidence it was stated that the woman had almost come to accept that the abusive behaviour was normal and she took a lot of guilt on herself. She endured the abuse for three years thinking that if she could get through it the men would accept her (Dyer, 1997b).

A Wren was successful at an industrial tribunal when complaining about four years of sexual harassment that led to her poor health and a suicide attempt. She said she had been bullied into miming oral sex whilst stood on a table surrounded by a gang of men. Complaining to the commander was like talking to a brick wall and no-one she told was interested. The tribunal said the award should be seen as a message to senior officers that such harassment would not be tolerated (Boseley, 1997).

A Wren was paid substantial compensation after she became bulimic and had to be winched off a Royal Navy ship to undergo psychiatric treatment after a sustained campaign of harassment and bullying by sailors. She suffered such severe trauma she had to retire on medical grounds after 12 years' service and was still on antidepressants two years after leaving the ship (Dyer, 1997a).

These extracts are set in the context of an extended debate in the 1990s in the UK on the place of women in the military, and especially whether women should serve on board Royal Navy ships. In the extracts, the terms harassment and bullying are both used with no real distinction between them. Neither are addressed as violences in spite of the women being seriously harmed with physical and mental health damage, often on a long-term basis. Bullying added to harassment suggests a more serious situation than citing 'harassment' alone but stops short of being designated as violence. This may inadvertently diminish the recognition of the seriousness of harassment, unless it is combined with bullying.

From Personal Experience to Campaigns

Attention has been drawn to bullying through the Internet. There are growing collective communities of victims/survivors of bullying, facilitated by the Internet. They may be geographically separate but socially relatively cohesive. The UK

Bully OnLine was created by Tim Field who had personally experienced a breakdown through bullying at work, before setting up a telephone advice line and publishing information on the Internet. Approximately 90 per cent of inquiries involve a serial bully; about 90 per cent involve professional or office-based employees, 5 per cent voluntary workers and 5 per cent manual or shop-floor workers (Field, 1999). Although Field's profile of a bully focuses on personal attributes and the idea that bullies bully because they feel threatened and insecure, he also suggests it is an 'epidemic' with causes relating to the reduced power of unions, recession, ruthless cost-cutting mergers and the disappearance of layers of management leaving other workers to cover (Field, 1996). These latter aspects are clearly organizational matters rather than personal characteristics. Bully OnLine suggests that bullies get away with it by exhibiting amoral behaviour, aggression and abuse of power in a climate of fear, ignorance, silence, denial, disbelief, evasion of responsibility and reward for bullying, whilst employment law is weak and secure jobs are scarce.

Other press release websites summarize bullying surveys and provides definitions and profiles of bullies (Field, 1996; Workplace Bullying Press Releases, 1999). The British IPD (Institute of Personnel and Development) survey of over 1,000 workers found that 1 in 8 reported bullying at work. Over half in the survey who had experienced bullying say it is commonplace in their organization and a quarter say the situation had worsened in the past year. The majority were being bullied by more senior staff; for almost a third the bully was a head of department or section, and for 16 per cent a chief executive or managing director. Over a quarter claimed the bully was a supervisor. It was not only junior staff who were targeted but also managerial and professional staff. A disturbing number of senior executives are abusing their power by condoning others' bullying; thus change should come from top management. Nearly three-quarters of victims had suffered from workplace stress; one-third did not raise the issue at work, as they did not think anyone could solve the problem, or thought they would not get a sympathetic response or they should deal with it themselves. Those who did raise it were dissatisfied with the response. Most organizations were regarded as 'blind' to the existence of bullying; 32 per cent said their organization did not believe bullying occurred or had not thought about it. 11 per cent said their organization disapproved of bullying but only dealt with reported cases reactively. A significant minority of victims took a stoic approach: just over a quarter agreed that 'it's only over sensitive people who complain about bullying – most people just accept it as a fact of working life' (Workplace Bullying Press Releases, 1999). Field also suggests that the figure of 1 in 8 is an underestimate, as bullying often goes on behind closed doors with no witnesses: 'bullying is behind all discrimination, harassment, prejudice, abuse and violence.' If there is a strong racial or sexual slant, it is all bullying. Field (1999) suggests that women are more likely to admit they are being bullied than men and more likely to be motivated to do something about it. He suggests the incidence of female bullies is probably due to the fact that teaching, nursing and social work have a higher than average percentage of female managers and that the percentage of female bullies seems to be increasing. He asserts that the only apparent difference between male and female bullies is that 'females make much better (or is it worse?) bullies than men', leading him to argue that bullying is not a gender issue.[13]

The Andrea Adams Trust also campaigns against bullying in the workplace and offers support to those bullied; training workshops on bullying; promotion of good practice; campaigning for effective legislation. The Trust factsheet (n.d.) defines bullying; outlines the effects of bullying; highlights the costs of bullying; lists typical bullying behaviour and gives the legal position. In addition the leaflet examines the fine line between managers taking a 'strong line' in the name of 'strong management' and bullying. This moves attention from the personal attributes of the bully and bullied to an emphasis on organizations. Corporate pride in strong management including bullying can be part of a company culture that shortsightedly emphasizes high levels of performance and productivity. The Trust suggests that bullying thrives where it is common behaviour across management hierarchies, especially in highly competitive environments where individuals regularly use bullying to motivate staff. While there is no reference to gender, this campaign material demonstrates the ongoing recognition and concern about bullying in the workplace, as well as being a resource for those being bullied. It can contribute to lifting the silence around workplace bullying and be a voice for employers to take notice and act. The theme of management failure to act or management participation in abuse remains central.

In October 1998 the Trades Union Congress completed a survey of bullying at work. This followed on from the TUC 'Bad Bosses' telephone hotline: 38 per cent of the 5,000 people who had rung said they were being harassed at work and almost half were men (TUC, 1998a; NATFHE, 1998). This suggested that in the UK up to five million people may be bullied at work sometimes with devastating consequences for their health. Women were just as likely to be bullied as men, with 11 per cent of those surveyed by the TUC reporting that they were bullied or had been bullied and a quarter indicating that they were aware bullying had taken place. Much of the blame was put on a generation of managers who were on the first rung of the corporate ladder during the Thatcher era and then wreaking havoc from positions of power. Many managers responsible for intimidation had suffered similar treatment when they were younger. This led to a TUC guide on how to tackle workplace bullying, *Bullied at Work?* (TUC, 1998b).

A UNISON study of union members in 1997 showed 66 per cent had either witnessed or experienced bullying at work. In 83 per cent of cases the bully was the line manager. In 84 per cent of cases bullies had bullied before and, while management knew about this, for three out of four they did nothing about it.

The UNISON study also revealed stark differences in the responses of those who were not being bullied and those who were. While only 5 per cent of those who had not been bullied said they would take no action, over 30 per cent who were being bullied at the time of the survey said they would do nothing about it. 36 per cent of those currently being bullied felt the best option available to them was to leave their job, compared to only 7 per cent who said if they were being bullied they would leave. (TUC, 1998a: 5)

This again points to the importance of management and the number of people subjected to bullying who remain silent.

Stress, Low Performance and Loss of Productivity

Bullying is sometimes subsumed under the category of 'stress' (Stress UK, 1999). Seventy-five per cent who had witnessed or experienced bullying said it had affected their physical or mental health, most usually stress, depression or lowered self-esteem. According to Cary Cooper, bullying accounted for between a third and half of employment-related absence due to stress. He estimated an annual cost to the economy of about £1.3 billion (TUC, 1998a: 4). Of safety representatives asked to identify the main hazard in their workplace of concern to their colleagues, 68 per cent identified stress as one of the top five health and safety concerns, with higher stress levels in the public sector than the private. The causes of stress included new management techniques (48 per cent); long hours (31 per cent); redundancies (24 per cent); harassment (21 per cent); shiftwork (16 per cent); bullying (14 per cent). Respondents could give more than one reply so it is unclear how many cited both harassment and bullying. 'New management techniques', such as quality circles and performance-related pay, can limit trade unions' ability to defend members from unreasonable managerial demands which may impose change making individual employees feel undervalued and lacking influence over their work. The language of 'downsizing', 'delayering', 'outsourcing' and 'outplacing' can mask violation and psychological harm (Collinson and Collinson, 1997). The Institute of Management reported in 1996 that 270,000 people take time off work every day in the UK through work-related stress, with a cost in sick pay, lost production and health charges of around £7 billion (TUC, 1998a: 4). IPD guidelines on harassment at work (IPD, 1998) begin: 'achieving high levels of performance from people is essential in today's competitive market place. Organizations should treat seriously any form of intimidating behaviour because it can lead to under performance at work.' It notes people cannot contribute their best when frightened and the damage brought to the image of organizations by bad publicity. Research by the Industrial Society has found that businesses that do not deal with bullying pay a heavy price in higher absence and sickness rates (McGhie, 1999).

Legal Aspects and Tribunals

In the UK the legal framework for addressing bullying is linked with legislation on sexual and racial harassment covered by the Sex Discrimination Act 1975 and the Race Relations Act 1976. These Acts do not specifically cover bullying unless it focuses on the race or sex of the person in which case it will be unlawful. The Disability Discrimination Act 1995 protects disabled people and the Criminal Justice and Public Order Act 1994 makes it a criminal offence to use threatening, abusive or insulting words or disorderly behaviour intended to cause harassment, alarm or distress. The Protection from Harassment Act 1997 which is aimed at stalking makes a course of conduct amounting to harassment both a civil wrong and a criminal offence, and introduces a criminal offence of putting a person in fear of violence.

Bullying is thus not specifically protected by statute though there is an EU recommendation to combat sexual harassment and a code of practice protecting people's dignity at work. EU policy gives employers a moral and legal obligation, a duty of care, to ensure the safety and well-being of their employees. Employers can be held liable for bullying behaviour arising from the duty at common law to provide a safe place of work and maintain mutual trust and confidence or by virtue of a claim for constructive dismissal in the event of inadequate protection from the employer. There may be some protection around potential health and safety hazards through the Health and Safety at Work Act, 1974, or if a person feels that they are intimidated through membership of a union through the Trade Union and Labour Relations (Consolidation) Act, 1992 (IPD, 1998; Andrea Adams Trust Factsheet, n.d.). Field (1996) notes that the law does not specifically address bullying and that the law on unfair dismissal and intolerable working conditions is so complicated that a complainant needs legal advice. Allegations of bullying have to be dealt with through the most appropriate legislation – typically sexual or racial discrimination or unfair dismissal – to obtain redress. Claims for personal injury can be pursued if illness or serious or life-threatening injuries have been sustained through prolonged bullying. Ishmael (1999) agrees there is little protection in law for workplace bullying and that the Health and Safety at Work Act 1974 is limited, though giving some indirect protection through the duty to provide a safe place and system of work for employees. The Act imposes on employees a general duty to 'take reasonable care for the health and safety of himself and other persons who might be affected by his acts or omissions at work. Whilst this falls far short of a prohibition against, it imposes an individual duty of care on the perpetrator of the bullying which mirrors the duty on the employer' (Ishmael, 1999: 200). Health and safety legislation does cover risks to mental and physical health at work. Prevention of stress is part of this, with bullying recognized as causing stress and requiring preventive measures.[14]

UK legislation does not hold out much hope of redress as it does not entail specific legislation but uses other legislation to address bullying. The Fairness at Work regulations cover better maternity and paternity rights, automatic union recognition if 50 per cent + 1 employees are union members and equal rights for part-time and full-time workers. It does not address bullying but raises the upper limit for unfair or constructive dismissal from £12,000 to £50,000 (Workplace Bullying News, 1999). The white paper suggested bringing unfair and constructive dismissal legislation into line with sex, race and disability discrimination but the government bowed to CBI pressure and did not include it.

A 1999 Industrial Relations Services survey of 157 employers from manufacturing, service and public sector organizations employing nearly 700,000 staff found that staff were very reluctant to blow the whistle on bullies with workers having little confidence that their claims would be taken seriously (Farquarson, 1999). De Maria's (1996) study[15] of punitive actions taken against 'whistleblowers' in Australia showed that many themselves were then harassed: 71 per cent experienced official reprisals, 40 per cent formal reprimands, 14 per cent punitive transfers and others received compulsory referrals to psychiatrists or other professionals; 94 per cent experienced unofficial reprisals and all experienced social

TABLE 3.2 *Studies on the prevalence of 'mobbing'/bullying (Salin, 1999)*

Country	Researcher(s)	Respondents	Prevalence (per cent)
Austria	Niedl (1995)	Healthcare professionals, N = 368	7.8–26.6
		Research institute, N = 63	4.4–17.5
Finland	Vartia (1996)	Municipal employees, N = 949	10.1
	Paananen and Vartia (1991)	Visitors at healthcare centres, N = 984	10
	Vartia and Hyyti (1999)	Prison officers, N = 889	4.8 (weekly)
	Björkqvist et al. (1994)	University employees, N = 338	16.9
Netherlands	den Ouden et al. (1999)	Healthcare workers, N = 2200	13.2
		Local council workers, N = 2700	13.8
Norway	Einarsen and Raknes (1991)	Union members, N = 2215	2 (weekly) 6 (now and then)
	Einarsen and Skogstad (1996)	14 different subsamples, N = 7986	1.3 (weekly) + 3.3 (now and then)
	Einarsen and Raknes (1997)	Male industrial workers, N = 460	7 (weekly)
	Einarsen et al. (1998)	Assistant nurses, N = 935	3 at that time 8.3 previous experience
Sweden	Leymann (1992d)	Representative sample of the Swedish working population, N = 2438	3.5 (weekly)
	Leymann (1992b)	('handicapped') employees in non-profit organizations, N = 179	21.6 (handicapped) 4.4 (non-handicapped)
	Leymann (1992c)	Politicians, N = 610	5.2 (weekly)
	Lindroth and Leymann (1993)	Nursery school teachers, N = 230	6 (weekly)
	Leymann and Tallgren (1989)	Steelwork employees, N = 171	4 (weekly)
UK	One in Eight (1997)	N > 1000	12.5
	Rayner (1997)	Part-time students, N = 1137	53 (ever subjected to acts of bullying)

Different researchers have used slightly different definitions of bullying. For discussion on the definitions and measurement methods used please refer to the original sources.

ostracism, with 80 per cent suffering some form of emotional deterioration. It remains to be seen whether the new Public Interest Disclosure Act (1999) will have an impact on bullying as opposed to other disclosures of misconduct.

Empirical Studies

The study of bullying is relatively recent in academia. The most developed research is from countries where there is strong public awareness, government-funded research and established anti-bullying legislation. There is now a considerable research literature on incidence in different organizational settings. This has been recently summarized by Salin (1999) (see Table 3.2).

Research Approaches

Quine (1999) suggests that there have been three main approaches to research into workplace bullying, including the individual characteristics of the bully and victim; epidemiological studies, usually descriptive and based on self-report; the interaction between the individual and the organization, particularly examining ways in which organizational structure and workplace climate may encourage a bullying culture. Swedish research has elaborated on the notion of 'mobbning' in several similar ways, including victimology and the characteristics of victims (Leymann, 1992d), the development of scapegoating processes (Thylefors, 1987) and the relation of 'mobbning' processes to wider, often very entrenched, organizational processes (Schéele, 1993). With some exceptions, the emphasis on organizational context is low and usually addressed in terms of loss of productivity and stress.

Hickling (1999) argues that much literature portrays the bully as a psychopath (Adams, 1992; Field, 1996). He argues this has been very influential, making the focus of investigation the personality or motives of the bully rather than organizational environments, structures and cultures. Hickling suggests that Field (1996) not only builds a personality profile of a bully but subtly introduces the notion of the 'psychopathic personality', quoting the Mental Health Act 1983 and interweaving this with reference to 'the bully'. He does not say that all bullies are psychopaths but implies this. Literature which profiles bullies to the exclusion of organizational matters ignores the issue that bullying is an integral part of organizational worlds recently emerging into public awareness. To what extent bullying is increasing or an 'epidemic' (Field, 1996) is unclear. Profiling of bullies and what contributes to them becoming bullies is important but should not distract from organizational context. Research suggesting that bullies can be inadequate or resent subordinates who are good at their jobs or have backgrounds as playground bullies or have authoritarian personalities (Adams, 1992; Field, 1996; Einarsen and Skogstad, 1996) cannot be divorced from the settings which allow such behaviour or give such opportunities to exercise power. Some organizations and managements encourage bullying through 'strong management', attempts to increase productivity or particular men's cultures.

The Recognition of Physical Violence

The growing recent recognition of workplace (physical) violence is different again. Its construction is, like bullying, usually not specifically gendered or sexualed. There is a limited but growing set of discourses around it, though the dominant one is probably that of clients who threaten or members of the public who are violent on isolated occasions. Physical violence in organizations, like much violence, is incidentalized (Hearn, 1998). The victims/survivors of physical violence in organizations are rarely constructed as identifying as such; they are probably more likely to identify as victims of crime regardless of organizational setting. There is less development of a community of victims/survivors of physical violence in organizations than of bullying.

Relevant subfields that have addressed the topic include: industrial relations; racial, sexual and personal harassment; interpersonal conflict; health and safety; anxiety, stress and avoidance; violence to women; organizational policy development; trade union action; as well as studies of particular organizations. Work organizations are in turn affected by the personal, social and economic costs of violence, so providing motivation for their study. There is a variety of motivations for studying the problem – employers' concern to take preventive action to improve personnel practice, avoidance of compensation claims and litigation, increased awareness of impact of stress, trauma and PTSD (Post Traumatic Stress Disorder) following violence, hostage taking, robbery (Hodgkinson and Stewart, 1991). Empirical research and increasing concern with violences in and around organizations has been policy-led rather than explanatory, and focused on single issues such as threats to employee safety, employers' preventive measures or the personal impact of violence.[16] UK research and policy interventions have often been within a 'personal safety' or 'health and safety' frame.[17] In Sweden and Finland research on violence has increased, with much located within an 'occupational health' frame.[18]

In the UK, key organizational actors have included the Health and Safety Executive (HSE), which carries a general responsibility and has produced many guidance texts, the Tavistock Institute, the Suzy Lamplugh Trust, the Home Office Crime Surveys, Victim Support and trade unions. The issue of 'violence at work' dominated the Health and Safety debate at the 1996 UK Trades Union Congress. The Society of Radiographers and the Chartered Society of Physiotherapy reported that risks to their members are increasing from long waiting times and staffing reductions. Staff on emergency night duty, often on their own, are reported at greater risk. Similar reports were received from Bifu, the banking union, of excessive stress caused by insufficient staff, unrealistic targets, inflexible work measurement techniques and other unreasonable new working practices.

The Suzy Lamplugh Trust, the National Charity for Personal Safety, has produced much guidance material for workers and employers. It commissioned two reports on existing literature (Joeman et al., 1989) and a survey of workers' experiences (Phillips et al., 1989). As the Trust's title suggests, the emphasis is on facilitating individuals' safety, especially at work. *Training for Personal Safety at Work* (Cardy, 1992), a training manual for working on these issues, was produced on behalf of the Trust. *The Review of Workplace-Related Violence* by Standing and Nicolini (1997) is an important document, summarizing research and highlighting methodological and policy issues. It develops the earlier Poyner and Warne (1986) model of violence in workplaces by distinguishing scenarios including incidents involving: (i) 'agents with no legitimate nexus to the organization'; or (ii) agents who are 'the receiver of some service of the organization'; or (iii) agents who are 'in some form of employment relationship (past or present) with the affected organization'. This is a useful development though it tends to reify the organization and not deal with violences by organizations as agents. The focus is on violence that is *unexpected* and *incidental* to work rather than *part* of work (see pp. 79–82).

The problem of physical violence in and around workplaces is also receiving increased publicity and media concern. Media reports of violence have covered a very large range of organizations, but certain organizations have attracted special and developing attention. Of these, three seem to be especially prominent: schools and institutions for young people, sports organizations, and transport organizations. In each case there has been a complex mixture of different types of reports. Often the stories of and about violence in and around these organizations appear to have an unfolding life and narrative of their own. There is a growing and complex series of events connecting violence, responses from staff and responses to these responses from management. In schools and institutions there have been reports of violence by teachers, disruptive pupils, attacks by 'boys' on women teachers, teachers' responses to exclude violent children, safety of school children, sexual abuse in children's homes (see Chapter 5), inquiries into schools and other institutions, the carrying and use of weapons by schoolchildren,[19] as well as high profile events such as Dunblane and the murder of the headteacher, Philip Lawrence. There is also growing concern with young men's violence, often drink-related, in college fraternities in the USA and elsewhere.

With sports organizations, there have been two major media narratives in the 1990s: the performance of 'excessive' violence in physical contact, and thus sometimes violent, sports; and the violence of famous sportsmen 'off the pitch' or in their 'private life'. In both these cases there is an issue of what are the limits of the rules and conduct of the sport in question. Specifically, there is often uncertainty about when does the control of the sport end and the control of the national or international law begin. This boundary has been open to negotiation in relation to such famous sportsmen as Mike Tyson (boxing), O.J. Simpson (American football), Eric Cantona, Paul Gascoigne (both soccer), Allen Iverson (basketball), and Philip Tufnell (cricket). There is also growing concern with the relation of sports violence, peer group support and sexual violence.[20]

Also in the 1990s there has been increasing media concern with violence in and around transport organizations. Supposedly isolated cases of 'road rage' and 'parking rage' have been accompanied by reports of bus and taxi drivers refusing to go into certain housing areas; taxi 'wars' between rival taxi companies; driving test examiners concerned for their safety from failed customers;[21] attacks on late night train travellers and staff; and most recently various accounts of 'air rage'.

Focus #6: Violence in Air Travel

In 1997 a fight was reported between two air traffic controllers at La Guardia airport, New York, following a 'racial slur'. An official inquiry followed ('Airport controllers land punches', 1997).

A drunk passenger terrified passengers and crew when he marched up and down the aisle, swearing and clenching his fist. He was overpowered, charged with endangering aircraft safety and being drunk on board, and jailed for two months (Harper, 1996).

A 'crazed' passenger burst into the cockpit at 30,000 feet and attempted to crash the plane down, shouting 'I'm going to bring you all down'. Police pressed charges (Hall, 2000).

The BA pilots' union Balpa's demands for action against violent passengers met with limited sympathy from the airline. BA said that it would be willing to withdraw frequent flyer rewards from offenders, if other airlines did likewise; otherwise punishment was up to the courts. It also opposed the informing of offenders' employers as urged by the union (Harper, 1999).

These three organizational settings have several common elements: all are heavily gender coded; they are dominantly and spatially male domains, if we consider boys' parts of schools; they operate with a complex mix of rules and constraints on the one hand and 'unrestrained' physical movement on the other; they are relatively 'enclosed' corridors within society; they pose complex uncertainties around the limits of organizational and managerial authority over violence within those organizational worlds. The media familiarize us not only with the performance of violence but also reactions to it, such as teachers' refusal to teach violent pupils or pilots' attempts to punish violent passengers, and then counter-reactions by organizations and management.[22]

One of the questions almost always asked in relation to violence and abuse is – how much is there? The extent of violences in and around organizations is difficult to assess. As discussed (pp. 16–18), violence can include force and/or violation, and may be physical, sexual, emotional, verbal, cognitive, visual, representational. The 1995 British Crime Survey definition of 'work-related violence' is as follows: 'Incidents of violence (wounding, common assault, robbery, and snatch theft) occurring while the victim was working. Incidents while travelling to and from work are excluded. Incidents not arising directly from the work are included. Incidents perpetrated by relatives or (domestic) partners are excluded.' Much of the focus on 'violence' has been on physical violence and threats thereof in and around work organizations. The definition of physical violence is thus closely bound to legal and criminal justice definitions and their distinctions between different kinds of assaults and worse. There is no unified gathering of statistics on such violence. Most research has comprised surveys of incidence, safety and/or risk in specific work sectors (see Cardy, 1992).

Incidence studies have been strongly directed towards particular sectors. Certain sectors and factors appear to present particular risks of violence: handling money, valuable goods and goods with street value; those in authority; lone workers; providers of care, advice, education and service; and those working with people who have been or are potentially violent people (Poyner and Warne, 1988; Cardy, 1992; Woods et al., 1993). Several comments might be made here: whether violence is at the workplace or when working; exclusion of travelling, which may be crucial for some workers; exclusion of relatives/partners who may be co-workers; exclusion of some forms of bullying and harassment. There is also the tendency to reduce violence to physical violence; this is something that has been noted as often occurring in men's accounts of violence, where the violent incident is described in relative isolation from its context and from social life more generally (Jukes, 1993; Hearn, 1998).

Physical violence and threats thereof in and around work organizations are relatively common: 1 in 10 Finnish government workers experiencing 'psychological molestation' (bullied at least once a week for at least six months) (Vartia, 1991); 1 in 4 Swedish healthcare workers afflicted by physical violence or threats at least twice a month, (Toomingas and Nordin, 1995).[23] Three-quarters of 130 Swedish medical staff in old-age nursing wards had been threatened by physical violence over the last year (Bergström, 1995). A particular concern is the rapid increase in (reports of) violence at work. There is evidence to suggest a rapid increase has occurred over the past ten years, along with considerable under-reporting. The 1988 British Crime Survey (BCS) found that about 25 per cent of all violent assaults and about 30 per cent of all threats against working people occur while at work. The 1992 BCS indicated that about a quarter of violent assaults at work involved other workers and the remainder members of the public, including members of other organizations. In the UK the annual rate of reported violent assaults doubled between 1981 and 1991 to 350,000 (13 per cent of all reported assaults) (Loss Prevention Council, 1995). Further large increases are reported from the 1995 BCS, though much of the increase may be due to respondents defining more experiences as violence. There are also increases in repeat victimization reported in the 1995 BCS. Reports of workplace violence have increased rapidly in Finland in recent years, with reports of such violence to women more than doubling between 1980 and 1993 (Lehtiniemi and Palmu, 1995). Homicide is now the second most common cause of death in US workplaces (VandenBois and Bulutao, 1996).

There are, however, larger issues still. According to the International Labour Organization, 1.1 million people, including 12,000 children, are killed at work every year – more than are killed by war, road accidents and AIDS. The figures are especially high in developing countries, where the death rate in the construction industry is more than 10 times that in the industrialized countries (Milne, 1999).[24] Historically, demonstrating 'corporate intentionality' or even negligence with regard to accidents and manslaughter has been difficult, particularly because of the problem of identifying accountability within hierarchical chains of command. Between 1986 and 1996 the deaths of 3,369 employees were reported to the Health and Safety Executive and local authorities. Yet in this period, just three individual employers were convicted of manslaughter and only two served prison sentences. The absence of corporate accountability may be changing. The number of manslaughter prosecutions against company directors is rising. The only conviction of a company, rather than individuals, for manslaughter so far recorded was in 1994, after four teenagers died in a canoeing trip in Lyme Bay. In 1996 against the background of growing disquiet at this lack of corporate accountability for a series of major disasters involving the UK (such as King's Cross, Pipa Alpha, Clapham Junction, Zeebrugge), the Law Commission proposed a new offence of 'corporate killing'. Here a death will be regarded as resulting from a company's conduct if it is caused by failure in the way the company's activities are managed or organized to ensure the health and safety of persons employed in or affected by those activities. These proposals suggest changes to render employers more accountable and provide greater legal recognition of organizations' responsibility in the reproduction of violence.[25]

The most important general conclusion of studies of both violence and organizations is the continuing significance of gender relations there. However, much research and commentary on violence in and around workplaces lacks a gender analysis. Swedish (Statistics Sweden, 1995) and Finnish (Ministry of Foreign Affairs, 1993; Ministry of Social Affairs, 1995; Veikkola and Palmu, 1995) official victim statistics indicate that more women report 'job-related violence' than men, as Field suggests they do with bullying. The 1993 and 1997 Statistics Finland surveys showed violence at work as the most common form of violence for women and the most rapidly increasing category of violence (Aromaa and Heiskanen, 2000). Aromaa (1993: 10) notes specifically that '(s)urvey research indicates that women are very seldom in a position in which they psychologically harass, violate or 'mob' men in the workplace'. He continues by adding that research results show that 'for women the experiences of work-related violence – physical violence or threats implicating violence – have increased'. This theme has also been explored by Haapaniemi and Kinnunen (1997: 57); they comment: '(o)ne explanation for the increase in violence and threats of violence at work, concerning mainly women, is the rapid expansion of occupations in the health and social service sectors and other service occupations.' The TUC (1999) report *Violent Times: Preventing Violence at Work* found that young women were twice as likely to be attacked at work than their male counterparts. Almost a quarter of women in the 25–34 age group had been threatened with violence at work, and 11 per cent had been attacked, compared with 6 per cent of men in the same age group.

Of special interest is the growing evidence of the risks of violence from non-members or temporary members of organizations, such as clients, customers and patients. Corporate commitments on customer service (whilst sometimes also restricting actual service) may increase public expectations, which if not met, may lead to frustration, anger and violence. At the same time, there is now the technology for greater customer and worker control and surveillance, through CCTV, swipe cards, security doors and so on, which may in some circumstances lead to similar outcomes, and the managerial facilitation of safety-related behaviour by workers. This can include the development of 'user-friendly' 'self-help' manuals that encourage or instruct the worker to look after themselves (self-surveillance). In many Suzy Lamplugh Trust publications, the focus is not on the violator, the propensity of certain people to be violent, on the workers themselves as violent, on social divisions, such as gender, nor on the greater risks elsewhere, such as at home – but on the potentially violated person who is given the responsibility to keep themselves safe. As earlier noted, socio-technological changes affect the gender–sexuality–violation complex in organizations in contradictory ways. They produce workplaces that are ever more like fortresses; they facilitate calming environments within them; and workers are increasingly given the responsibility to monitor their own behaviour in most minute ways. Violence and potential violence 'at work' may thus paradoxically create both more docile workers and more active citizens.

Towards Organization Violations

The relationships between gender, sexuality, harassment, bullying, violence, violation and power are complex. It is important to recognize both the special features of each category of sexual harassment, bullying and physical violence, and the differences. Definitions and connotations of sexual harassment and bullying differ significantly, with the former emphasizing touch, sexual advances, jokes, use of pornography and sexist language, and implying men's power over women. Lists of bullying behaviours are usually much more work-orientated, with unwanted behaviour focusing on the work task and emphasizing stress and loss of productivity. This formulation is more subtly gendered.[26] 'Violence' is usually more focused on physical attacks and behaviours not usually associated with workplaces, apart from 'violent settings' such as prisons. In making comparisons, there is a danger of presuming a linear progression and ranking, with physical violence at the 'top' and more likely to be perceived within a criminal framework. Harassment is often not seen as severe as physical violence, so ignoring harassment being violence. Joking around sex or race might be (falsely) described as 'mild' and seem far removed from physical violence. Seeing each as a separate category compartmentalizes them and detracts from addressing their interconnections with gender, sexuality and organizational power.

There are clear overlaps between harassment, sexual harassment, bullying and physical violence. Not all bullying is sexual harassment, though arguably all sexual harassment is a form of bullying and violence to the individual. Bullying and violence are not just 'associated with' harassment; rather harassment is a form of bullying and violence linked with the gendering of organizations and part of men's violences. Similarities between the categories, such as physical and psychological harm, intimidation, persistence and unwantedness, need to be recognized. All appear endemic in many workplaces, though unrecognized in most organizational analyses. The processes by which harassment, bullying and physical violence have been named and voiced have been outlined. For each, processes of voicing and silence are in a dynamic relation. Naming and voicing do not automatically lead to policies and practices that then create less violent working environments. There is often a less clear process with many remaining silent, through fear of losing jobs, little confidence in management, difficult legal procedures or further intimidations. All have been addressed by trade unions and legal means of redress have been sought in each case.

Campaigns around each have had different impacts on public perceptions with high-profile cases attracting publicity through campaigns and trusts or high-profile, almost celebrity, status given to individuals such as Lisa Potts, severely injured when protecting nursery-school children from a machete attack. The persistence of his family led to the Stephen Lawrence case having continuing coverage and an inquiry pointing to the endemic racism in the police force, which was initially not addressed as violence but rather the actions of a few incompetent officers (McPherson, 1999). These examples are generally not seen as part of organizational hierarchies but more to do with hazards associated with certain jobs, with being black, or with clients or members of the public causing harm.

TABLE 3.3   *Conventional categories of violation in organizations*

	Non-physical and physical violation	Primarily physical violation
Gendered/sexualed	Sexual harassment	Sexual violence (or men's violence to women)[*]
Not gendered/sexualed	Bullying	(Physical) violence

[*] Usually a missing category.

There have also been high-profile cases in the media around violence, such as those on whether sportsmen should be prosecuted when they go beyond the usual use of force in boxing or rugby or football, or attack members of the crowd who insult them. It is more difficult to find cases of bullying and sexual harassment with similar public profiles. This may say something about the relative publicity given to physical injury from physical violence, as against the psychological harm from harassment and bullying. These distinctions make it difficult to see them all as violation, even though all subjected to harassment, bullying or violence have been violated. We might speak of the violation of each or violation caused by each, though this is itself not unproblematic.

Harassment and bullying have been understood as wide-ranging phenomena that may include both physical and non-physical violations. Violence is generally, though not always, focused on physical abuse. Only sexual harassment is specifically seen in relation to gender and strongly influenced by feminist theorizing. This is despite the fact that feminist analyses of sexual harassment focus on men's violence to women and descriptions of harassment frequently use the term 'bullying' to account for the experience. This means that there are several missing categories in the usual classifications. There is generally an absence of a gendered/sexualed category of violence, paralleling sexual harassment (see Table 3.3).

Sexual harassment, bullying and physical violence are to be understood in the context of the gendering and sexualing of organizations. If this is only acknowledged for sexual harassment, the gendering of bullying and violence is ignored. This is not an essentialist argument in which women are categorized as victims and incapable of harassment, bullying and violence, and men as perpetrators. Indeed some bullying surveys (Quine, 1999) have found more female bullies being reported than male bullies. Field (1996, 1999) argues that bullying is not gendered. That women as well as men can bully does not mean there is not a gender dimension; instead the significance of gender needs to be examined. Cardy (1992: 2) considers 'aggression and violence in the workplace is a people problem not a gender problem'. To support this the claim is made that twice as many men as women suffer from assaults at work. Such approaches have several shortcomings. First, surveys show that women experience most sexual harassment, usually perpetrated by men to known women as colleagues, managers, customers. Second, violence by men to men, or between men, is related to the social construction of men, masculinities and men at work. Third, most violence in and around workplaces is perpetrated by men. Gender and sexuality are clearly linked with sexual harassment. With bullying, the ways in which organizations are constituted through gender make it impossible for bullying to be understood outside this gendering. Fourth, these claims ignore the masculinism of most organizations and management.

An emerging theme is the importance of hierarchical managerial power. As men still dominate management, their opportunities to exercise power in negative, violating ways are greater than those of women, as is their ability to silence complaints. Some women are accessing higher positions, bringing opportunities to exercise power negatively, as suggested in some bullying surveys. Men have dominated hierarchies in organizations throughout history and the exercise of management power. There is a growing number of studies of powerful male cultures and women's consequent difficulties.[27] The masculinization of workplaces sets the norms by which women who seek to join must behave, hence the phrase 'becoming one of the boys'. This may be essential to survive in an environment where the greatest insult to a man would be to be seen in any way 'soft' or like a woman. For men, to point the finger at women who bully and harass is convenient in distracting attention from masculinist environments and their responsibilities. In our earlier presentations on sexuality in organizations, we grew to expect the first question or comment would be from a man giving an example of a woman who harassed or asking us to comment on women who do. This is not to deny the possibility and presence of harassment, bullying and violence by women; this may be an important issue in workplaces dominated by women and for some women in work environments that are especially ruthless.

All the phenomena discussed here are violations of the person. They violate what is called 'human dignity', a concept that itself needs to be gendered and sexualed. Focusing on violences as violation brings together debates on different forms of violence that have usually been kept separate – sexual harassment, bullying and physical violence. While the conceptual framework of 'organization violence'[28] has been used, we now consider the term 'organization violation' as analytically more useful. This includes not only what is recognized as harassment, bullying and physical violence (each of which are still generally seen as something contrary to the ordinary life of the organization), but also other violations, whether mundane or structural. In indicating that each form of 'violence' violates and damages the person, the concept of 'organization violation' contradicts any presumed linearity. While notions of a continuum or continua of violence are useful, they need to be treated with caution. Their overly behavioural focus may neglect the experiences of violation and play down both more structural relations of oppressions and mundane experiences of violation in organizations that would usually not be labelled harassment, bullying or even sometimes physical violence (see Figure 3.1). Violations occur within routine organizational processes, in managerial and work cultures, the ordinary enactment of authority, in the very existence and ordinary functioning of organizations, whereby certain people are demeaned and violated. Such structural relations of oppression and mundane experiences of violation are not mutually exclusive; they may violate without resort to physical violence. Violations do not occur along a neat progression of increasing severity. Organization violations refer to the simultaneous structural presence, operation and social enactment of organization and violation.

Taken-for-granted violations, not recognized as violations:

Mundane Violations within Organizations

Intermediate violations, becoming recognized as violations:

(Sexual and Other) Harassment, Bullying, Physical Violence

Structural violations, recognized or not recognized as violations:

Structural Oppressions

FIGURE 3.1 *Levels of violations*

A broad framework and a broad conceptualization of violations are needed to explore violations in specific organizations. This involves bringing together the conceptualization of harassment, bullying, violence, structural oppressions and everyday/supposedly mundane violations. This becomes a more central issue as the boundaries of violation are extended, the social construction of violence is more fully understood and theorizing of violence/gender/sexuality/organization increases. It is important in understanding workplace violation transnationally and developing a wider comparative perspective, including the globalization of processes around sexuality and violence. Part of the power of violation is it being presented as separate from the rest of social life, including organizational life. To put organizations and violation together, as in 'organization violation', assists these analyses.

4

Theorizing

Organizations and Organization Violations

This chapter addresses violence and violation in relation to organization theory. Following a review of some contributions from organization theory, a theoretical framework for analysing organization violations is outlined. We conclude with a discussion of the interconnections of organization violations.

The Perspective of Violence and Violation

While it is widely accepted that organizations are centrally concerned with power, domination and control (Morgan, 1986), it may still seem strange to talk of organizations, violence and violation together. Yet many concepts in organizational analysis – 'power', 'domination', 'control', even 'authority' – can be euphemisms for violence and violation. This is most obviously so in analysing organizations where there is legitimated use of violence, as with the police, military, prisons and state custodial organizations (Scraton et al., 1981). We have noted how violence and violation have been even more marginalized from the mainstream than gender and sexuality. An analytical perspective on organizations through the lens of violence and violation does not mean movement away from concerns with gender and sexuality. To focus on violence and violation means dealing with gender and sexuality, as made clear in the notions of gendered violence and sexual(ized) violence. Organizations do not only respond to violent acts, they may also contribute to, construct and reproduce violence and violation.

This is not of course to suggest that all organizational life can be reduced to violence and violation. Indeed, this perspective may be limited in directing attention away from other organizational perspectives, such as that emphasizing mutual cooperation. This perspective may also leave as relatively open questions such as the extent to which organizations are distinct from other areas of social life in terms of violence; and violence, in its non-physical or less directly physical senses, is distinct from power in organizations. Rather, this perspective argues that the question 'what is happening in organizations?' can be answered more fully by bringing violence and violation into the picture. Putting 'violence', 'violation' and 'organizations' together problematizes what we understand by organizations.

Developing organizational analysis through the lens of violence and violation provides a framework for theoretical development and a research agenda, opens up new research questions and acts as a guide to the empirical analysis of particular organizations. Throughout, special attention needs to be paid to men's power as a major element in structuring violence, violation and organizations.

Organizational Theories: Towards a Violation Perspective on Organizations

Rereading Mainstream Theories

The importance of violence is slowly being recognized within organization studies. In one sense, many mainstream theories of organizations can be reinterpreted as commentaries on violence, especially if violence is seen broadly as violation. Organizational and management theories can be reread as, for example, ways in which violence and violation, especially managerial violence, are organized, managed and sometimes legitimated. In its crudest forms, Taylorism has provided the means to reproduce managerial violation to workers, through the legitimated control of the workers as functional agendered bodies. The absence of consideration of violated bodies can itself be violating.

In contrast, the idea of 'human relations', as used in organization theory, might seem to suggest the need for fuller attention to gender, sexuality and violation. Human relations have rarely been constructed as gender(ed) relations or sexualized, let alone violating, relations. 'Human relations', as conceptualized in Human Relations Theory, becomes problematic when considered in relation to gender, sexuality and violation. It is no longer self-evident what 'human relations' are to mean. Human relations perspectives could be a means to controlling the worst excesses of physical violence or unrestrained management. Yet despite the apparently 'humanist' predelictions of Human Relations Theory and its managerialist successors, there is much room left to 'negotiate' whether violence is at all relevant to the managerial task. Moreover, such approaches have facilitated the development of a focus on teamwork and organizational cultures, which can be more or less violating. This is especially so with contemporary possibilities of creating subtle psychological violations.

Human Relations Theory was one of several influences contributing to the establishment of the system as a central paradigm for organizational analysis. In one sense, the system reduces social divisions, including gender, sexuality and violence, to systemic language; in another, systems thinking reproduces gendered dualities, such as between goal attainment and system maintenance. This can obscure gender, sexuality and violation, including managerial violence, and justify and perpetuate women's 'maintenance roles' in less powerful organizational positions. Systemic theorizing also highlights processual aspects of organizations, which can be very important in understanding dynamics of violation over time.

In the UK much of the Tavistock Programme's work on organizational analysis can be seen as centrally concerned with violence. At the most general level, it has attended to the destructive aspects of individual and group dynamics, the death instinct and 'the violence and intensity of feeling' (Menzies, 1970: 7). More particularly, there was the practical work with the survivors of violence, prisoners of war and psychological casualties of war in and after the Second World War. Action research on high anxiety institutions can be understood as partly about people's experiences of violation in organizations. Jaques's and Menzies's analyses of deeply distressing tasks and events led them to focus on collective defence mechanisms, most often through the use and reinforcement of organizational rules, procedures and formalities; the routine organizational mode co-exists with the severely distressing *and* its avoidance. The Tavistock Programme's contribution to 'the government of subjectivity and social life' (Miller and Rose, 1988) included the place of violation and defences against it within organizations.

Organizational Forms and Structures: Bureaucratic and Post-bureaucratic
Another important strand of organization theory focuses on differing organizational forms and structures. Within the modernist project the dominant model of organizational form has been that of bureaucracy. This is part of the process of transforming 'premodern' societies into modern societies, with organizations operationalizing principles of scientific rationality (Reed, 1993). It can provide the organizational infrastructure to overcome nepotism, brute force and violence, yet can be harnessed for the most violent purposes, as in the institutionalized violence of the Third Reich. Bureaucracy can be one means to the production of routinized, military, institutional violence (Johnson, 1986). Local bureaucracies can be violent and violating in mundane ways, in the state, capitalist or 'partnership' sectors.

Gibson Burrell (1999: 402) goes so far as to suggest that:

> Modernism is about the death camps in a fairly uncontentious way even though its apologists seek to distance the likes of Auschwitz from the achievements of the modernist society ... . Ritzer's (1993) ... *The McDonaldization of Society* shows how the high achievements of modernity such as the Big Mac are still heavily redolent of the mechanized death of large numbers of creatures. ... we know that the trains into Auschwitz were made up of cattle trucks; and we know that the efficiencies of the Ford motor plants relied heavily upon lessons learnt and technology drawn from the abattoirs of Chicago. The attainments of the organized world of modernism are, in fact, built upon the flesh and bones of the dead and the methods of their speedy and cheap execution.[1]

There is a large literature questioning and critiquing the bureaucratic organizational form.[2] A specific problem is the way in which gender and sexuality may be 'added on' to non-gendered, non-sexualed models of bureaucracy, Weberian or otherwise. 'Adding on' sexuality and gender is unsatisfactory (Sheppard, 1989), and this also applies to violence and violation. Organizational analyses, concepts and models need to speak of sexuality, gender and violation. Bureaucracy has itself been analysed as clearly gendered. Within bureaucratic patriarchies, women may be marginalized from inflexible male cultures of efficiency, rationality and instrumentality, and male managers may be expected to be unemotional, objective, impartial, efficient and rule-bound (Burris, 1996).

Bureaucracies, specifically patriarchal bureaucracies, can easily constitute sites and forms of violence and violation.

Understandings of organizations have indeed fundamentally changed over time. Formerly organizations could be understood as based in single places as opposed to now being organized across space and cyberspace. Globalization and global change, including multinational corporations and information and communication technologies, are rapidly impacting on organizations. Organizational forms and structures are changing to meet the demands of global capitalism and international communication. This often involves lateral and networked control, diversification of operations, interdisciplinary liaison, differentiated service and multi-skilled teamworking rather than production line processes (Mullender and Perrott, 1998). There has been widespread delayering of organizations and some moves 'beyond hierarchy' with team-based organizations and 'adhocracies' (Dawson, 1996). This is sometimes thought of as the postmodern organization operating in the context of globalization.

Information technology can facilitate production control and performance monitoring from remote sites leading to reductions of middle management. However, this should not be confused with lessening the need for control and co-ordination. New technology creates the possibility for new forms of violation, as in Internet pornography and trafficking in women, and email abuse, whilst sometimes simultaneously being non-abusive face-to-face. There is growing interest in the impact of new technologies and work intensification processes on the physical and mental safety of employees. Lean production, intensified targets, performance-related-pay and inflexible management techniques can result in intimidation and excessive tension, leading to violating conduct by managers, co-workers and/or customers within abusive workplace cultures (Wright and Smye, 1997).

Thompson (1993) characterizes these new organizational forms and structures as:

- large companies eliminating bureaucratic structures because of cost;
- decentralization;
- federal organization: central business functions disaggregated to small independent units;
- initiative, drive and energy coming from the parts, not the centre;
- firmly anti-hierarchical: flat organizations with no more than four layers with 'downsizing' and 'shrinkage of middle layers which not only narrows status differences but enables more effective and direct ways of communication;
- networking: informality, equality and horizontal links;
- breakdown of bureaucracy.[3]

Leonard (1997) has discussed moves to less hierarchical and more community-based organizations and participative forms of welfare organization but is cautious about how far they indicate a replacement of modern organizations with late capitalist forms. Different structures, with less hierarchy and joint decision-making, have arisen in helplines, community projects and organizations supporting women surviving violence. Mullender and Perrott (1998) suggest that funding sources are changing this with insistence that the smaller become like the larger, and moves from equal status to hierarchies and directors (Oerton, 1996a). However, Thompson (1993) argues that it is premature to herald the end of bureaucracy.[4] Organizations may become leaner and decentralized but remain bureaucratic. Global decentralization of labour processes and production decisions may combine with increased centralization of power, control, research, planning and strategic management at corporate headquarters over the spatially dispersed, interdependent units. Control is maintained at the centre with information technology systems in the control of senior decision-makers. Increased operational autonomy in lower and local management may be within more tightly controlled frameworks. Such emerging forms do not challenge existing power relations and in many senses are not postmodern. Thompson (1993) argues that many 'spend their time and resources rationally calculating which firm to swallow up, which market to move into and what to spend cash on. In other words any decline in instrumental rationality is strictly in the minds of the postmodernists' (p. 191). Parent corporations continue hegemonic control over satellite firms and suppliers. Such organizational forms and structures thus represent rather contradictory conditions for violation, both more flexible and more subtly controlling.

Bringing Violence into Organization Theory

Rereading organization theory texts and examining the implications of organizational forms can provide valuable insights in the study of organization violations. It has, however, generally been rather rare to bring violence and violation into organization theory. Three examples of such direct engagements are noted here.

A well-known example is that of Poyner and Warne (1986), who proposed an Individual–Interaction/Situation–Outcome framework, described as '... a guideline for most of the UK and international studies ever since' (Standing and Nicolini, 1997: 30). While this may be an overstatement, the influence of their model has been great, perhaps by virtue of its simplicity (see Figure 4.1).

There are, however, several shortcomings to this model, and three of them are summarized by Standing and Nicolini (1997: 31) as the basis for their own 'enrichment' of Poyner and Warne's model:

1 Shifting the focus from the individual assailant/victim towards the organisational context.
2 Introducing a distinction between different types of violent incidents.
3 Differentiating between constrained/invariant and manipulable aspects of the organisational context.

All these three criticisms are important, and are drawn on to spell out three different scenarios of 'incidents' or episodes of work-related violence:

Type 1 scenarios include incidents involving agents who have no legitimate nexus to the organization (for example, till snatchers, gangs attacking fire crews on call). Standing and Nicolini (1997: 33) state that in such episodes '(b)oth assailant and context characteristics will combine with preventive actions by the organisation and the employees to determine a specific level of risk' (Figure 4.2). The likelihood of the occurence of violence and the extent of violence depend

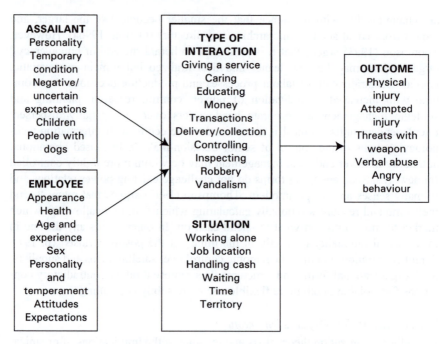

FIGURE 4.1 *Poyner and Warne's model of violence in the workplace*
(Source: *Violence to staff: a basis for assessment and prevention, 1986*)

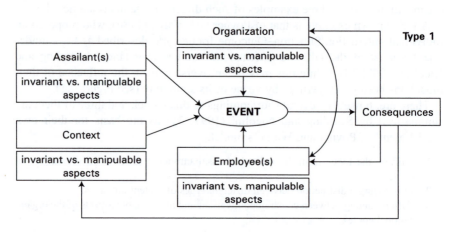

FIGURE 4.2 *Scenarios for incidents involving agents who have
no legitimate nexus to the organization* (Source: *Standing and Nicolini, 1997*)

partly on the course of action taken 'by the organisation' (p. 33). This includes
attention to the organizational context, support programmes for employees,
reporting systems and diffusion mechanisms.

*Type 2 scenarios include incidents where the agent is the receiver of some
service provided by the organization.* 'Most of the offences against public sector

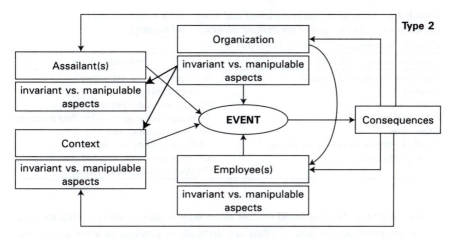

FIGURE 4.3   *Scenarios for incidents where the agent is the receiver of some service provided by the organization* (Source: *Standing and Nicolini, 1997*)

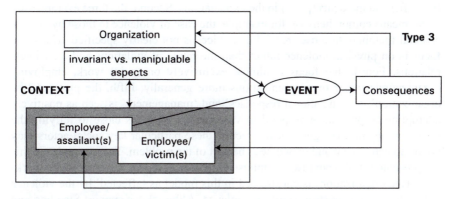

FIGURE 4.4   *Scenarios for incidents where the agent is in some form of employment relationship (past or present) with the affected workplace* (Source: *Standing and Nicolini, 1997*)

and service provider employees belong in this category. It also includes retail organizations where the violence is the result of the service encounter itself' (p. 35) (Figure 4.3). It is argued that organizational response is important here, and that a lack of reaction may reinforce the recurrence of this type of incident.

Type 3 scenarios include incidents where the agent is in some form of employment relationship (past or present) with the affected workplace (Figure 4.4). It is argued that the nature and dynamics of the violence is different in this scenario from the other two. 'The organization' is both an important antecedent and context of the violence. The implications of the employment relation are emphasized, as is the way that 'the organization' handles apparently 'minor' episodes and/or 'near misses', including the circulation of information and experience.

TABLE 4.1   *Main invariant/constrained and manipulable organizational
contextual factors emerging from current literature and research*
(Source: *Standing and Nicolini, 1997: 39*)

Invariant/constrained factors	Manipulable factors
Organizational purpose and task	Management style and culture
Location	Staffing levels
Relative size	Recruitment and selection procedures
Cash handling	Working process and cash-handling procedures
Client base	Risk-assessment routines
Ascribed characteristics of an employee,	Staff expectations and awareness
e.g. gender, age	Organizational awareness and proactivity
	Degree of organizational isolation

Standing and Nicolini build on this three-way model to set out what they call
'invariant/constrained factors' (that are difficult to change, at least in the short
term) and 'manipulable factors' that can be changed more easily (Table 4.1).

There are still, however, various problems with Standing and Nicolini's revised
formulation. First, there is a confusing switching between scenarios, episodes
(p. 33 ff.) and incidents (p. 32) in the explanations. Second, the three examples are
by no means comprehensive; for example, the case of violence to those by organizational members to those 'receiving service' is not clearly specified. Third, the
focus is on physical violence rather than the range of violations and their interrelations. Fourth, the focus is almost exclusively on (paid) work, employing
organizations rather than organizations more generally. Fifth, the place of 'the
organization', 'organizational responses' and 'management' is seen as positively
attempting to prevent or respond to violence. This comes close to reifying the
organization and management. In practice these particular key social actors may
not be so benevolent and may indeed be part of the problem. Two examples of this
are presented in the next two chapters. To put this slightly differently, the workplace (the organization) is constructed in this model as 'affected' by the violence
rather than being constitutive of the violence. Although we support Standing and
Nicolini's (1997: Ch. 4) emphasis on the importance of strategies for preventing
violence, there is a clear managerialist perspective in their understandings of the
development of violence in and around (work) organizations.

A third example of an attempt to bring violence into organization theory is provided by Salin (1999) in her examination of the kinds of factors that may be
important in explaining the occurrence of bullying. Here a more embedded
approach is taken to the analysis. The major factors are summarized as follows:

- 'enabling factors', which include perceived power imbalances, low perceived
  costs of violence to the organization, and dissatisfaction or stress;
- 'motivating factors', which include the reward system and expected benefits,
  and the presence of very high or very low performing colleagues or subordinates; and
- more specific 'triggering factors', which include restructuring crises, other
  organizational changes, changes in the workgroup and changes relating to
  individual employees (see Figure 4.5).

Even though this approach is focusing on bullying, we see this kind of think-ing as a broader and more useful way forward for the analysis of violations more generally. The relationship of these 'factors' to each other and to major social divisions is, however, obscured within a certain eclectism.

Gendered, Sexualed Power, Resistance and Violation

While questions of power are clearly present in all these examples of organiza-tional theorizing of violence and violation, the explicit theorizing of power and indeed resistance is not developed in any detail. Yet questions of power and resis-tance are central in analysis of gender, sexuality and violation in and around organizations. Ongoing debates on power and resistance are clearly relevant in developing critical perspectives on organization violations.[5] It is thus necessary to insert a brief discussion of their relevance here before theorizing organization violations more fully.

Power remains a contested concept (Lukes, 1974) in organizational analysis as elsewhere. There is a very wide range of words and concepts available to analyse the field, including: various understandings of power (*Macht*) (perhaps with the threat of sanctions) and resistance themselves, authority (*Herrschaft*),[6] domi-nation, control, regulation, influence,[7] manipulation, persuasion, coercion, force, violence, abuse, strategy, tactics, oppression, exploitation, hegemony, sover-eignty, ideology, false consciousness, rebellion, protest, collective action, struggle and conflict, as well as macro analyses of societal power and, beyond, transnational/global power.

Power has been traditionally construed as a capacity and the ability to domi-nate or influence others through reward or punishment (Dahl, 1957; Weber, 1958; Wrong, 1979). Following Lukes (1974), a second dimension of power sees some people's interests as never reaching the formal level of decision-making or agenda-setting (Bachrach and Baratz, 1970). A third dimension of power views people's 'real interests' as distorted by ideological conditioning (Lukes, 1974). One-, two- and three-dimensional views of power also provide commentaries on resistance. Lukes's approach is set firmly within the mainstream/malestream tra-dition of non-substantive analyses of power. His third-dimensional approach pro-vides one model of structural analysis. There are of course many other possible aspects and approaches to structural analysis. These include:

- the recognition of collective actors, with their own agency;
- the normality, persistence, even inevitability, of social conflict and resistances;
- the intersection of material and ideological powers;
- the interplay of the technical and the social relations of production.

All these elements are important in Marxist and neo-Marxist analysis. Indeed in such approaches one can hypothesize resistance, conflict and even certain violations as indications of differences of interest and thus democratic or proto democratic impulses. Such resistance and conflict resists dominance and submis-sion. Significantly, resistance may sometimes take the form of harassment, bully-ing, violence and violation. In some cases, this may also be enacted in

---

Triggering factors:

Restructuring and crises (e.g. downsizing, increased internal competition and stress)

Other organizational changes (e.g. delegation of control and sanction mechanisms)

Changes in the workgroup (e.g. new employees, new manager)

Changes relating to individual employees (e.g. benefits, 'privileges')

Motivating factors:

Reward system and expected benefits (e.g. more favourable performance appraisal or improved career opportunities through sabotage)

Very high or low performing colleagues/subordinates (e.g. 'getting rid of threats and burdens')

Enabling factors:

Perceived power imbalance (e.g. hierarchical differences, victim and perpetrator characteristics, exposed position, outnumbering)

Low perceived costs (e.g. weak leadership, large and bureaucratic organizations)

Dissatisfaction (e.g. low work control, role conflict, poor social and communication climate, strained atmosphere, little time for conflict-solving)

FIGURE 4.5 *Enabling, motivating and triggering factors in the work environment explaining workplace bullying* (Source: *Salin, 1999*)

resistance to structural inequalities and oppressions in relatively localized sites; in other cases, this resistance to inequalities and oppressions may take the form of more collective action. Thus, it is not always possible to neatly separate dominant and resistant power and power relations from each other. Violation *in resistance* can be experienced as no less violating by those receiving it than that enacted *in domination*. These complications and multiplicities of power relations are part of contemporary concerns in theorizing power and resistance.

In recent years major critiques of both non-substantive and structural(ist) approaches to power have been provided by poststructuralism, postmodernism and feminism. Poststructuralist conceptions of power see individuals as constituted by their discursive environments so that 'objective' interests do not exist waiting to be defined (Foucault, 1980, 1981; Barbalet, 1987).[8] These theories have become especially important in the analysis of particular social divisions such as class, gender, race and permutations thereof. Feminist, along with postcolonial and radical multiculturalist, work on power and resistance has major implications for bringing gender, sexuality and violation, and their intersection with other social divisions, towards the centre stage in organizational analysis.

Genderic organizational power can be conceptualized not only as the ability of men to prevent women's entry to and advancement within organizations on an equal basis through covert and overt material means, but also through the part discourses play in dissuading women from resisting such situations. Additionally, men in lower occupational positions, though subordinated by other men, often continue to misogynize, harass and devalue women in equal, lower and sometimes higher organizational positions (Cockburn, 1983, 1991; Gutek, 1989). It therefore cannot be presumed that marginalized men (for example, by racialization), even those who may be seen as feminized in the context of the dominant culture (Hamada, 1996), do not reinforce gendered hegemony or are devalued in a similar way to women. Although women might correspondingly enact 'hegemonic masculinity' and some do attain high-level organizational positions (Collinson and Hearn, 1996; Ledwith and Colgan, 1996), only very few women reach the highest echelons of organizations.[9] It is not only the formal doing of gender (Butler, 1990; Gherardi, 1995), but the culturally assumed biological sex of the performer, more precisely the ascribed presence or absence of being male, that is usually important.

A focus on sexuality, as in 'organization sexuality' (Hearn and Parkin, 1987, 1995), shows how interlinked sexuality and gender are, and how sexualities are often subsumed under and are core, if not defining qualities, of gendered identities. Hegemonic masculinity is often defined by its hierarchically heterosexist masculinism. Femininities and alternative masculinities are often subordinated and derogated because they are seen to be linked to women and 'passive, receptive' female sexuality (Reynaud, 1983; Hearn, 1987), which is negatively connoted (Addelston and Stiratt, 1996). Some commentators suggest it is the sexing or sexualizing of gender, in particular the sexing of females, that defines the female gender (MacKinnon, 1982, 1983) or leads to their domination through compulsory heterosexuality (Rich, 1980, 1983). Indeed if gender is not only sexualized but sexuality is also gendered, then it may be very difficult, if not sometimes impossible, to strictly separate them, particularly if they are organizationally institutionalized. Just as it is impossible to 'add on' gender to sexuality in an uneasy combination, once each is recognized as fundamental to the other, so bullying, harassment and violence cannot be so easily categorized separately. All are products of and contribute to gender/sexual power relations in organizations. Gendered, sexualed power provides the material and ideological backcloth to organization violations – the range of violations including direct physical and emotional harm and damage, and the pervasive experiences of oppressions more generally.

A Theoretical Framework for Organization Violations

Violation, Violence and Oppression

Different forms of violation are understood very differently, whether in organizations, campaigns, research or analysis. Harassment, bullying and physical violence are often the primary ways in which contemporary understandings are organized. These are usually conceived as distinct from interpersonal workplace conflicts, industrial relations disputes, work process, exploitation, oppression, class conflict and gender conflict. The struggles that have developed around the specific recognition of 'violence' have generally constructed a social phenomenon distinct from, say, exploitation, oppression or class/gender conflict. The presentation of violence and other violations as separate from gender, class and other social divisions is itself part of their significance and their reproduction. The contemporary focus on harassment, bullying and physical violence is clearly vitally important, but there are major categories and forms of organization violation that are neglected. What forms of violation are missing from current concerns? The broad violations of patriarchy, capitalism and nationalism are rarely considered in the literature on bullying and physical violence, as if they occurred in a world without gender, class and racialization. Also, the multitude of mundane, everyday violations that occur in, construct and constitute organizations are not seen as significant in these debates.

To go beyond this and develop a broader framework, it is necessary to bring together these organizational worlds and the conceptualization of 'violences' and 'oppressions' as violations. As noted, the notion of a continuum of violence can be clearly useful but on its own it may be overly behavioural in focus and neglect wider experiences of violation. Also a behavioural continuum may play down the importance of more structural relations, including relations of oppressions, that may operate without use of direct violence. Iris Marion Young's (1990) plural catgorization of oppression as exploitation, marginalization, powerlessness, cultural imperialism and violence is relevant here, as one way of contextualizing violence within oppression. Violences and oppressions are both violations, just as organizations are sites of oppressions and violations such as physical violence, harassment, sexism and racism. Hickling (1999) suggests that bullying is part of the harassment of oppressed groups but is also outside current categories of oppressed groups and their movements for change. It can thus fall outside known categories of oppression, occurring, as it does, at many levels of organizations and occupations. Violence and oppressions are usually dealt with separately in sub-fields. Instead they need to be brought together – as organization violations. This follows from the recognition of organizations as fundamental to the operation of power and the 'mobilization of bias' (Schattschneider, 1960). Thus we do not wish to create a separate paradigm for violation in organizations, any more than for sexuality as distinct from gender (see pp. 14–16). The recognition of the connectedness between forms of oppression and their fundamental links with violence, violation and organization is vital. Violences and violations are ways of maintaining oppressions and subtexts in the enactments of work, organizations and management.[10]

Social divisions of oppression, such as age, ethnicity, disability, gender, sexuality and class, have all been the focus of processes of politicization. These have voiced concerns about inequalities and have in some cases stimulated anti-discriminatory and anti-oppressive practices. Such practices may seek to recognize harm caused by oppressive practices with attempts to prevent or redress such damage. Hopton (1997)[11] suggests there is a need to move

> beyond simple identity politics to offer an explanation of how a person's self-esteem and self-confidence can be undermined by an adverse social, cultural, economic and political environment. The acknowledgement of complex interrelationships between political structure, ideology, culture and individual mental well-being/distress demands that any attempt to ensure substantive equality for those previously isolated on the margins of mainstream society should be accompanied by a radical change in cultural values. (p. 44)

This recognizes the ongoing damage caused by organizational exclusions, abusive use of language and the power of mainstream cultural values, and structural dominations. To call this 'violation' articulates in stark terms ongoing, often 'very ordinary' oppressions and exclusions, and the distress and damage caused. The ordinary and extraordinary tactics perpetuating oppressions – bullying, isolation, exclusion, harassment, physical violence, emotional assault, demeaning actions, along with cultural, ideological and symbolic violences – need to be named as violations. Furthermore, dominant power relations bring their own resistances, sometimes with violations, sometimes localized, sometimes collective.

A useful way of analysing this vast range of organization violations is in terms of macro, meso and micro organization violations,[12] conceptualized as both overt 'violence' and more general 'oppression':

1 *macro extra-organizational structures*, including the impact of structural violations and the place of violation in the existence, context and formation of organizations;
2 *meso organizational domains*, including organizational domain orientations of particular organizations to violation;[13]
3 *micro intra-organizational processes and practices*.

It is also necessary to consider the relations between these levels of analysis.

Macro Extra-organizational Structures

The Existence of Organizations

Violence, violation and oppression are both interpersonal and structural. Violations are very closely linked, but not totally determined, by structural power differences, particularly but not exclusively those around gender and sexuality. These include:

- macro-patriarchal structural violations: patriarchal social structural relations;
- macro-economic structural violations: systems of capitalist and imperialist exploitation;
- macro-cultural structural violations: national exclusion, structural racism and xenophobia.

While gender and sexuality are empirically significant in the explanation of violence, particular violences are mediated through other social divisions, such as age, race and class. Structural power differences are very closely linked to the production of structural violations, which include:

- the structural pattern of individual and interpersonal violence, such as the societal patterns of men's violence to women in the home;
- the violent acts and effects of social institutions such as the state – more accurately referred to as institutional violence;
- the violent effects of inequalities, including those on a world scale, such as distributions of famine;
- the violent effects of warfare and inter-nation and inter-community violence;
- the social structural relations of institutions that have historically been violent or underwritten violence, as in the social relations of fatherhood or capitalism (Hearn, 1998: 16).

The very structuring of such social relations can itself often be violating to some and a form of violence/violation, even with the incredible variety of social and cultural formations and practices that are called organizations. The very production and reproduction of organization(s) can be a form and location of violence. What is particularly interesting is the extent to which the basic activity of organizing, of forming and maintaining organizations, is violence or involves violence. Organizations depend for their continuation upon obedience to not just authority, but authority that is at least to some degree unaccountable and unjustifiable. Apparently neutral forms of organizational 'efficiency' (Jackson and Carter, 1995), 'effectiveness' and 'business competition' (Sievers, 2000) can be violence and violations. It is difficult to think of an organization that is not violating at all, whether in terms of managerial expectations of obedience to rules, non-intervention when violence is named or silencing of those seeking to expose violation.

An avenue for theoretical and empirical development is the examination of the extent to which particular organizations, and forms of organizing, make explicit the forms and sources of authority in use, and how these authorities are gendered. In most cases the unaccountable and unjustifiable authority of organizations is men's, and it is that which is violating. In terms of how this works in particular organizations, there may be several paradoxes. For example, organizations and organizing which rely most explicitly on physical violence for authority may both need to only periodically justify such general authority through violence and yet routinely not need to justify that particular authority through the very force of the violence. On the other hand, organizations and organizing which rely on non-violence for authority may routinely need to justify such particular authority and yet periodically may not need to justify the general authority through the very absence of explicit physical violence. Indeed in some organizational settings a norm of 'non-violence' may mean that social exchanges employing heavy persuasion and other techniques of authority are experienced as violating by those with less power. This may help to explain why, although coercive power may tend to be associated with alienative involvement with organizational members

(Etzioni, 1961), in some correctional institutions social deprivation and anti-staff culture may be *negatively* correlated (Cline, 1968).

A further consideration in theorizing organization violations is how violence and violation is different in organizations, both behaviourally and experientially, from other social contexts, most obviously in the house/home or in the street. Insights from both 'violence to known others' and 'street violence' need to be brought together as violation in organizations can involve both those known closely, even intimately, to each other and relative strangers in public places. An important question is how does violation in and around organizations bring distinct responses from others – onlookers, workers, clients, as well as managers and policy-makers? These violations and the responses to them are in a sense 'public', and thus likely to be different from those where the violation is constructed as 'private'.

The Context and Formation of Organizations

Violation also figures in the contexts and formation of organizations. Social structures provide the societal context of organizations, whether in state, business or other locations, which in turn form the context of particular organizations. Organizational formation typically takes place *in the context of* the structural relations of domination, control and violation. The formation of organizations also contributes to the reproduction of those structural relations and may only be understandable in that context, whatever organizational relations of violation are operative. Organizations can thus be understood as means of (re)creation of oppression and exclusion.

Such processes are most apparent in the historical formation of the state, and the historical development of the political and economic systems of slavery, feudalism, capitalism, imperialism, communism, and so on. The formation of states and political and economic systems have frequently involved violation. States, especially nation-states, have been established in competition with others, primarily by men to maintain rule, albeit historically temporary rule, over women. States retain the ability to use force through military and paramilitary organizations. Streets, land and buildings in a given area usually belong to the state if that need arises, as in wartime. Capitalism and capitalist organizations may not be actively violent at a given point in time. Yet the system of capitalism depends upon the obtaining of property both in the past and in other parts of the world. Thus, for example, food or minerals may be 'peacefully' consumed in the First World following organized violence in, say, South America. For these reasons, organizations need to be understood in the context of histories of patriarchy and especially public patriarchy (Walby, 1990; Hearn, 1992b), of patriarchal relations of violence, of the patriarchal state (Burstyn, 1983; MacKinnon, 1989; Connell, 1990) and of patriarchal capitalism and other economic systems (Mies, 1986; Waring, 1988). Patriarchal systems are based not only on men's domination over women, but also on some men's rule over other men through organizational hierarchies, by age, class, 'race', or other social divisions (Hearn, 1992b).

Specific organizations may be formed through processes or acts of violation. A prisoner of war camp is understandable by the violence of war preceding its formation. Alternatively, organizations may be formed by non-violence, for example a pacifist organization, or by some combination of processes involving violation, non-violence and ambiguous actions, for example a psychiatric institution. The conditions of formation of an organization may have lasting effects on organizational processes, not only in formal structures, but in continuing resentment, guilt and anxiety. To understand the place of violation in particular organizations, it is necessary to consider their relation to other organizations with their own agendas of violation, as in arms manufacturers' relations to the military.

In addition, historically changing organizational contexts and conditions are likely to shape the nature and extent of violation. Particular organizations have their own distinct histories in terms of perceptions, experiences and handling of violence. In some cases these histories go back a long way.[14] There is also a long history of violence in workplace resistance, sabotage and on picket lines, documented in industrial relations literature. Such histories enter into contemporary structurings and constructions of violation. This moves us on to the meso organizational level of analysis.

Meso Organizational Domains

Social Relations, Organizational Power Relations and Organizational Categories

Organizations occupy certain social domains, where particular structured social relations around violation operate in terms of gender, class, ethnic and other social relations. Typically structured organizationally defined power relations constitute a meso level of organization violations. Two aspects are considered here: first, the social relations of exploitation and oppression that constitute organizations, including the relevant organizational categories that are so formed and contribute to organizational structural violations; second, the broad organizational orientations to violence and violation. These aspects are constitutive of presence or absence of organization violations themselves.[15]

These organizational social relations effectively construct different categories of people who are collectively significant in the reproduction of organization violations. Indeed if organizations are the focus of the creation and re-creation of oppression and exclusion, then different categories of people are more or less subjected to forms of violation, through harassment, bullying, managerial controls, labour processes, cultural and ethnic exclusions, and so on. This brings us directly to the question of violations by organizationally defined categories, including, most obviously, particular managements, particular organizational groups of men and particular organizationally defined ethnic or cultural groups.

Several general analytical distinctions may be made between different social relations, all of which are likely to be gendered/sexualed. First, we may consider meso-patriarchal organization violations. These include the structured relations and power imbalances between men and women in organizations, and the associated violations. The inequality and rigidity of gender, sexual and other related social divisions (Gwartney-Gibbs and Lach, 1994) and the structured gendering of organizations are central issues here.

Second, there are meso-capitalist organization violations. To examine these involves a rethinking of the operation of structured economic class relations in organizations as violations, and the interpretation of at least some forms of capitalist work exploitation as violation. The importance of considering such exploitation in a globalizing context should be stressed (see Chapter 6). The point was made clearly by Friedrich Engels in an early discussion of what would now be called occupational injury and disease:

> If one individual inflicts bodily injury upon another which leads to the death of the person attacked we call it manslaughter; on the other hand, if the attacker knows beforehand that the blow will be fatal we call it murder. Murder has also been committed if society places workers in such a position that they inevitably come to premature and unnatural ends. ... Murder has been committed if society knows perfectly well that thousands of workers cannot avoid being sacrificed so long as these conditions are allowed to continue. Murder of this sort is just as culpable as the murder committed by an individual.[16]

Third, and more generally, it is important to take account of meso-cultural, ethnic and national organization violations. These have been less fully recognized than class and gender violations in organizational analysis. They include structured ethnic relations in organizations (institutional racism), collective violating actions of cultural majorities and the range of structured cultural exclusions in organizations. These may be defined by ethnicity, race, locality, language, culture, religion, citizenship or other cultural exclusions relating to bodily definitions, such as disability. These organizational categories of people may well overlap and interlink, for example, where there are strong connections of dominant white ethnic groups, men, management and organization violations. Where there are clear power imbalances between organizationally defined categories, it is likely that there will be low perceived costs of violence to the organization. These power imbalances may well be accompanied by high levels of dissatisfaction or stress. In such ways violence and violation may be normalized.

Organizational Orientations

A more specific set of questions concern organizational orientations to violation. It is necessary to be clear and specific about the various relationships between organizations and violation, and the *place of violence in aims and task of the organization*. Some organizations are more obviously orientated towards 'violence' and 'violation' than others, with, for example, some implicitly oriented to violence through the use of violence or control of violence (Hearn, 1994). Others are implicitly orientated to violence even when this is not an overt issue. Organizations are thus sites of violations, and one way of conceptualizing organization violations is to recognize that organizations can have an *explicit* or an *implicit* relation or orientation to violation (see Figure 4.6). In some organizations this involves the reproduction of institutional violence and violations.

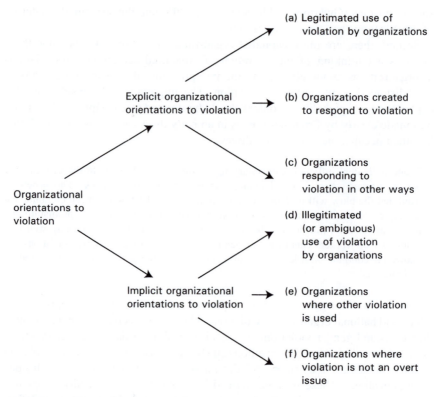

FIGURE 4.6   *Types of organizational orientation to violation*

Explicit relations include:

(a) the legitimated use of violence and violation by organizations (for example, the state, sport, schools);
(b) organizations created to respond to violence and violation (for example, criminal justice system, anti-violence/peace organizations);
(c) organizations explicitly responding to violence and violation in other ways.

Implicit relations include:

(d) the illegitimated use of and violation by managers/controllers/owners (for example, capitalist, counter-state);
(e) organizations where other violence and violation are used (for example, resistance);
(f) organizations where violence and violation are not overt issues.

These differentiations apply to both different types of organizations and different parts or aspects of given organizations. It is quite possible, indeed more than likely, that there will be more than one orientation to violation within an organization. In each type of organization or organizational aspect, different organizational structures, functions, operations and processes are likely. These include matters of hierarchy, accountability and discretion; professional and occupational constructions; negotiations ('a zone of uncertainty') around what constitute different forms of violation; forms of client–organization relations (for example, 'batch', single); talk about violation in work cultures (Hearn, 1994). We briefly consider six broad types of organizational orientation to violation.

(a) *Legitimated use of violation by organizations*   In organizations where violence is legitimated (though not legitimate), an important question is how this is articulated and framed within the goals and objectives of the organization. The organizational forms of *routine* social processes or social activities as overtly or physically violent may be relatively rare outside military, paramilitary, sport, pornography, criminal, sado-masochistic and genocidal organizations. There is a large literature here from studies of the military, the police and organized crime (for example, Harries-Jenkins and van Doorn, 1976; Ryan and Rush, 1997). Such organizations are simultaneously engaged in the doing of violence, the maintenance of the potential for violence and the justification of violence. Such legitimated use of violation needs to be located within a broad social framework, and particularly men's use of violence (Morgan, 1987; Karner, 1998). Such organizations are characteristically created, dominated and staffed by men; the form they take is typically very closely entwined with the dominant actions of men and the construction of very particular forms of men's practices and identities. The dominant way of enacting these is through the reproduction of hierarchy, often a strict hierarchy. In many such organizations there may often be the risk of the extension and elaboration of violence into further forms, either within the organization, as in prison suicides, or externally, as in rape in war. However, even in such organizations, there are great variations in the extent to which overt physical violence is part of organizational routine. A military organization may not necessarily routinely engage in overt physical violence. A martial arts organization may be routinely involved with controlled violence within the rules of that activity, while the dominant goals may be the making of profit. With sport, routine organizational activity may often be characterized as ritualized violence. In some cases a major element of organizational activity is the watching of violence, as in, for example, professional boxing promotions and pornography cinemas.[17]

An outstanding example of the analysis of the dynamics of institutional violence in organizations of this kind has been produced by Robert Johnson (1986). In a wide-ranging review of the literature on war, the military, massacres, concentration camps, torture, police, prisons, as well as some industrial workplaces, he sets out some of the major organizational and social pyschological processes by which violence is reproduced. He argues to some extent for a naturalistic model of human behaviour in that for such violence to be done repeatedly and routinely it has to be underwritten by authorization. The means to this 'dehumanization' include bureaucratic organizing, procedures and rules; isolation of the organization from mainstream moral values and regular external review; and insulation of workers or agents of the institution (p. 188 ff.). Organizational isolation can be physical (behind walls, etc.) or social. In both cases it is also psychological for those concerned. Such organizations also socialize and train their personnel '... to insulate them from awareness or appreciation of the moral dimensions of their behavior' (p. 184). Responsibilities can be dispersed and impersonal rather than clear and personal. An important part of these organizational processes is the reproduction of transcendent and mundane authorizations (Kelman, 1973). The first are vague justifications of the expendability of people; the second are more specific justifications of how stipulated ends will be achieved. Both constitute organizational ideologies. Those likely to receive violence can be constructed as less than human, as numbers, as not-people, as when bomber pilots use psychological devices to convince themselves that their work does not involve harming others. Despite these and many other insightful points, and some attention to issues of class and race, Johnson avoids issues of gender and sexuality.

A problematic issue that particularly concerns military, paramilitary and similar organizations is the difficulty of maintaining the potential for physical violence to others outside the organization while minimizing, or reducing, that violence to each other (and the self) within the organization. This classic dilemma for armies is examined in Dixon's (1976) *The Psychology of Military Incompetence*. He argues that the primary anxiety is redirected by and controlled through organizational devices, such as rules and procedures. However, the most important element of organizational process in such organizations is that they produce and reproduce violation, pain and damage. Accordingly, people with such experiences may remain in the organization, be expelled from it or even be killed. This issue has been the subject of increased study in recent years in terms of the intersection of such processes and masculinities (Bowker, 1998; also see Bourke, 1999). For example, Huggins and Haritos-Fatouros (1998) have examined masculinities among Brazilian police torturers and murderers, comparing the 'lone-wolf' and the 'institutional functionaries' as different organizational forms and masculinities.

There is also a major set of studies on the reactions and agency of those who are the objects of violence in concentration camps and other similar organizations. Following Bettelheim (1960, 1979) and Arendt (1963), there have developed very powerful debates and disagreements on the social compliance and/or resistance of those violated in these most violent organizations. There is a growing recognition of the importance of survivors' accounts and resistances in response to processes of cultural duping.[18] The accounts and resistances of those murdered, such as 'the missing ones', are clearly less easily retrieved.

(b) Organizations created to respond to violation   In organizations created to respond to violence and violation, 'violence' becomes both an element in the achievement of goals and an element in the routine performance of work. This is most clearly seen in psychiatric institutions, criminal justice agencies, the probation service and anti-violence/peace organizations. In some cases, violation, particularly physical violence, may be transformed into a file or a case. Such definitions may be overlain by professional ideologies that are either tolerant, even accepting, of violence,

or are unambiguously opposed to violence. The resort to procedures and proceduralism is perhaps not surprising. The processing of violence and violation interrelates with diverse organizational processes, including the construction of rules on how violence and violation are handled in the organization. In studying men's violence to known women, that violence outside the organizations in question was often 'reduced' to an element of the organizational structure, function, operation and process (Hearn, 1998). The way this happens and continues to happen involves interrelations between the men's violence to women, men's explanations of that violence, organizational/professional–client relations within worker culture, formal organizational goals and talks, and violation in the organization more generally. Through these kinds of interconnections we are not only concerned with the links between client relations and work-group cultures, but the links between client relations and patriarchalism/anti-patriarchalism in organizations.

In such organizational situations, responses to violation are often part of organization–client relations. This is likely to involve engaging with the pain and damage from violence, past or present. The place of the violated is undervalued and undervoiced in most organizational contexts. There may even be a sense in which organizational process is (usually) antithetic to the recognition of the full experience of pain from violence. On the other hand, organizing around pain and damage can produce very powerful organizational processes, not least in the movement from violation to anger to action. Such organizational dynamics and contradictions may be especially important in survivors' (of violence) organizations. Organizational responses to violence, past or present, may develop ambiguous social processes between destructive violating experiences and 'de-violenced' structures and modes of being.

(c) Organizations explicitly responding to violation in other ways Explicit responses to violation and indeed threatened and potential violation are found in many other organizations, in the form of policies and procedures on violation and sexual violence, for example sexual harassment and 'campus rape'. This is becoming increasingly common in welfare agencies, sometimes prompted by physical and verbal threats from clients to workers. It is also becoming an increasingly important issue in commercial organizations, particularly in terms of the safety and security of staff. There are a number of organizational considerations which may highlight these questions, including workers working alone or in small groups, the handling of money or other valuable goods, the entry of women into organizations and occupations that have been 'men's domains', work in high risk areas of cities and other organizational activity that is unpopular or perceived as hostile by others.

(d) Illegitimated (or ambiguous) use of violation by organizations Whereas some organizations appear to rest on the pursuit of violent goals with an explicitly legitimated orientation to violation, others have an illegitimated or ambiguous relation to violation. Thus, violation may not be part of official goals but may be officially sanctioned or may be an ambiguous phenomenon, as in the use of corporal punishment and other violation in schools. Elsewhere, violation may become part

of the unofficial goals or at least taken-for-granted practices of the organizations. This could be argued to have been the case in the Pindown episode (Levy and Kahan, 1991), where violent regimes became institutionalized, even though physical violence was not part of the official organizational aims or practices. In such situations, violence and violation may express and reproduce hierarchies. In some organizations, for example prisons, violence between peers (inmates) may be used as a form of control by managers, staff or others in authority.

(e) *Organizations where other violations are used*   Violation may also occur in a number of other ways in organizations. These include the use of physical violence to resist authority, hierarchy or even presence in the organization at all. Thus the organizational relationship between the violator and the violated is a crucial issue in understanding how violence and violation relate to organizational dynamics. Such relationships might include violence between workers and managers, between organizational peers and between clients and professionals.

An important and intensely practical issue is how organizational members maintain organizational relations when physical or other violence does occur in or around organizations. This is especially important when violence is relevant to the task of the organization. This is one of the challenges examined by Baron (1987) in *Asylum to Anarchy*. Following a violent incident in a therapeutic community, in which a patient is badly injured and two staff are punched in the face, the staff move on to discuss the violence as an instance of differing perspectives on the ideology of the organization. This includes differences on how staff respond to violence and reinterpret, through psychodynamic or other frameworks, other staffs' positions. In particular, a key area for attention is the interrelation of administrative and therapeutic concerns. To collapse them into one 'system' of authority and control opens up the way for totalitarianism (whether by totally administrative or totally therapeutic modes); a partial solution is the creation of separate modes by time, place or personnel.

(f) *Organizations where violation is not an overt issue*   In some, indeed many, organizations, violation does not appear as an overt issue at all. This may be because violation does not occur, because talking about violation is not part of the dominant discourse(s) of that organization, or even because violation does occur and is experienced as such, but it is in the interests of the violators not to recognize this as an overt issue. Of special interest here is Johnson's (1986) commentary on institutional violence in some industrial workplaces. He argues that similar processes can operate there in dehumanizing workers as in those found in military, prison and police organizations where violence is, in some senses, more openly legitimated. In situations of great work and production pressure, managers and supervisors may push workers to work in ways that are dangerous, exhausting or in other respects health or even life-threatening.

Micro Intra-organizational Processes and Practices

While the place of violence and violation within organizational domains and orientations, with their broad patterns of organizational structure, function and operation, is very significant in providing the main contours of organizational life, it does not necessarily determine the local complexities of violations within organizations. To do this involves attending to micro processes of organization violations. The notion of organizational process(es) is immensely important in considering both the temporal aspects of organization violations and the impact of intensification. Organizations can be understood as social processes, as sites of organizing and as accumulations of organizational practices rather than fixed organizational structures. Such social processes include small group interaction processes, management styles of control, flows of information and the reproduction of organizational cultures over time. These processes may contribute to or undermine the goals and tasks of the organization. The specific processing of violations is part of the general social processes of organizations and organizational worlds, and as such has several elements:

- organizations process violations;
- violations are processed within organizations;
- organizational processes are themselves violations in some organizations;
- violations are not just 'incidents' but ongoing processes – they have a processual character;
- violations develop through their own complex processes over time, including the enactment of violations and the responses to them, that themselves may constitute violations, and their interrelations.

At this level of analysis useful distinctions can be made between relatively given and more variable organizational conditions. Standing and Nicolini (1997) point to certain factors of organizational life that are, in the short term at least, relatively fixed or as they call them 'invariant/constrained'. These include: organizational purpose and task, location, relative size of the organization, the extent of cash handling, client base, ascribed characteristics of employees, for example their gender or age. On the other hand, other factors are more 'manipulable', even in the relative short term. These include: management style and culture, staffing levels, recruitment and selection procedures, working process and cash handling procedures, risk assessment routines, staff expectations and awareness, organizational awareness and proactivity around violence, and degree of organizational isolation.

Such contrasts are, however, not always clearcut; moreover, they do not articulate the micro-organizational processes and practices of social divisions within organizations. Micro-patriarchal violations often entail particular groups of men routinely producing violations, for example through perpetuating men's dominant organizational cultures. Violating, usually masculine, organizational cultures that reproduce violent, bullying, harassing and conflictual behaviours and experiences are crucial here (Parkin and Maddock, 1994). Organizational responses to violence are also significant. Sexual harassment research suggests that inadequate managerial responses can reinforce rather than resolve sexual harassment claims (Collinson and Collinson, 1996). The nature of these responses may be related to the gender profile of management.

Micro-economic violations include both managerial violation and work and labour processes themselves that can be violent/violating or likely to lead to violence/violation. This may be through monotony of work (Appelberg, 1996), the rigidity of organizational hierarchies and task allocation, and work intensification and work pressure. Similarly, as noted, several sectors and factors appear to present particular risks of physical violence, such as handling money and/or valuable goods, those in authority, lone workers, providers of care, advice, education and service and those working with potentially violent people and in 'dangerous work' (Cardy, 1992; Woods et al., 1993). The local organizational construction of time and space can have specific implications for the production of violence. Similar effects may result from the increasing pressure on employees to work longer hours as part of the '24-hour-a-day economy'. Late-night opening of retail outlets can render employees, especially women workers, vulnerable to intentionally harmful behaviour, for example robberies or sexual attack. Lone workers, such as taxi drivers, may be particularly vulnerable to violence.

Critical literature on power and organization theory, particularly on managerial practices and organizational cultures, suggests a detailed approach to the analysis of organization violations. This points to the critical examination of effects of managerial and organizational processes on the reproduction and construction of violations. Critical studies of management and organizations, such as labour process theory and debates thereon, highlight the detrimental effects on employees of management control systems (Leidner, 1993) in 'dangerous working environments' (Jermier et al., 1989) and with particular technologies (Zuboff, 1989). Managerial power and control can often be reconceptualized as violation or tending to increase violation. While such systems and motivations might not intend to generate directly harmful or violating effects, they may contribute to work cultures that in turn increase tension and/or vulnerabilities and facilitate intentionally harmful behaviours at work. Wright and Smye (1997) have identified three kinds of corporate abuse: extremely competitive, win/lose corporate cultures in which people strive against their colleagues rather than with them; blaming cultures in which people are frightened to step out of line; and sacrifice and overwork cultures which involve people putting their jobs and their work above their personal and social lives and well-being to the extent that they become ill (see Johnson, 1986). These processes and practices may be exarcerbated where there are distinct 'front' and 'back' regions, for example in commercial kitchens.

More specific factors which can increase violence and violation include restructuring crises and other organizational changes. Of relevance here are organizational changes such as customer care initiatives, work intensification, expansion of contract work and internal markets, quality initiatives and business process re-engineering, technological innovations, restructuring and downsizing, surveillance and new forms of managerial control. Reorganizations can be fruitful grounds for violations. Organizational crisis, work stress, strong internal competition and time pressures may be associated with bullying, scapegoating and other violations (Einarsen et al., 1994; Vartia, 1996; also see Kivimäki et al., 2000). Teamworking can generate conflict between co-workers where intense pressure to meet deadlines leads to aggression towards those who have difficulty complying with required production levels, especially where increased work pressures impinge on group cohesion (Klein, 1996).[19]

These kinds of organizational processes and practices interlink closely with other micro-cultural, broadly ethnic violations involving local organizational exclusions of 'outsiders'. Workplace cultures are important in constraining or facilitating the emergence of violence. Possible 'motivating factors' (Salin, 1999) towards violation include the nature of the reward system and expected benefits, the presence of very high or very low performing colleagues or subordinates, as well as changes in the workgroup that lead to dominant subgroups engaging in resistance to those changes. The literature on workplace resistance (Jermier et al., 1994), drawing on poststructuralist analyses of subjectivity (Kondo, 1990) and emotion (Fineman, 1993), has highlighted the significance of the 'non-rational' and the 'emotional' in organizational behaviour and questioned overly rationalist assumptions about human behaviour that have dominated the organizational literature. Violence may also be an outcome of perceived injustice (for either subordinate or dominant groups) within or from organizations. Resistant violations may sometimes take the form of the unjust appropriation of parts of the organization: time, work, products (Ackroyd and Thompson, 1999); but not all 'organizational misconducts' can be considered violations. Violations, that are analytically understandable as arising from conscious or unconscious resistance, may paradoxically and unfairly be enacted towards those in less powerful organizational positions, some would say through processes of interpersonal projection. Violations towards the more powerful may be performed in the name of resistance, however morally justifiable they may be. In the most extreme form, sacked employees, particularly in the USA, have responded by shooting their superiors and/or colleagues. Violence may also be targeted against oneself, for example drug abuse. In Japan, the term *Karoshi* has been coined to describe employee suicides as a result of overwork (Collinson and Collinson, 1997).[20] Where (usually gendered) workplace cultures are characterized by heavy drinking and/or intense competition between employees within or between organizations, violence may be more likely. Heavy drinking also can be a means of workers dealing with feelings of intense conflict, guilt or shame (Johnson, 1986: 196) – in extreme cases in the military, death camps and other organizations specializing in violence.

The details of how violation episodes develop over time and how organizational life is lived and experienced by organizational members in relation to violation deserves much further research. The qualitative dynamics of such organizational situations may develop over long time periods and take complex forms. It is here that Standing and Nicolini's (1997) work on scenarios is of value (see pp. 79–82). In distinguishing different kinds of relationships between participants, though admittedly not in a fully comprehensive way, they lay the foundation for further detailed studies of the dynamics of violations. Rather similar insights have been suggested by Gwartney-Gibbs and Lach (1994) on gender and workplace disputes. Their approach addresses origins, processes and outcomes of such disputes; in each phase they emphasize the importance of the patterning of gender roles, sex segregation in jobs and institutionalized work structures.

Leymann (1992a) has looked at the developmental processes of bullying episodes in workplaces and how they often move through various stages – from conflicts and unethical communication, targeting of individuals by psychological violence, violating responses by personnel staff, to expulsion. Sometimes the process may recommence with other targets. Another example is the place of insults in organizational life, with their dynamics of apology, commensurate or disproportionate retaliation and escalation (Gabriel, 1998). In such dynamics audiences may be of special significance. Insults provide means for the development of domination and subordination; sometimes resistance; finer gradations of status and power relations; and alliances and coalitions.

There is also a definite need to recognize the impact of these mundane processes upon individuals, as either violators or violated. Organizations provide many social and psychological resources for the reproduction of individual psychologies of violation. These include the processes of rationalization, distancing, following organizational 'role' and authority, and trivialization, perhaps through humour. For example, bomber pilots and crew may adopt trivializing, casual, ironic and supposedly humorous psychological and linguistic methods, such as 'There goes the cookie', in continuing their bombing without too much direct thought for the impact of their bombs (Johnson, 1986; Smith, 1993). This is a more extreme case of routines of organizational defence against violations to those that may occur in what are usually considered more peaceful organizations and workplaces (Menzies, 1960). Similarly, there is the importance and impact of the presence of individuals and groups of people who are more (or less) likely to be violent/violating. This may be because of their previous enactment of violence, or their membership of a social category that is more likely to be violent, for example the social category of 'men'. In some organizations the work of the organization is routinely concerned with people who are likely to be violent. For some individuals – managers, employees, users – dramatic organizational changes may be significant in understanding violation, as in the examples of shooting and suicide.

These detailed work processes and practices operate at the level of everyday discourses and consciousness, as in the following example on the relation of violation to the reproduction of masculinities and men's power. At several points in research on men's violence to women (Hearn, 1998), 'horror stories' were told to the researchers by men workers. These were either about particular horrific cases of men's violence to women or men's threats on men professionals. The stories seemed to have several meanings; they conveyed a sense of both voyeurism and bravado. They confirmed a certain kind of masculinity ('I can take it'), while at the same time admitting an emotional response to violence. Past events were objectified and externalized, and simultaneously the worker said something for his benefit, dealing with the feelings that persist. This kind of talk can of course easily slip into a verbally or even physically violent work culture, as when clients are characterized as 'full of shit'. Such forms of men–men talk have been examined in factories (Cockburn, 1983) and sport (Curry, 1991).[21] For the men, such as probation workers, solicitors and social workers, there was often a profound ambiguity between a routine 'straight' masculinity (set within a conventional homosexual subtext) and a less obviously heterosexual, more ambiguous sexuality that is saying 'I'm not like that'.

Of particular interest was the way in which accounts given by individual men and accounts of staff in agencies that deal with them often mirrored each other. For example, men in contact with the Probation Service tended to see their violence to women as secondary to other crimes and often talked at length of their violence to men; probation officers often did not focus on violence to women as the main issue in their work with the men. In contrast, men in men's programmes usually accepted that violence to women was the central problem and sometimes developed relatively sophisticated explanations thereof; workers in those programmes similarly saw violence as central and developed complex understandings of it that related both to general questions of power and control, and the individualities of individual men. Working on and responding to violence involves not just dealing directly with violence but also constructing accounts and explanations of violence. Definitions and explanations of violence by agencies and agency staff are themselves often dominated by men. The way that men who have been violent provide definitions of, and excuses and justifications for, their violence is often mirrored in the accounts of staff in agencies that deal with men that are also dominated by men (Hanmer and Hearn, 1999). While both individual men and agency men may avoid the topic of violence, both may also reproduce it by treating it as a strictly separable activity (Jukes, 1993): this separation of 'violence' from men's power and control in general can become part of the problem of violation in organizations.

Interrelations of Violations

Finally in this chapter we need to address a number of kinds of interconnections. First, there are many interconnections between macro, meso and micro levels of analysis. One major theme of connection is the form that organizations take, the kinds of organizational worlds created. In the next two chapters we consider two very different kinds of organizational forms and worlds: the closed institution and the global network. The interrelations of coercion, violence, abuse and confinement are particularly important areas for study within total institutions (Johnson, 1986). Such organizations are frequently, perhaps characteristically, bound in a profound paradox whereby they are separated off from the rest of society for specific purposes and yet that separation creates the conditions for other purposes to be pursued there. This may mean that societal or official purposes of violence/violation may be subverted, or official purposes of non-violence may be subverted so that violence is enacted. These issues are especially significant where the residents are not there voluntarily.

Second, there are the complex links between organizational structures, policies, occupational constructions of violence/violation, relations with those who have been violent, and teamwork and other organizational processes and practices. It is likely that the greater the violence, and the more immediate the contact with violence, the greater the likely range of coping strategies used by staff. This also entails issues of stress and anxiety for the violent and the violated, managers, staff and users.

A third kind of interconnection is between violation by organizations, violation in organizations and organizational responses to violation. These are conceptually distinct but may in practice be simultaneous and overlapping. Organizational responses may be part of the goals of organization, including, for example, the extent to which violence and restraint are used. Furthermore, all these aspects of the relationship of organizations and violation are, or at least may be, contested. This is most easily seen in contestation around talking about violence, for talking about violence may be a means for further violation by the violator of the violated. In these and other ways, organizations are also engaged in the process of constructing and defining violence and violation. These practices and processes of organizational construction apply to all three aspects – violation by organizations, violation in organizations and organizational responses to violation. All three are in part cultural constructions, and contribute to the cultural construction of violence and violation. Such cultural constructions contribute to the reproduction of masculinities and femininities in organizations and elsewhere. For example, masculinity may be defined through the performance of violence, the potential for violence, the emulation of others' violence, the denial of violence or even sometimes opposition to violence.

This chapter has approached organizational analysis through a focus on violation. In some ways this builds on the tradition of the Tavistock School, exemplified by Jaques's (1976) analysis of the psychological dynamics of bureaucracy. He argued that if accountability and authority were not clearly specified, delegitimated power will develop, so that '(i)f the situation becomes widespread it is a potential source of energy for social violence' (p. 68). While this does seem an overly deterministic (and prescriptive) formulation, it does highlight the way in which (social) violence can be intrinsically embedded in organizational processes and practices. Whereas Jaques sees accountability, authority and organizational rules as necessary to control and deflect 'social violences', we see such organizational structures and processes as a means to managing, masking and obscuring the pervasiveness of violence. There remains a need for conceptualizations of the relationship of organizations, violences and violations, including the extent to which organizations can be understood as violence/violation. By this we do not mean that organizations are simply violent and violating by virtue of their direct use of violence and violation, both within and beyond themselves; rather we are thinking of the extent to which organizations depend for their continuation upon obedience to unaccountable or unjustifiable authority (see Lessnoff, 1986). For these and other reasons, organizations, violences and violations may overlap; organizations may be forms of violation, may use violation, may house violation, may respond to violation and may be characterized by organizational processes and practices around violation.

5

Enclosure

Organization Violations and Institutionalization

with Lorraine Green

Organization violations occur within different organizational forms and through different organizational processes. A fundamental aspect of the form of organizations is the extent of enclosure and openness, while central elements in organizational processes are development, change and sometimes intensification over time. These features have major implications for gender, sexuality and violation. In this and the next chapter we explore two contrasting organizational forms and organizational processes, including their relation to organization violations. First, we examine closed organizations, and the ways in which violations, as part of organizational processes, are contained and intensified within given institutional boundaries, in relative isolation from the outside world. In the next chapter, the expansion and transformation of organizations and violations in the globalizing world is discussed.

Focus material on children's homes and other institutions demonstrates how institutionalized settings may facilitate regular violations of the person and the silencing by stigmatization of residents. Residential care organizations, particularly those supposedly caring for children, are considered. Inquiries into abuse and violence in such settings have tended to focus on identifying the person or persons responsible or in changing rules, regulations, policies and procedures rather than examining organizational forms, structures and processes which may contribute to the situation. The relationship between organizational forms and those living and working there is explored in terms of broad inequalities and oppressions.

Organizational Worlds, Forms and Processes

Organizational worlds often produce hegemonic dominations of the situation. Dimensions of power, not easily correlated with, but still inseparable from, formal structures exist, along with more fluid aspects of culture and discourse. These are key matters for the material reproduction and construction of gender, sexuality and violation. For example, the imposition of heterosexual norms through formal and cultural aspects of organizational life underpinned by hegemonic masculinity is a powerful silencing of other forms of sexuality and gender.

Organizational worlds exist across macro, meso and micro levels, and in the previous chapter we have outlined these elements in the construction of organization violations. While these have introduced the questions of organizational form and organizational process to some extent, some additional exploration of these concepts is necessary here. There are several aspects to organizational form but one that is crucial is the extent of organizational openness and closure from the world beyond the organization. Thus we see organizational form as distinct from organizational structure or organizational hierarchy. Most organizations are characterized by some degree of closure from the outside. However, specifically closed and isolated organizational forms are of special interest in relation to violation.

The notion of organizational form also cuts across the macro, meso and micro levels of analysis previously used. Closed and isolated organizations operate within historical, extra-organizational conditions that form the organizations, create the possibility of their separation from the outside world and construct the social categories of people that are placed and often indeed confined within them. For example, in the eighteenth and nineteenth centuries, many Western societies applied the principles of large-scale factory organization to 'people-containing organizations' for definite segments of the population. People were contained in large orphanages, asylums, almshouses and workhouses as sites of totality and institutionalization. Indeed most closed organizations are in fact the creation of previously existing organizations. These extra-organizational conditions link with the meso organizational domains of such 'total' organizations. These organizational domains also have special features in terms of fields of power and responsibility, organizational boundaries, structures, hierarchies, regimes and often very specific orientations to violation.

These broadly structural conditions provide the organizational context for micro intra-organizational processes and practices. These often appear to involve intensified organizational dynamics, not least in the creation, conduct and resistance to violation. Organizational closure and isolation often seem to be accompanied by intensification of organizational processes. Closed organizations can be seen as archetype, historical legacy, relic and contemporary realities, even within rapidly changing globalizing forces. Closed organizations say and show what we often take organizations to be. Closed institutions are the paradigm case of the organizational, especially within traditional and modern conceptions. Such relatively isolated organizational units are often subject to strong internal controls, whilst being difficult to control externally.

Total Institutions, Closed Organizations

We have already noted (pp. 93–4) the work of Johnson (1986) on the possible dehumanizing effects of closed, isolated organizations and the organizational and social psychological processes by which violence is reproduced. He has emphasized 'the institutional arrangements that ... structure situations and, to a lesser extent, develop dispositions and perceptions that (1) neutralize normal moral restraints against violence and (2) supply the motives and mechanisms necessary to carry out violence or to permit violence to occur, on a regular basis' (p. 184). Johnson goes on to examine the situational constraints effecting authorization to harm, whether transcendent (general, often vague, akin to value-rationality) or mundane (specific, means for achieving stipulated ends, akin to instrumental rationality). Organizational crises, bureaucracy and organizational isolation are all examined in this light. He then focuses on situational socialization in and around organizations that may assist such authorizations and dehumanizations. Bureaucratic policies, statutes, legal decisions, training, procedures, routines, dispersal of responsibility and divisions of labour are all invoked in the reproduction of both the organizational conditions and the immediate psychological perceptions that facilitate violence. While Johnson's work provides a very powerful and compelling account, it can be criticized for presenting an overly humanistic model of both persons and violation: non-violence is seen as 'normal' and 'violence' is seen as contrary to that 'normality'. It also neglects class, ethnic, gender, sexual and indeed other social relations. However, it does clearly point to the power of bureaucracies, large impersonal institutions, heavily structured, strictly hierarchical, militaristic organizations and isolated total regimes in the construction of organization violations.

Closed organizations or total institutions involve the total or attempted control of bodies of residents, including their sexuality, as people eat, sleep, work and play under a unified organizational structure. They are defined by barriers – physical, social and/or psychological. Total institutions are not random in their recruitment across these boundaries, tending to gather the old, the young, the sick, the criminal, the poor and sometimes the very rich. The dominant divisions between public and private domains, found in many other societal arenas, are less clear or are abolished. Indeed issues of sexuality, and its possible control, are almost always significant in total institutions. Goffman's (1961, 1969) studies of processes of institutionalization in large psychiatric hospitals and other closed organizations demonstrate how structures of control, surveillance and totality affect individual and collective behaviour.[1] Compounded by isolation and separation from the outside world, they can produce conditions that contribute to violations within them, including around sexuality, gender, race and other social divisions. Processes of degradation, mortification and 'stigmatized status', along with resistance, adaptation and mutually hostile, if often symbiotic, staff/inmate cultures, lead to the construction of individuals with little or no voice. They are organizationally constructed as unable to 'speak' of the violations inflicted by the processes themselves and by those working there. Such institutionalized worlds are 'unspoken': those living there do not usually have a voice. This may lead to abuse continuing undetected and unchallenged over long periods of time. Violences against them have for a long time been unspoken and unheard, whether in long-stay hospitals (Martin, 1984), asylums or prisons.

Interestingly, total institutions have occupied a special place in recent mainstream, generally non-gendered, social theory. In addition to Goffman, well-cited male social theorists who have addressed this issue include Bauman, Bettelheim, Foucault and Giddens. Rather paradoxically, Goffman's work on systemic processes of humiliation, depersonalization, dispossession and degradation within institutionalization stands in tension with his own methodological stance on the micro-social processes of self-presentation and reality construction. Such totalizing perspectives relate closely to Bauman's (1989) analysis of exclusion leading to depersonalization, dehumanizing and moral invisibility in the Holocaust or 'final solution'.[2] When the task of organizational members is reduced to obeying or refusing to obey a command then action is removed from the sphere of morality and becomes a matter of organization or technique.[3] This also link with Foucault's (1977) work on 'panoptic' monitoring of the person qua body in organizations, including those formally labelled as 'caring'.

Varieties of 'Total Institution'

The term 'total institution' may not only refer to large-scale organizations. First, elements of totality can also occur in organizations that are not obviously perceived as total institutions. Relatively closed or 'total' worlds, such as armies, ships and the fire service, often have ideologies and cultures operating within strong physical or social barriers, creating forms of closure which can inhibit speaking out on how the organizations treat women, gays, lesbians, black people and other subordinated groups. Such institutions are forms of 'social total institution', within which closed, frequently masculinist cultures reproduce racial and sexual harassment. In one sense it is 'understandable' that violence is part of the organizational worlds of prison, army or police, as they are either controlling violent individuals, preparing for or engaged in warfare, or dealing with acts of violence. Violence manifests itself in obvious ways as part of the job but also in other ways in which the organization deals with members of subordinated groups that join. The ability to leave the organization and access to compensation through tribunal or courts varies according to the type of organization and the people involved. Even with possible recourse to litigation, there is violence inherent in such systems through the labelling of those who complain as 'whistle-blowers', the blaming of victims, suspension from work, destruction of careers, further persecution and physical and mental ill-health.

Second, such processes of institutionalization and violation can recur in both small organizations and those created for 'caring'. In many countries large long-stay institutions have been closed in recent years with people moved into smaller community homes and hostels. Such shifts from 'containment' to 'care', whether in community 'homes' or smaller residential establishments, do not necessarily stop voices of the residents being 'unspoken'. It is not so apparent that these smaller organizational forms and structures, with their emphasis on being 'homelike' settings caring for vulnerable and dependent people, can also be described in terms of totality and institutionalization. Forms of totality, closure and control of bodies can occur in such small units and can be particularly dangerous when they merge with notions of home and domesticity. Whatever the organization's size, totality and closure concern the control of time, space and bodies and usually control of sections of the population often least able to defend themselves or gain public sympathy. The people so housed are still often isolated and invisible from public gaze, and have little voice in the world outside their 'homes' to demand how they should be cared for. It is not just being categorized as vulnerable through being old or sick or young but being placed in residential care as a 'last resort' when all else has failed, as with the admission of an older person who can no longer be sustained in the community or a child with difficult behaviour. Such groups are particularly vulnerable to abuses of power and not likely to have their protests heard even if they dare 'speak' them. Recent scandals about violence to older people, children and people with learning needs suggests that the smallness of the organized 'home' does not necessarily solve these problems.

Scandals and Corruption in Residential Care

Residential care settings are places where people live together. Official inquiries into scandals in long-stay hospitals in the UK in the 1970s initially focused on the 'bad apple' assumption that the scandals were explicable in terms of the corrupting influence of particular individuals (Wardhaugh and Wilding, 1993). Subsequently the focus has moved towards the organization in which the corruption had taken place. To some extent this reflected the impact of Goffman's work who had seen the corruption of institutional care produced by the very nature of the institutions. In discussing scandals and corruption in closed institutions, Wardhaugh and Wilding drew on Kelman's (1973) paper 'Violence without moral restraint', in outlining eight propositions which contribute to the corruption of care. Kelman suggests that the focus of any inquiry into violence should not be on the *motives* for violence but on the *conditions* in which the usual moral inhibitions against violence become weakened. The propositions are summarized as follows:

> The corruption of care depends on the neutralization of *moral* concerns in that residents and patients come to be viewed as beyond the normal bounds of moral behaviour and less than fully human.
>
> The corruption of care is closely connected with the balance of power and powerlessness in organizations whereby the vulnerability of 'inmates' is furthered by issues of gender and ethnicity but also where staff who have absolute power over residents are themselves powerless within the organization.
>
> Particular pressures and particular kinds of work are associated with the corruption of care and this is linked to working with people who lack worth and value in the eyes of society and who are depersonalized. Official aspirations and standards, especially staff training, are not resourced.
>
> Management failure underlies the corruption of care with comprehensive failure of management to act in spite of numerous complaints from residents and staff. There was a frequent lack of clear guidance and direction.

The corruption of care is more likely in enclosed, inward looking organizations where there is a degree of isolation along with a strong sense of group loyalty and criticism and complaints were easily stifled along with routinised and conservative practice. Within these closed worlds few would dissent.

The absence of clear lines and mechanisms of accountability plays an important part in the corruption of care exacerbated by the lack of status of users and their families and distance from community or other outside safeguards.

Particular models of work and organization are conducive to the corruption of care citing professional, hierarchical factors as well as size of units and types of difficulty encountered with residents.

The nature of the client groups encourages the corruption of care with children, older people and those with learning difficulties sharing common characteristics in that they are seen as less sentient beings because of their difficulties or age. Violence could be excused on the grounds that 'they don't understand' or as part of the wider context which accepts forms of violence towards children. This is exacerbated by societal indifference towards many groups as well as the day-to-day difficulties they may present to carers.[4]

Wardhaugh and Wilding (1993) also suggest that 'particular models of work organization … promote inward-looking and narrowed models of internal reporting; attention is drawn to the stifling of self-criticism and complaint, professional isolation, routinization and undue hierarchy'.[5] For example, Aitkin and Griffin (1996) have explored abuse in hospitals and residential settings for older people, noting this is usually regarded as distinct from abuse in the home.[6] They identify features of abuse and violence in residential settings for older people, starting with the recognition of the frequency with which victims can be ignored or sidelined by finding excuses for perpetrators. This lack of solidarity with the victim is itself an act of *ideological* violence and an indication of the power of discourse which legitimates violence, stigmatizes victims and treats people not as active agents but as material for social policy (p. 80).[7]

An important gendered aspect of abuse in some residential care is the recognition that the abuse may be by women against women. This contradicts constructions of women as non-violent and men as violent. Carework is still very much the province of women and constructed as part of the 'domestic' realm. Paid carework and 'people work' (Goffman, 1961) are widely not considered as 'work', reinforcing tacit assumptions about its nature. These include assumptions that women are sympathetic, are equipped to deal with bodily substances, are able to provide for others emotionally, enjoy work as an extension of their 'natural'/domestic role and engage in it by choice. Yet workers also resist, as in their, whether women's or men's, subcultures of 'toughness'.

In Lee-Treweek's (1997) nursing home study, rather than doing care, the auxiliaries themselves saw their work in instrumental terms and survived by dehumanizing the patients and ritualizing their work.[8] The materials and matter of care are the recipients of care, the wards and the bedrooms. Although residents' privacy may be supposed to be respected, their 'private' areas of the bedroom can become workers' workplaces. With hierarchical power exerted on auxiliaries, they can exercise power over residents. Work is as much about order as in a factory or office, with the end product being a 'clean, orderly quiet resident'

(Lee-Treweek, 1997: 54). Lee-Treweek describes 'situational withdrawal' when nursing home patients, as 'end products', were sat in total compliant silence. This contributes to the processes of keeping violences 'unspoken'. Thus violation in workplaces cannot be separated from the nature of the work itself and their particular organizational worlds. Those perpetrating violence may themselves be powerless in the organization but have absolute power over residents. This is particularly so with the female auxiliaries who held complete control of residents' private bedroom space where the pressures of the work led to mechanistic and dehumanizing practices in order to survive.[9]

Many staff were defined as 'unskilled', and work to survive financially. The overall emphasis may thus be on economic relationships which 'transform(s) relations of potential equality into ones of domination and submission when the exchange seems unequal' (Kappeler, 1995).[10] This dehumanizing process also constitutes violation towards residents who could also be violent towards staff on a daily basis. In settings where pay and status is low and the work is physically demanding, it is perhaps not so surprising that institutionalized violation, including woman to woman violence, is sometimes evident.[11] Other aspects of residential care that may contribute to abuse or in themselves be abusive and violating include denial of autonomy, imposition of institutional regimes, power differences between staff and residents, and difficulties of staff and residents complaining about violation. In order to explicate such violating processes in a particular setting in more detail, we now set out focus material on children in public care. In doing so, we should make it clear that we are certainly not criticizing the existence of public care for children *per se*, nor are we arguing for a pro-family position on childcare, as has been well established, by feminist work, families can be violent and violating places. Rather we are outlining some important organizational processes that may occur in these organizational worlds of these particular organizational forms.

Focus #7: Children in Public Care

Children's Homes

Children in public care have become the focus of considerable media attention in the UK through scandals around abuse in residential homes. Along with foster care, one of the 'refuges' or 'places of safety' for children harmed in their homes has been residential facilities or 'children's homes'. Children living in contemporary children's homes are increasingly characterized as coming from families with great material deprivation and significant histories of abuse and neglect (Bebbington and Miles, 1989). Recent policy initiatives have focused on the need for foster care or smaller children's homes in ordinary houses for ten or fewer children. Children are placed there because it is assessed that their own homes could not provide care and safety for them, whether because of harm to children there, parents' inability to care for them or children's behaviour difficulties (Kahan, 1994; Madge, 1994). Importantly, children's homes are increasingly being seen as an undesirable 'last resort' and places of caring for difficult-to-place teenagers with various challenging behaviours (Aymer, 1992; Madge, 1994).

There is repeated evidence demonstrating the existence of longstanding abuse, violence and violation in these settings presumed to be places of care. As with prisons and asylums, there is a population hidden from the public gaze, in spite of newspaper coverage, police investigations, inquiries and reports (Bowcott, 1997; Sheffield, 1997; Utting, 1997). As one journalist summed it up: 'No one is listening. For years the muffled sound of scandal has been leaking from the closed world of Britain's children's homes, sometimes through the trial of a careworker who has turned out to be a child rapist, sometimes in rumours about paedophile rings and cover-ups and connections in high places. Whispers of nightmares, never the whole story' (Davies, 1997). In February 2000, a three-year tribunal of inquiry, The Waterhouse Report, *Lost in Care* (HMSO, 2000), reported on very extensive and long-term physical and sexual violence and abuse by staff, particularly to boys but also to girls in children's homes in North Wales. One hundred and forty former residents made allegations of abuse between 1974 and 1984.[12] Twenty-four former workers were sought by police. The obvious question is why did this take so long to make fully public, especially as one of the senior 'childcare' officers was imprisoned in 1990? The growing acknowledgement of decades of abuse and violence points to the previously 'unspoken' nature of much violence, the disbelief of residents' testimonies and the difficulty of making organizational processes explicit and setting up responsive systems. This is not just a matter of identifying abusers and paedophiles but examining the organizational processes which allow the continuation of their violations. The long history of scandals in residential childcare settings follows the ignoring of complaints and the further punishment of children and staff who have dared to protest.[13]

In order to understand such violence and its cover-ups, it is essential to explore the organizational worlds of staff and residents. This is done through two studies. The first, the 'social work' study, was undertaken with 40 social work students on residential placements and explored their experiences in settings providing care for different groups (Parkin, 1989). The second study, the 'residential childcare' study, explored residential childcare in over 100 establishments covering 14 different local authorities, and involved interviewing over 100 staff and past and present residents, and prolonged ethnographic studies over nine months within two settings (Parkin and Green, 1997a, 1997b; Green, 1998; Green and Parkin, 1999).

Gender Relations

Children's homes initially appear to be atypical of public realm organizations.[14] For the children, like other groups in residential care, the settings are their homes where they expect nurture, care and the meeting of physical and emotional needs. Until recently children's homes had 'houseparents', 'aunts' and 'uncles', using the language of the family. The creation of smaller units in houses may also contribute to this notion. However, these organizations are clearly the product of public care, clearly located as public realm organizations, however funded. Children in them are subject to staff rotas and regimes of care with considerable emphasis on control rather than care. For example, in the residential childcare study there were instances of children's bedrooms being used by staff for meetings, demonstrating a lack of privacy.

Gender is a major structural feature in many ways in children's homes, for example carework is done by women, largely untrained, in lowly paid, low status jobs. While some unit managers are women they themselves tend to be controlled by male managers. Some women reproduce caring female discourse with little or no questioning of the assumption that they will make tea or breakfast for male colleagues and under-take most of the domestic tasks in the units. This is overlain by the notion of the 'maternal', in which mothering is seen as part of the 'female role' and a substitute for any form of training on the assumption that 'natural' maternal skills will be all that are needed to deal with the disturbed children in their care. However, the residential child-care study demonstrates the limitations of this approach, with some staff indicating their concern that the children might disclose abuse to them with which they were inadequate to deal.

'Homes', Sexuality and Public/Private Dilemmas

The social work study involved a group of social work students on a range of residen-tial placements who shared their experiences of dealing with issues of sexuality. This 'opened the floodgates' with numerous accounts of students and staff involved in situations where sexuality was an issue. These ranged from the regular day-to-day inti-mate caring tasks for very vulnerable residents through to male staff being required to deal with distraught female adolescents but not daring to be alone with them or be seen giving any form of supportive touch.[15]

Children's homes often cater for children already sexualized by past abuse and who might approach staff sexually. This outpouring of concern was more understandable when agency policies on sexuality were explored. Of the 40 organizations examined, only one had any written guidelines on sexuality, leaving the staff in the others in a situation with no rules or guidelines or training on how to act. It was an 'ever-present' issue for staff and a 'never-present' issue for formal organizational processes. More recent research demonstrates little change, with a lack of rules and guidelines leading to reactive decision-making on issues of sexuality. An example of this was the discov-ery of two male adolescent residents in the same bed, which led to phone calls to management and the reactive removal of both residents, in an unplanned way, to other homes. Another was the frequent denial of teenage pregnancy as a problem, by moving pregnant girls out of the homes and into flats. The only advice was on contraception which was usually too late. There was no formal education for resi-dents around sexuality and no training for staff other than that under the auspices of AIDS training.[16]

Apart from the violence of being contained in a setting, perceived as a last resort, with placements often made with no consultation or planning, another form of violation concerned expectations that a child would be cared for and kept safe translating into realities around control, punishment, even abuse. The language of homes and care might lead to the expectation of safety and protection in a small unit with staff trained to care. Instead both inquiries and this research demonstrated that containment is the norm and that further abuse is perpetrated against vulnerable children who over the years have not been believed when attempting to complain (Jones, 1993). Thus the violations of Pindown regimes (Levy and Kahan, 1991) are exacerbated by the violations inherent in the setting itself and its anomalous position between public and private. Here relations of power around gender and sexuality can be played out in a setting where public realm rules and private realm rules co-exist in an ambiguous organizational form which is nei-ther public nor private but both. The emphasis now on establishments which look like any other house compounds this and possibly makes the residents more susceptible to violence not being detected than in large organizations which are more obviously 'public' and open to formal scrutiny.[17]

The social work study provided much evidence of people living in homes where many of the processes were around control and totality, and the co-existence of notions of 'home' and associated language with aspects of totality (Parkin, 1989). The naming of these settings as homes might indicate a location within the 'private realm' though they are clearly public realm organizations. This ambiguity contributed to abuses of power with the need to pay attention to this particular form of organization and the ways in which they differ from more open/obviously public world organizations. Confusions and ambiguities around the nature of settings could arguably render residents less safe. Assumptions of residents and those involved in arranging places could be around being cared for in a homelike and safe environment which could mislead those living there about the reality. It could be even more misleading if those observing think there could be no cause for investigation because people are in a 'home'. Thus the ambiguous nature of settings becomes even more dangerous, as living in a 'total' setting regarded by many as a safe 'home' can be a double trap.

Institutionalization

It has been suggested that institutionalization is no longer relevant for understanding childcare settings (Bonnington Report, 1984; Berridge, 1994). Institutionalization might be understood as a feature of large Victorian orphanages, and it might be thought that the move to smaller units would eliminate this feature. This is not, however, borne out by the residential childcare study. From all sources there were almost unanimous references to institutionalization of varying intensity. Staff in children's homes were treated similarly when concerns were voiced: 'numerous reports of inquiries into abuse in residential settings ... refer to other staff suspecting or knowing what was going on, but not reporting it, or not being listened to, or being frustrated by management's unwillingness to act. Staff who did break ranks were not infrequently left feeling their careers had suffered because of it' (Utting, 1997).

Goffman (1961, 1969) described total institutions as 'storage dumps' where official, 'rational' aims contradicted with 'inmates' actual treatment. In such 'batch living' human needs tended to be subjugated to organizational needs, and people were organized and responded to not as individuals but as 'blocks' of people. There was much evidence that children's homes are not dissimilar to the institutions Goffman examined in the late 1950s and early 1960s, in terms of their uniform, objectifying treatment of children in their care. Children's homes were frequently referred to as 'storage dumps' by residential workers. The often-used staff colloquialism – 'heads for beds' – expressed the belief that children were placed indiscriminately in residential homes without attention to their needs or wishes, staff needs or other children in the home. Many of the children's homes studied were characterized by concerns around control and measures to aid this. Regimes tended to be rigid, promoting conformity, with fixed menus, locked cupboards and punishment by food deprivation. Many staff were preoccupied by locked doors and alarm systems. Both children and staff continually made analogies between the children's homes and their perceptions of prison. Children talked of feeling subject to constant scrutiny, having no privacy and being clocked in and out of the building by staff writing down their movements in logbooks every time they came in or went. The children were often seen as 'less sentient' beings through their difficulties, youth, isolation or enclosure. Managers spoke about the homes as either good or bad for surveillance purposes. Military language was often used, such as children being 'marched' to the family planning clinic, staff being on the 'wakeful watch' or referred to as 'captains'. One home was described by staff as akin to 'Fort Knox with guards on duty on the bridge'. Many staff carried keys conspicuously as might prison warders.

Staff in charge often used the language of 'my' by referring to 'my' home, 'my' kids, 'my' carpet or spoke of 'kingdoms' implying ownership and control. Residents spoke of living in a 'goldfish bowl' and the home becoming their whole world as a 'world within a world', totally cut off from wider society. There was often little family contact, sporadic contact from social workers and few contacts outside the home other than with other groups such as pimps and drug-pushers. The children's isolation was also exacerbated by poor school attendance (Jackson, 1987). There was isolation from the communities within which the homes were placed and isolation from the rest of the organization. Staff spoke of feeling cut off from the organization, with limited channels of communication imposed by outside managers. Internal managers reported that communication from outside managers was rarely via personal contact and consisted mainly of written memoranda and telephone calls. Staff spoke of being as 'institutionalized as the kids'; they might have power over the children but little other in the organization.[18] Institutionalization of staff helps to explain the situation of those trying to expose abusive regimes from within or those who recognize the abuse but feel powerless to act or are so culturally absorbed that abuse and violence are no longer recognized.[19]

Goffman (1961, 1969) described two cultures as mutually interdependent, with little 'mutual penetration' and very different, often stereotypically hostile 'world' perceptions and views of each other. Staff saw 'inmates' as 'untrustworthy, bitter and secretive', and ' inmates' saw staff as 'condescending and mean'. In children's homes such viewpoints were continually reinforced and reproduced. There was also mutual interplay between them. The more controlling and repressive were staff, the more the children rebelled and resisted. This was followed by further attempts at control and punitive sanctions and further counter-resistances from the children. This resulted in a self-perpetuating spiral of escalating oppression with the prejudices and grievances of each culture continually fuelled by the behaviour and responses of the other. Some of the children's behaviour can be seen as a product of regimes imposed on them rather than earlier experiences or 'inherent' deviance, as often perceived by staff.

The processes of children's adaptation and resistance to institutionalized regimes echoed Goffman's categories but often manifested themselves in different ways. 'Situational withdrawal' (temporary or long term from the immediate physical environment) could mean emotional withdrawal or use of drugs. 'Rebellion' (when the institution is rejected and rules flagrantly flouted) was not short lived, as for long-stay prisoners or patients, as the children were often short-stay with frequent changes of residence and the impetus for rebellion constantly renewed. Colonization (whereby the institution is embraced) was rare and took the alternative form of colonization outwards to other subcultures of drugs and prostitution, where the children felt accepted even when exploited. Conversion (when inmates ally themselves with the staff, accepting their view of them and playing model inmates) was extremely rare.

Along with adaptation to institutionalized practices went forms of resistance. These included overt rejection of institutionalization, through absconding, stealing, refusing food and generally behaving in ways unacceptable to staff; covert manipulation, by procuring money by false pretences and involvement of sexual activity in the homes without detection; material destructiveness, which was frequent with purposive damage to property and graffiti about particular staff; psychological 'wind-ups' and sabotage often involving sexist, homophobic and racist abuse to staff, particularly those perceived as having control and authority, contrasting with children being pleasant with cleaning staff not perceived as having power over them; self abuse/'buzz living', where rejection of the institution and its dehumanizing processes led to residents searching for a 'buzz' often through drink and drugs; counter-resistance, whereby cycles of control and resistances would occur with staff trying to prevent, for example, sexual activity, with residents finding alternative places and staff retaliating by removing locks from doors and residents then barricading themselves in until resistance on that issue came to an end; combined resistance and compliance, where rebellion and compliance occurred simultaneously, such as prostitution taking place alongside compliance at mealtimes.

Children's Homes, Institutionalization and Violations

The two research studies summarized here did not set out to study violence and violation but these issues recurred throughout them. They will remain unspoken until named and made explicit. The system itself in which both children and staff are caught in cycles of control and resistance within an isolated and ambiguous setting is a form of violation. Violence could be physical, sexual, emotional and/or psychological. Violences could occur between staff and children or staff and staff or amongst the children themselves. There were examples of staff's intentional harm to children through sexual violence and physical harm in corrective regimes. Other examples include food deprivation and a 15-year-old boy made to eat off a plate on the floor after being told he was behaving like a pig so could eat like one. Between staff and staff there were hierarchical power differences often used to intimidate staff who could be threatened with dismissal or the imposition of extra duties if they did not go along with the regimes in place or threatened to 'whistleblow'. Misogynist, racist and homophobic language and behaviour was communicated from staff groups to resident groups. In some respects staff were as much a product of the same isolated totalizing cultures as the children – cultures which were often characterized by sexism, racism, harassment, bullying and homophobia.

Not only was there intimidation and control from staff to children but also considerable violence and intimidation within the both male and female children's own cultures. Weakness and difference were punished and individuals bullied. 'Top dogs' who had power and status over other residents used bullying and intimidation to maintain their position and were also used by staff to control other residents. The inquiry into Castle Hill private boarding school, which formally aimed to offer therapeutic help to children, demonstrated the power and violence of the 'top dog' system: 'children in residential institutions were not only vulnerable to exploitation by adults entrusted with their care but to abuse by children older and/or physically stronger than them' (Jones, 1993: 83). The Castle Hill Principal was imprisoned for 12 years in 1991 for prolonged and systematic abuse of boys in the school. Many of the boys were in care and/or rejected by mainstream education. Part of the abuse was the initiation by the Principal of a system of 'Joeing' where physical abuse and organized bullying were used from those older boys, nominated by him as 'top Joes', to younger boys. Money and cigarettes were used as rewards to encourage the beating up of younger boys and the carrying out of the Principal's orders. He had complete charge of boys and staff and was a well-respected member of the local community. The children were also isolated from their own communities (Jones, 1993).

In the residential care study, violence within the children's group was also often initiated from the top and clearly part of power relations between adults and very vulnerable children. Other examples of 'top dog' cultures suggest that they arise in organizational contexts characterized by isolation and vulnerability. There were many other examples of physical and emotional violence within the children's groups. Teenage boys were often very physical with the girls. Resulting bruising was often dismissed by the girls who saw it as 'friendly', 'playfighting' or as signs of affection. There was frequent bullying, including cigarette burning and name calling, sometimes encouraged by staff, especially around sexism, racism and homophobia. All these processes were present to a greater or lesser degree in the establishments studied. In the homes with less institutionalized regimes there was less difficult behaviour on the part of the residents which might reflect less need for resistance.

Reforms

Suggestions for change range from the abandonment of residential care as an option; reform of social services; provision of 'hotlines' for children (Sylvester, 1998); appointment of children's rights officers; more inspection; rapid investigation of allegations of abuse; formation of groups to provide a voice for children in care; wider access to police checks on people working with young people; extensive training programmes for staff working with children and foster carers; breakdown of the isolation of residential services (Utting, 1997; Brindle, 1998a, 1998b; Little, 1999). Other possibilities include the need to listen fully to children; policies and practices against bullying and harassment; provision of therapeutic help; more contact with friends and relatives; and more leisure activities (Sinclair and Gibbs, 1996). Recommendations for change attend to many issues arising out of inquiries and reports and have led to some policy changes, though still paying little attention to the organizational setting and, therefore, arguably, limited in their effectiveness. The Waterhouse Report (HMSO, 2000) makes 72 recommendations, including a much more proactive local authority stance on complaints and whistleblowing from residents and staff.

Wardhaugh and Wilding's (1993) propositions go beyond more superficial changes to recognize the deeper-seated problems within residential care organizations. This includes recognizing the problems of the organizational setting and its ambiguity, especially when a 'care' setting called a home is actually a place of totality with the emphasis on control and surveillance thus overwhelming aspects of care. Institutionalization was the prevailing organizational form for children's homes with their silencing in regimes and discourses. Until these questions are addressed, such settings, whether for children, older people, disabled people or people with learning difficulties, are likely to be places where the regimes themselves are forms of violation within which other violations involving sexism, sexual harassment, racism, homophobia and adult power can flourish. Violations in these settings are part of wider oppressions of gender, sexuality, age, disability, ethnicity and class, all intensified through their location in particularly oppressive organizational systems.

Closure, Violating Processes and Oppressions

Our focus in this chapter has been on the organizational worlds of closed institutions and the operation of power, social divisions and multiple oppressions there. In such locations there are many organizational elements that may maintain groups of people in near permanent silence and exclusion. Hegemonic domination of organizational definitions of the situation suggests dimensions of power not easily correlating with, but still inseparable from, formal structures. This is thus in keeping with the notion of organizational worlds, which, while recognizing relatively fixed structures of power and authority, also attends to the movement of organizations in time and space and more fluid aspects of culture and discourse. It is also of key importance for gender, sexuality and violation, especially with the difficulty of recognizing and 'speaking' such issues. Organizational worlds, especially those characterized by totality and closure, often act as sites for the (re)creation of oppressions.

Social Divisions

There are many paradoxes in such organizations. Total institutions are usually created by previously existing organizations, and are usually structured specifically around one or two major social divisions, such as age and sex, ethnicity and sex, disability and age, or wealth and age. These organizationally defined social divisions define the institution in relation to the outside world; they are also constructed and reproduced within the organization through organizational structures and processes; and they construct the person. The organizational person, whether resident or staff, is constructed through these organizational social divisions – either as resident defined as a member of these categories or combinations of categories of social division, or as staff implementing and enacting these categories on others and on themselves. All of these aspects of social divisions can constitute organization violations.

Violations in 'Caring' Organizations

Many closed organizations are sites of violation – prisons, asylums, long-stay hospitals, and so on. Semi-closed or 'social total institutions' demonstrate high levels of bullying and harassment frequently linked to masculinist cultures. Prisons, the army and police could be seen as likely arenas of violence and violation, either through the populations with which they deal and/or the nature of the job itself. What may be less expected is that organizations set up to care for vulnerable people would also be arenas of violation. These have been even more hidden from public view because structures of totality are not usually associated with caring and the domestic. The focus material has outlined ways in which other forms of totality exist in settings not obviously perceived as closed. The lack of recognition of residential homes as closed contributes to the silencing and unspokenness of what is happening. Bringing together totality and 'caring' reinforces the operation of power and oppression there. The primacy of the organizational setting is seldom recognized as a key aspect of cover-ups and the silencing of residents and staff. Placement in a care setting may well be the ultimate silencing or social exclusion as all the various powerful forces, spoken or unspoken, come together. This returns us to Wardhaugh and Wilding's (1993) first proposition of people being regarded as beyond the normal bounds of moral behaviour. The neutralizing of moral concerns and the creation of moral distance leads to corruption in care. Dehumanization can clearly occur in formally 'caring' as well as controlling and custodial organizations (cf. Johnson, 1986; Bauman, 1989).

Violation through the Stigmatization of Residence

Goffman (1961, 1969) suggested the end result of institutionalization was the creation of the 'stigmatized status' which was not necessarily around social divisions of stigmatization and oppression but a product of organizational processes. The residents could be perceived as at the bottom of the organizational hierarchy. At the same time they are 'users' or 'consumers' of organizational services yet excluded from organizational power decision-making and influence. In isolated settings residents can adapt or resist but have little chance of being believed. This stigmatized status, originally applied to prisoners and hospital patients, has been recognized and applied here to settings and categories of people defined by virtue of the need for residential care. The difference is that those in residence in the name of care may be even further disadvantaged and silenced through the non-recognition of their places of residence being perceived as in any way dangerous and violent. The need for care does not necessarily overlap with wider social divisions. When they do, such as with older or disabled people, then there is a double stigmatization of 'resident' with other social divisions which could also be in some ways 'stigmatized'. Their double stigmatization is a further dimension of their silencing. Children and older people are not seen as having a voice; some people with learning difficulties and other disabilities literally cannot easily voice their own concerns. The users of organizational services have recently increasingly been categorized as consumers, and empowerment of users and oppressed groups has been promoted, in theory at least. The language of empowerment and user participation remains problematic in the context of the stigmatized statuses in and of these settings.

Violations, Social Divisions and Oppressions

Total institutions are typically, perhaps always, founded in relation to a particular social division or divisions, such as gender, racialization, age and disability. The specific violations described in this chapter are powerful in themselves; however, they only take their full force when considered within the broader context of social divisions and oppressions. By oppression(s), we mean the multiplicity of ways in which certain people within and as social categories are excluded from organizations or discriminated against within them (Hearn and Parkin, 1993). Thus social divisions easily become oppressions. However, the combined presence of totality, residence and indeed 'caring' provides the opportunity for oppressions other than those that are formally defined as organizationally paramount. Indeed paradoxically the organizational exertion and enactment of particular social divisions and social categories in the creation and operation of total institutions creates the conditions for not just other oppressions but the obscuring of these other oppressions. Again this paradox can be reinforced in 'caring' total institutions, whether officially defined as closed or not. Furthermore, these organizational conditions provide the grounds for the obscuring of the interconnections that exist between oppressions, as people, especially residents but also staff, come to be defined by one or two 'major' organizational social divisions or their combination.

Organizations as the (Re)creation of Oppressions

These paradoxical and often unspoken intertwinings of totality, social divisions and oppressions raise questions about the place of organizations as sites of the creation and re-creation of oppressions. This, however, leads on to a more general point. Forms of organizational oppressions have often, firstly, not been acknowledged at all, and then, secondly, sometimes been seen as separate and subject to different legal and policy initiatives, with 'subfields' around gender, race, age, class, sexuality and disability. Oppressions may each be experienced as unique but are related to other oppressions. The interconnectedness of oppressions is crucial to their maintenance. Indeed we have previously argued that

> ... both the analysis of multiple oppressions and postmodernism show up the inadequacy of organizational analyses that rely on either (a) a single dominant set of social categories, be they those of economic class, occupational status, institutional hierarchy, gender etc. or (b) fixed, unproblematic versions of such social categories.
>
> Instead both the analysis of multiple oppressions and postmodernism rely on assumptions of the *complexity and interrelations* of social categories and social categorizations, and the changing nature of such categories and categorizations. Thus the social categorizations are at the very least *relational* within discourses. This relationship applies in the construction of specific discourses; for example, the way in which 'women' and 'men', 'femininity' and 'masculinity' are constructed relationally to each other. It also applies in a much more complex way in terms of the relationality of different oppressions to each other. By this we mean that specific oppressions – for example, age – are maintained as such not in isolation but only through their interrelations with other oppressions. This mutual reproduction and reinforcement of oppressions thus occurs in all cases. All oppressions contribute to the reproduction and reinforcement of all the others. They are all bound in systems of difference and differance. More particularly, social divisions and oppressions are continually reproduced through organizational hierarchies and interrelations with such hierarchies. Organizational hierarchies are the routine, formal means of reproducing the variety of social divisions and oppressions in patterns of mutual reinforcement. (Hearn and Parkin, 1993: 159–60)

Organizations are sites of various oppressions, which have long been silenced. The emergence of the various subfields of oppression, such as race, gender, sexuality and class, has been part of the 'speaking' of organizational processes of discrimination and oppression. The recognition of the interconnectedness of oppressions further contributes to their 'spokenness' beyond separate subfields, as separate categories are linked together and acknowledged as fundamental parts of organizational power dynamics previously kept even more powerful through their silencing. Part of this process has been the gendering and sexualing of organizations and the opening up of new fields of organizational analysis. The 'speaking' of and politicization of other subtexts such as age and disability, and their relations to other subtexts, has developed more slowly. The point of view of those directly violated is the least likely to be heard, especially those socially excluded and silenced, whether through categories of oppression and/or confinement in residential settings. The very difficulty of exposing such organization violations is part of their power and persistence.

6

Globalization

Organization Violations, Multinationals and ICTs

Towards the Global?

In the last chapter we addressed the enclosure and intensification of organization violations that may take place within firm organizational boundaries. In contrast, this chapter is concerned with organization violations within the context of 'globalization' – and that complex, simultaneous and contradictory combination of the global and local summed up in the term, 'glocalization' (Robertson, 1995). Though these terms have no fixed or incontestable meaning, they may assist understanding how contemporary rapid developments impact on organizations and their locations in time and space. Globalization and glocalization are short-hand references to contemporary substantial historical social change; they are an attempt, however flawed, to talk about that.

Two fundamental aspects of global change are the impacts of, first, *the expansion of multinational corporations* (MNCs) *and other transnational corporations* (TNCs), and, second, *the growth of information and communication technologies* (ICTs), including the expansion of the Internet and access to it. These developments are closely interconnected, most obviously in transnational financial and ICT corporations and commerce. The rapid growth in ICTs and e-business has also changed organizational structures within transnational corporations. MNCs, TNCs and ICTs are difficult to control and police, though for apparently very different reasons from the closed organizations examined previously. They suggest a very different model of power and organization, highlighting transformations of boundaries, boundarylessness and pervasive, expanding organizational forms and transformations, rather than organizational closure. They in turn prompt and demand new ways of understanding, for both members and analysts. This is not a restatement of the established contrast of closed and open organizational systems; it is a contrasting of difference, of two forms that are not opposites.

Globalization and glocalization may be characterized in many ways. For our purposes, important features include the transformation of clear organizational boundaries. This creates increased possibilities for expansions and extensions of pervasive organization violations, so reinforcing glocal multiplicities of social divisions and oppressions. Glocalization produces new, complex social divisions and oppressions. The interaction of new social divisions and oppressions with transformations of organizational boundaries is of growing importance in the construction of organization violations. Organization violations are thus liable to qualitative transformations.

Before specifically discussing globalization in more detail, it is necessary to say something of the dominant way of addressing these questions of place and space – namely 'culture'. Secondly, the broad context of globalization is examined. Interestingly, there is a strong need to relate globalization and glocalization to the interrelations of gender, sexuality and violence. We outline some of the major theories of and approaches to globalization, and consider their relevance for understanding changing forms of gender, sexuality, violence and sexualized violence. Thirdly, attention is directed to transnational corporations, and their patterns of gender, sexuality and violence. Fourth, we discuss the form and impacts of ICTs, including focus material on the contemporary implications of ICTs for the construction of sexualized violence at a global level.

Culture as a Way of Talking about Place and Space

Organization studies, like much of the social sciences, is often less comfortable with the spatial features of social reality than the social features of spatial reality. It has frequently not been noticed that the social exists in time and space, leading to current quandaries on how to relate organizations to the changing dimensions of time and space under glocalization. The most popular way of talking about place and space in the social sciences has gone under the broad title of 'culture' and the equation of culture with 'a people' – as in the 'archipelago' notion of culture (Eriksen, 1997;[1] see Wright, 1998) and the cross-cultural paradigm more generally. Culture is one of the most complex concepts in the social sciences, with a multitude of meanings within different traditions (Williams, 1976). The (cross-) cultural framing debate remains very powerful. It tends to reduce place and space to the non-spatial social set *within* particular places and spaces, rather than see culture as 'a political process of contestation over the power to define concepts, including that of culture itself' (Wright, 1998: 12).

The question of culture figures in many ways in the analysis of organizations – as context, societal norms, organizational culture, and so on. The question of national culture is particularly significant in the study of international management and transnational organizations. Much cross-cultural research on organizations and management has not considered issues of gender, sexuality, violence and violation. On the relatively rare occasions when gender has been brought into the equation (for example, Hofstede, 1980, 1991, 1993, 1998), it has been through an emphasis on varying cultural *values*. This has tended to operate on a model of comparing management within different national cultural environments. Gendered culture is reduced to values rather than contested, material discourses, practices and processes. Interestingly, in studies of international business, culture often remains an unproblematic category that is available to explain global variation and managerial difficulties in organizing more globally.[2] There is a clear danger here of using a restricted and society-bound notion of culture, even within cross-cultural studies, rather than more complex conceptualizations of culture found within contemporary organization studies, social anthropology, sociology and cultural studies (Martin, 1992; Wright, 1994, 1998). Over-simple conceptualizations of gender parallel over-simple conceptualizations of culture (Harlow and Hearn, 1995). The notion of specific (national) cultures needs to be understood in a very critical way, not least because of the impact of transnational and global processes.

In addition to cultural approaches to organizations, there is a growing literature that connects notions of culture to or contrasts with questions of race, ethnicity and racialization. Sometimes this has been set within the frameworks of 'ethnic diversity' and 'managing diversity' in organizations. Such approaches in many ways reproduce some of the problems of comparative cultural paradigms within organizations, sometimes through the assertion of the essential cultures of 'identity groups' within it (see Calás, 1992). In contrast, Stella Nkomo (1992) has more critically investigated gender in organizations and management through the lens of 'race', contrasting an ethnicity (incorporating) paradigm and new 'power-conflict' models.[3] She argues strongly against essentialist views of 'race' and in favour of far-reaching structural and historical analysis. Women and men are not just that; they are 'racialized' and constructed through other social divisions. These debates are likely to increase in global studies of organizations, not least through contemporary returns in many parts of the world to notions of national, religious or linguistic 'ethnicity', as a sign of racialization, and their necessary critique.

Globalization

What is Globalization?

Contemporary debates on and interest in globalization and the economic, political and cultural processes that characterize it are huge. However, globalization is not new: it has been part of the world story since the beginings of exploration.[4] The historical intensity of global developments increased greatly with the growth of more organized conquest, mercantilism, colonialism, imperialism, long-distance capitalist trading and integrated production. What is important is that the contemporary era has brought a further intensification, with the advancement of technologies of transport, communication, refridgeration, mass production, information and media. Through these social and technical processes, place and space have new meanings. Indeed Malcolm Waters (1995: 3) defines globalization as: '(a) social process in which the constraints of geography on social and cultural arrangements recede and in which people become increasingly aware that they are receding.'

The recent major growth of literature on globalization and global change has failed to produce a consensus on what constitutes globalization. There is considerable variation in how theories of globalization have analysed contemporary economic, political and cultural change. However, even within this variation, some key themes can be discerned. Some commentators have emphasized the development of transnational economic units. Robertson (1995) asserts the importance of the greater material interdependence and unity, but not the greater integration, of the world; greater world consciousness; (while it is a single system) the promotion or 'invention' of difference and variety in globalization; and indeed 'clashes, conflicts, tensions and so on constitute a pivotal feature of globalization' (Robertson and Khondker, 1998: 29). Giddens (1990) highlights the importance of the nation-state, modernity (capitalism, surveillance, military order, industrialism), time–space distanciation and reflexivity. Lash and Urry (1994) emphasize the transcendence of the nation-state, and the increasing importance of signs and symbols, and transnational cultures more generally.

Waters (1995) has reviewed such theories and argues that globalization affects the movement or not of: people, goods, services and information through material, political and symbolic exchanges. He writes:

1 Material exchanges tend to tie social relationships to localities: the production of exchangeable items involves local concentrations of labour, capital and raw materials; ... Long-distance trade is carried out by specialist intermediaries ... who stand outside the central relationships of the economy.
2 Political exchanges tend to tie relationships to extended territories. ... Political exchanges therefore culminate in the establishment of territorial boundaries that are co-terminous with nation-state-societies. The exchanges between these units ... tend to confirm their territorial sovereignty.
3 Symbolic exchanges liberate relationships from spatial referents. Symbols can be produced anywhere and at any time and there are few resource constraints on their production and reproduction. Moreover they are easily transportable. Importantly, because they frequently seek to appeal to human fundamentals they can often claim universal significance. ... symbolic exchanges globalize. (Waters, 1995: 9)

In each case, however, there are contradictions. Economic change is increasingly global, but the immediate production of material goods is favoured to some extent, albeit very unevenly, through international transportation costs. Waters may well be overstating the tendency towards local material exchanges, as there are many ways in which the economic realm is also becoming more global in the form of its transactions. For example, textiles and plastic bag production are tending to move to low labour cost countries, as savings outweigh transport costs. The nation-state remains a crucial unit of social and political organization (especially if you happen not to be a citizen of a particular nation-state), and in the contemporary era is continually both further affirmed and transcended. Symbolic exchanges are both global and have local uses and meanings, with degrees of self-referentiality not reducible to global communication. A fundamental aspect of all these social forms is the development of ICTs and other new technologies (White, 1987). There remains a danger in separating the material economic from the non-material economic, as ICTs become of growing importance both economically and materially.

Globalization and glocalization are not one set of things. It is important not to reify or overstate (or indeed understate through naive relativism) the grand narrative that globalization has become. In all sorts of ways, lives, including organizational lives and the lives of organizations, persist in complex contradictions, not simply through the lure of one particular version of 'globalization'. Many other discursive and material realities may be further subordinated by talking simply of globalization. Yet, to talk of globalization opens up many possibilities for speaking subordinated realities. Locating globalization simply within debates on postmodernism, or at least the more apolitical versions of postmodernism, is certainly a danger. What is called 'globalization' needs to be deconstructed not as an exercise in postmodernist musing but as a means of critique to show and change these discursive and material realities. Though we use the term 'globalization' as a shorthand, its critique is vital.[5] Globalization is a matter of value, capital, exploitation, profit and accumulation. These are all gendered, sexualed, violenced, and constructed through and constitutive of age, class, disability, ethnicity and racialization.

Gendering Globalization

The dominant literatures on globalization, MNCs and TNCs have generally been relatively ungendered, presented as 'gender-neutral', reproducing an implicit male narrative. They have also developed in relative isolation from those on gender relations in organizations (Calás and Smircich, 1993; Hearn, 1996a). Most theories of globalization have been remarkably lacking in their attention to gender and gender relations, let alone sexuality and violence. There is a special and specific need to gender globalization, and there is a growing interest in the gendered aspects of global change and development, including the gendering of globalization.[6] All the social trends and theoretical challenges already noted, as well as their complex interconnections, raise question marks about how to locate organizations within a more fully gendered understanding of the complex changes subsumed under globalization.

There has also been a substantial growth of political and research interest in gender equality and inequalities worldwide. This has been prompted partly by a wide range of international and transnational feminist and gender-aware researchers, increasingly in association with NGOs, INGOs and governmental and transgovernmental organizations, including the UN, UNESCO, the ILO (International Labour Organization) and the Council of Europe. There is now a mass of easily available information from these and other organizations. UN initiatives include: the 1979 Convention on the Elimination of All Forms of Discrimination against Women (CEDAW), the World Conferences on Women, and the UN Human Development Reports (1996–2000). Such information can inform gendered analyses of globalization and of national and societal inequalities between and within 'North' and 'South'.

Recent research sponsored by the UN, reviewing gender equality and inequalities throughout the world (Human Development Report, 1996–2000), draws on national data and presents several different perspectives on the gendered aspects of social, political and economic development in most countries of the world. This includes the assessment of 'gender-related development': the life expectancy, adult literacy, educational enrolment and the share of earned income for females and males respectively. This shows both the incredible persistence of gender inequalities in such 'development' worldwide, as well as the huge range and variation in the extent and form of those inequalities.[7] A second series of measures produced by the UN concerns 'gender empowerment': the proportions of parliamentary seats, administrators and managers, professionals and technical workers, and earned income held by women.[8] These kinds of measures are highly instructive at a broad level of generalization, though of course ridden with limitations, technically, empirically, politically and epistemologically.[9] The UN material also gives information on gendered time-use. In a sample of developing countries, 34 per cent of females' time on SNA (System of National Accounts), 66 per cent on non-SNA work, compared with 76 per cent of males' time on SNA work, 24 per cent on non-SNA work (53:47 females:males of total). In a sample of industrial countries, the equivalent figures were 34 per cent and 66 per cent for females; 66 per cent and 34 per cent for males (51:49 of total). This remarkable persistence of global inequality in gendered distributions of paid and non-paid work and time-use sits alongside the material differences between the more and less wealthy parts of the world. It can be read as the persistence of patriarchy and/or global gendered convergence.

There are of course many other gendered aspects of globalization, for example gendered patterns of migration and movements of refugees, the gendering and sexualing of global symbolic systems and the emergence of gendered (male-dominated) transnational polities and governances. In many of these global processes it is men, particular groups of men, who are the main purveyors of power (Hearn, 1996a). As Connell (1993: 606) suggests: 'Since the agents of global domination were, and are, predominantly men, the historical analysis of masculinity must be a leading theme in our understanding of the contemporary world order.'

Sexualing and Violencing Globalization

Not only is globalization gendered, it is also sexualed, that is having meanings and needing to be understood in relation to sexuality. Analyses of globalization need to be subject to sexualing, just as they need to be gendered. It has been unusual for globalization theories to address questions of sexuality and sexualized violence as central concerns. So what are the implications of globalization for sexuality? Processes of globalization are gendered and sexualed in specific and identifiable ways. Following Waters's characterization of globalization, it is not material sexual 'exchanges' or the political control of sexuality or symbolic sexuality *in general* that are globalized but particular forms of men's sexuality and men's sexualized violence that are dominant and particular forms of women's sexuality that are so dominated.

While sexuality has not been a central concern within much globalization theory, there is a wide range of issues around sexuality that are strongly affected by and bear on global development and change. These include trafficking in women; militarism and prostitution; global pornography; computer sex; new technological developments in computer imaging. Later in this chapter we focus more specifically on sexualized violence and ICTs. Just as cities are characteristically organized sexually and spatially, so the world is organized in specific sexual-spatial and sexual-geographical ways. A clear example is the close association of the European and US imperialism and militarism, mass prostitution and sex tourism in South East Asia (Enloe, 1983). In the face of such globalizing and glocalizing forces, sexuality, as the social expression of, social relations of or social references to physical, bodily desire or desires, is liable to considerable historical transformation. Povinelli and Chauncey (1999) have gone further. They have criticized the literature on globalization for often proceeding 'as if tracking and mapping the facticity of economic, population, and population flows, circuits and linkages were sufficient to account for current cultural forms and subjective interiorities, or as if an accurate map of the space and time of post-Fordist accumulation could provide an accurate map of the subject and her embodiment and desires' (p. 445).[10] Sexuality may often be understood in terms of that desire which is *felt* to be 'primordial' (MacKinnon, 1982), felt to be mostly one's own. Globalization disturbs this naturalism socially and geographically in ways whose consequences are difficult to predict.

If one is interested in gender, sexuality and globalization, then one has to be also concerned (in both senses) about violence too. Many of the social relations described within the narratives of globalization involve violence and violation. Global political economic developments and connections are not 'without' violence and violation; they may involve slavery, indentured labour, child labour, trafficked labour and other exploitative practices and human rights violations. Many legitimate global economic institutional arrangements and transactions depend for their reproduction on violence and violation. These violations may be institutionally embedded in the exploitative economic and political arrangements between those with very unequal power, whether they are nations, companies, owners, employers or workers. Sometimes this is a matter of the specific and persistent use of physical and other violences by those with the power to do so 'legitimately', that is, with few repercussions for them. Sometimes there are blatant uses of sexuality in the symbolism and practices of global militarism, for example in the sales presentations, the 'new pornography' (Peretti, 2000), of the arms trade. Moreover, the extension of global technologies of 'communication' can also be re-seen through the eyes of violence and violation. Global models of persons, images and cultural artifacts can all constitute violence and violation to local symbols and meanings. They are not innocent: they may comprise cultural violence and violation.

Multinational and Transnational Corporations

From the Nation-state to Transnational Organizational Management

Processes of globalization and glocalization, however large in scale and impact, are immensely contradictory. Divides in power and wealth persist between the so-called 'industrial' and 'developing' countries, the 'North' and 'South'. The nation-state still functions as a, and often the, dominant local political unit, especially and paradoxically for people who are migrants, newcomers, refugees or outside it. New and resurgent nationalisms and nations are being promoted, while others are challenged. At the same time, the dominance of local and national bureaucracies and nation-states are problematized by the growth of transnational corporations, as part of powerful globalizing processes.

Multinational and transnational corporations have a long history in extending, transcending or attempting to transcend the nation. This is especially so in the imperialist nations of Europe, North America and Asia, not least through the development of trade within the former British Empire. This, coupled with the hegemonic power of the USA and the growth of the Internet, has meant that English has in recent years become, even more than previously, the 'lingua franca' in many transnational organizations. This is being reinforced daily through the Internet and e-commerce. The nation-state is subject to decomposing political and economic forces, through MNCs, TNCs and ICTs. There has also been rapid growth in the number of INGOs (Mathews, 1997),[11] anti-militarism, organizing against trafficking, trade boycotts, fair trade movements, green campaigns and ethical consumerism.

The Enormity of MNCs and TNCs

The nation-state is no longer necessarily the most important economic or political unit. Transnational corporations constitute collective social actors that may transcend the nation, being in some cases larger in size than individual nations. Their ever-growing importance stems particularly from the fact that they operate across national boundaries, rather than simply within one or even several nations. In recent years there have been major expansions of USA, Japanese and European multinationals. The GNP of some nation-states is exceeded by the assets of many supranational corporations (Bauman, 1995: 152). Five hundred companies now control 42 per cent of the world's wealth. Furthermore,

> The world's 500 largest industrial corporations, which employ only five hundredths of 1 per cent of the world's population, control 25 per cent of the world's economic output. The top 300 transnationals, excluding financial institutions, own some 25 per cent of the world's productive assets. Of the world's one hundred largest economies, fifty are now corporations – not including banking and financial institutions. The combined assets of the world's fifty largest commercial banks and diversified financial companies amount to nearly 60 per cent of *The Economist*'s estimate of a $20 trillion global stock of productive capital. (Korten, 1998: 4)

Of the 100 largest economies, half are corporations, half are countries. The ten biggest companies turn over more money than the 100 smallest countries. The top ten companies account for 11.7 per cent of the total revenues of the top 500, 15 per cent of profits and 13.6 per cent of employment.[12] Only 27 countries now have a turnover greater than Shell and Exxon combined; Shell – the second largest company in the world – owns more land than 146 countries (Vidal, 1997).

The International Labour Organization reports that 31 of the 50 most profitable firms, and seven of the top ten, are US companies. They continue:

> The most profitable, however, was Shell (the Netherlands) – with profits of $8.9 billion. Shell's profits increased by 28.7 per cent over 1995. In 1996, the top 500 companies did not get bigger, they got richer. Their profits increased by 25.1 per cent, while revenues increased only by 0.5 per cent, assets by 3.5 per cent, and the number of employees by

1.1 per cent. Most of the largest American and European companies in terms of revenues are also the largest in terms of foreign assets. The largest American companies, by revenue, are GM, Ford and Exxon. By foreign assets, the largest American companies are Ford, GE, Exxon and GM (data of the United Nations Conference on Trade and Development, UNCTAD). Shell, which is the only European company among the ten largest by revenues, also had the largest foreign assets ($79.7 billion) in 1995 (*Fortune* Magazine and UNCTAD). (ILO, n.d.: 2–3)

These concentrations of wealth and power are increasing.[13] John Korten has reviewed the situation and noted that while the largest companies are often shedding people through 'downsizing', they are not shedding control over money, markets or technology. He explains:

Concentration of control over markets is proceeding apace. *The Economist* recently reported that in the consumer durables, automotive, airline, aerospace, electronic components, electrical and electronics, and steel industries the top five firms control more than 50 per cent of the global market, placing them clearly in the category of monopolistic industries. In the oil, personal computers and media industries the top five firms control more than 40 per cent of sales, which indicates strong monopolistic tendencies.

Downsizing is really about consolidating the firm's monopoly control of markets, technology and money in a small, well-paid headquarters staff. Everything else is contracted out to smaller firms that are forced into intensive competition for the firm's business. The contractors – commonly located in low-wage countries – compete by hiring workers at substandard wages under often appalling working conditions. For example, the popular Nike athletic shoes that sell for US$73 to $135 around the world are produced by 75,000 workers employed by independent contractors in low-income countries. A substantial portion of these workers are in Indonesia – mostly women and girls housed in company barracks, paid as little as fifteen cents an hour and required to work mandatory overtime. Unions are forbidden and strikes are broken up by the military. In 1992, Michael Jordan reportedly received $20 million from the Nike corporation to promote the sale of its shoes, more than the total paid to the Indonesian women who made them. (Korten, 1998: 4)[14]

Multinational and transnational corporations not only have economic effects on national economies via investment strategies, the stock markets, mechanisms of market development and organizational and management methods. They also have various social and cultural effects at national and transnational levels on gendered practices and practices that construct wider gender relations as defined at the transnational corporate level (Carty, 1997).

Gendering Multinational and Transnational Organizations[15]
Although international research in the field of gender relations in organizations has expanded greatly over the last twenty years, most has addressed gender relations in local national contexts. The dominant focus of even critical, gendered literature has usually been on individual organizations in one particular country. While the largest global corporations continue to grow and extend their activities, transnational companies are still not at the centre of organization studies, even less so in terms of gender relations. There are still, however, few gendered studies of international management, either at top levels or more generally (Adler and

Izraeli, 1988, 1994). Current literature on gendered organizations and gendered practices in organizations suggests many possible approaches to and questions in gendered studies of transnational corporations. A focus upon their gender relations – their dominant patterns and structuring, their gendered labour forces, management and global impact, their policies and practices on gender – is especially important. The concept of the 'glass ceiling' may be extended from individual organizations to complex sets of transnational organizations. The position of women and indeed men as gendered actors in multinationals is far from clear (Dallalfar and Movahedi, 1996).

A focus on gender relations does not only need to address 'women', but also the gendering of top managerial positions, including the analysis of men and masculinities there (Collinson and Hearn, 1994, 1996). Much research on gender relations in organizations has not considered the gendering of women and men in organizations equally thoroughly. An explicitly gendered focus on men is very important in the analysis of managers and managements, in what might be called a 'men in management' literature. Few studies have examined men in transnational management from a critical gendered perspective (Woodward, 1996). Men continue to dominate business management, comprising about 95 per cent of senior management in the UK and the USA. This is especially so at the very top and more highly paid levels of the business sector, where men comprise as much as 98 per cent of 'top managers'. Davidson and Burke (2000: 2) report that 'in the European Union countries fewer than 5 per cent of women are in senior management roles and this percentage has barely changed since the early 1990s'. According to the official Labour Force Statistics, the relative percentage of women and men in senior staff and upper management in Finland was also constant from 1990 (21:79) to 1995 (22:78) (Veikkola et al., 1997: 83). By 1990 of 100 top Confederation of British Industry companies, only 3 per cent had women on their boards at all (Hansard Society, 1990). In some countries, such as Australia, the figure is even lower (Sinclair, 1995). Men's domination is even more pronounced in the boards of directors of large companies. The 1998 UK Institute of Management survey found that 3.6 per cent of directors were women (Institute of Management/Remuneration Economics, 1998; also see Collinson and Hearn, 1996). This compares with a figure of 17 per cent of directors who were women on the 114 Finnish stock exchange-listed companies in 1995 (Veikkola et al., 1997: 83–4). Two of these companies had women CEOs (Chief Executive Officers). There is evidence of some increases in women in middle management and small business ownership, and thus management overall (Davidson and Burke, 2000; Vinnicombe, 2000). However, at director and the highest executive levels the numbers may actually be reducing, static or increasing very slowly indeed. (Calás and Smircich, 1993; Institute of Management, 1995; Veikkola et al., 1997; Institute of Management/Remuneration Economics, 1998).

Organizational restructuring processes, such as downsizing, re-engineering and redefinitions of core functions, have direct and indirect effects on gender relations. Changes in internal structures of transnational corporations and organizations may create differences in gender relations in management and throughout organizations. Relationships between different companies within larger transnational corporations may have further impacts, depending on whether they are highly integrated globally, locally run networks or strongly centralized. Transnational corporations with a strong central office may contrast with polycentric transnational corporations, where head offices issue looser guidelines for subsidiaries, for example on corporate policies on equal opportunities. Centralized TNCs may be more likely to develop some sort of EOPs, in response to demands from local areas, even if these are insignificant at high levels. Decentralized TNCs may be more likely to respond to local conditions and develop more autonomous and variable structures within local or functional units.

Concepts and theories in organization studies based on the assumption of the single organization within the single country need to be critiqued and reformulated. Questions of career, organization, management, the relation of the economic and the cultural, and relations of government and economy need to be re-examined. Interdependence between national economies and transnational corporations appears to have increased and been restructured, in turn affecting gender relations. Analyses of transnational organizations and management need to address the complexities of gendered organizational interconnections, structures, processes and interactions.

Sexualing and Violencing MNCs and TNCs

We have already discussed some connections between globalization and sexuality – connections that are rarely articulated in mainstream analyses of globalization. Equally, transnational corporations can be very powerful institutions in the construction of sexuality – for their own managers and workers in different national locations, for their actual and potential sexual partners, in the reproduction of corporate sexual regimes and ideologies, in the circulation of sexual images in advertising, promotion and business-to-business marketing, and sometimes in the provision of 'sexual entertainment', prostitution and sexual services for customers, managers and employees. Questions of sexuality need to be recognized in both theorizing on and practice in transnational corporations.

Most MNCs are characterized by organizational and managerial cultures, policies and practices that assume heterosexuality. Related important issues include assumptions about sexuality that lie behind the managerial policies and practices of transnational corporations, such as corporate policies on family leave, childcare, transnational mobility and 'postings', and their implications for personal life. This concerns both the nature and effects of those policies and practices, and the processes of decision-making on them. Such policies and practices can also raise very difficult decisions for partners and spouses, often women, whether or not they are relatively dependent on men. Further complications surround the differential social position and experience of women and men working abroad, and the kinds of business, social and social-sexual networks that most easily develop in those situations.

Transnational corporations increasingly have to decide on their policies and practices on not only sexual harassment but also on the practice of different kinds of sexuality amongst their employees. There have also been various relatively high-profile cases around sexuality and sexual harassment involving top managers in transnationals, among which the Mary Cunningham case (Cunningham, 1984) and the Lars Bildman case (Hauserman, 1999), are particularly well known examples. This raises the question of whether the same policies on sexuality apply throughout the company or vary according to local conditions and decision-making. More specifically, heterosexual hegemony may be challenged and perhaps changed in one country of a TNC but in other participating countries lesbian, gay and bisexual sexualities and partnerships may be persecuted, even illegal. There are also significant exceptions and variations to general patterns of heterosexual hegemony. In her research on an international airline company, Sarah Rutherford (1999) found a strong presence of gay men amongst the air cabin staff and a low presumption of heterosexuality in that division. This seemed to exist alongside a much less sexist and sexually harassing heterosexual environment than in the other sections of the company. She concludes: '... where there is no presumption of heterosexuality and there is a high proportion of homosexuals, relations between men and women were statistically better than in other divisions in the airline ...' (p. 304). In the airline, travel 'perks' extended to partners of employees of either sex.

There is growing recognition of links between some transnationals and provision of sexual entertaining for customers, managers and employees. Rutherford (1999) has collected evidence of 'sexual entertaining' as part of corporate 'entertainment' in the financial sector, along with sports entertainment of clients and potential clients. She notes the significance of men-only dinners, hostess clubs and nightclubs in the social round of some London 'City gentlemen'. She continues: 'The restaurant School Dinners has long been a favourite for client lunches. The waitresses dress as schoolgirls and boys who are naughty might get blanch-mange smeared all over their faces. Another City favourite is the Circle Line, called the Titty Circle by people who go there, because the waitresses don't wear much. Women are allowed in but not allowed to go into certain areas, like the bar! There are many clubs, both private and public, where hostesses look after customers and overseas trips have been known to include the procurement of prostitutes for clients, particularly Far Eastern trips' (pp. 274–5). Allison (1994) has studied in more detail relations between sexuality, pleasure and corporate masculinity in Tokyo hostess nightlife. Such practices exclude, marginalize, sexualize and violate women.

At the same time, images in advertisements of transnationals are continuing a long tradition of corporate use of sexuality in marketing (Hearn and Parkin, 1987, 1995). Unfortunately, this is in itself something that is no longer surprising. What is more novel is the production of both blatantly sexist and increasingly ambiguous sexual messages in advertising, their diffusion through the Internet and multimedia, and their easy availability throughout much of the world. Thus there is the possibility of increasingly complex intersections of local and global sexual meanings in what might be called 'glocalized sexualization'. The use and misuse of email and the Internet, by both employees and management, are matters of increasing legal, policy and social concern for MNCs and TNCs, in terms of use of company time and resources; sexual, racial or other offence(s), such as pornography use; and cyberliability. Derogatory remarks can lead to suing from individuals or companies. Norwich Union paid £450,000 to a rival insurance firm after staff were found to have sent libellous emails. In May 1998 the USA Justice Department filed an antitrust lawsuit against Microsoft, in which emails from Bill Gates and others were crucial evidence of attempts to exclude Netscape from the market: 'Screw Sun ... Let's move on and steal the Java language' (Kehoe, 1998). Companies have disciplined or sacked employees for sexist and racist email use, have been sued by employees for allowing or condoning sexually or racially harassing workplaces, and are increasingly introducing systems of surveillance of email and Internet use. This raises complex legal and policy issues that transcend national boundaries (see pp. 152–4).

The significance of TNCs in relation to violence and violation is also complex. The size, concentration of wealth and associated power of some TNCs means that they are able to marshall huge resources transcending national borders and local legal controls. Contemporary TNCs have had a special place in the organization of violence, cutting across the lines and responsibilities of nation-states, forming new 'cartographies of violence' (Shapiro, 1997). Transnational organizations have become a central organizational means to large-scale destruction of both human and natural environments. Their violating effects can be obscured through the complexity of their corporate organization, including sub-contracting to local companies for the performance of direct organization violations. At the same time TNCs operate in a world with huge variations in the extent of risk of violence, as in kidnappings of executives, in different parts of the world.[16] Some old organizational forms of violence have remained and even expanded, as with modern mercenary organizations servicing TNCs,[17] alongside newer forms, such as insurance companies providing cover against kidnapping.

Multinational Monitor, founded by Ralph Nader, produces its Internet *Corporate Rap Sheet*. In the December 1996 issue, Russell Mokhiber wrote of 'The Ten Worst Corporations' of the year, including Caterpillar, Disney, Gerber, Mitsubishi, Seagram and Texaco (http://www.ratical.org/corporations/mm10worst96.html). This describes the USA Equal Employee Opportunity Commission's (EEOC) filing of a major sexual harassment lawsuit in Peoria, Illinois against Mitsubishi Motor Manufacturing of America. This alleged that sexual harassment has been ongoing at their Normal, Illinois plant since at least 1990, victimizing hundreds of female employees, including corporate retaliation against and forced resignation of a number of women who opposed the discrimination. The EEOC Vice Chair, Paul Igasaki, reported to journalists how the working environment at Mitsubishi was characterized by continuous physical and verbal abuse against women, including the following:

> Male employees repeatedly grabbed female employees' breasts, buttocks and genital areas. Apparently at least one male employee put his air gun between a female's legs and pulled the trigger. Drawings of genitals, breasts and various acts of sexual intercourse, labeled with female employees' names, were made on car fenders and cardboard signs along the assembly line. Male employees and supervisors constantly called female employees sluts, whores, bitches and other names ... 'I cannot repeat in front of TV cameras.' Females were routinely asked questions about their sexual habits and preferences.[18]

There have also been various recent high-profile examples of allegations of and campaigns against corporate violence. The Shell Corporation has been prominently accused by MOSOP (the Movement for the Survival of Ogoni People) of environmental devastation, oil spills and gas flares over 40 years in the Ogoni region of Nigeria, violent political opposition to local organizing by the Ogoni people and support for those murdering nine political dissidents, including the playwright Ken Saro-Wiwa (http://www.ratical.org/corporations/Cmurder Prof.html). Recently, Shell has gone to lengths to present itself as a socially responsible global corporation (*The Shell Report*, 1999, 2000; Sklair, 2001: 184–91).

Another example involving an oil company is the campaign against alleged environmental and human rights violations by Union Oil Company of California (Unocal). This is alleged to include: '...ecocide; environmental devastation'; 'unfair and unethical treatment of workers', 'aiding the oppression of women'; 'aiding oppression of homosexuals'; 'enslavement and forced labour'; 'forced relocation of Burmese villages and villagers'; 'killings, torture and rape'; 'complicity in gradual cultural genocide of tribal and indigenous peoples'; 'usurpation of political power'; and 'deception of the courts, shareholders and the public'. Some of these allegations stem from close business ties with the Burma and Taliban military regimes, with their own human rights' violations (http://www. heed.net/charter/doc2.html).

On the other hand, it is clearly important not to paint MNCs and TNCs as necessarily or essentially violent; that would be inaccurate. There is a growing debate on not just 'ethical investment' but 'ethical globalization' and 'ethical global corporations'. In some cases some MNCs and TNCs have produced positive corporate policies and practices against violence. The third annual 'Work to End Domestic Violence', 1 October 1998, involved the participation of hundreds of US businesses and other organizations:

> On this day, Bell Atlantic Mobile introduced a toll-free link to the National Domestic Violence Hotline. They also continue to provide awareness cards to employees and customers and work with police and social service agencies to provide wireless phone and voicemail boxes to victims of domestic violence. At Limited, Inc., human resource and security managers have attended domestic violence education and response courses led by a women's shelter director. In addition, associates receive information on violence against women and have access to an internal company domestic violence hotline number. Numerous other companies, including Liz Claiborne, Inc., Levi Strauss, Blue Shield of California, Gap Foundation, Marshalls, Wells Fargo, Polaroid and Time Warner, sponsored the programme, [and] have taken measures to educate managers about violence against women, and provide support for employees who experience abuse. (Yodanis and Godenzi, 2000: 123)[19]

These initiatives are not simply important at the practical level. They intersect with the growing awareness of the business, working life and other economic costs of violence (see pp. 62, 69–70), and its likely increasing contribution to the creation of policies in the workplace that support rather than punish women who experience violence (NOW Legal Defense and Education Fund, 1996; Yodanis and Godenzi, 2000). On the other hand, such corporate practices, however welcome, do not mean that the wholesale reform of policies on gender and sexuality, as illustrated by the sexist advertising by some such companies. What is most interesting is that just as an individual man can be sexist and violent and yet still be 'respectable', so too many large corporations have reproduced sexist, sexually violent and violating practices and are still regarded as 'respectable' organizations. This is being challenged more and more by various organized oppositions. Recent concerns with 'corporate social responsibility' need to be seen as variable forms of 'corporate responsiveness' to changing social conditions.

Information and Communication Technologies

A second key aspect of global change is the development of ICTs. They involve the use of multiple complex technologies and have several characteristic features. These include: time/space compression, instantaneousness, asynchronicity, reproducibility of image production, the creation of virtual bodies, the blurring of the real and the representational. Importantly, these technologies are not to be understood as just texts but exist within and indeed create material social relations. They are also ever-changing and expanding, becoming cheaper and more widespread though still beyond the reach of the many – hence the increasing split of the haves ('netizenship') and the have-nots, those in cyberhomes, those who are not. They also contribute to fundamental change in the form and process of organizations. ICTs raise increasingly complex issues around political control and democracy. There is the technology for both decentralized TAZs (temporary autonomous zones) and strong centralization and surveillance. Thus ICTs can be understood as both 'free space' unfettered by moral codes and the most surveilled social arena yet (Shields, 1996). The growing interest in governance (Loader, 1997), power, order and control (Smith and Kollock, 1999: Part 3) and violating conduct (McLaughlin et al., 1995) in research on ICTs is sometimes, though often not, gendered.

Gendering, Sexualing and Violencing ICTs

ICTs as a key aspect of globalization have a wide variety of implications for the gendering of organizations. However, it is important to emphasize how the 'gendering of information technology takes specific forms in different times, cultures and places' (Vehviläinen, 2000: 19). One basic issue is the pattern of ICT use. In the USA in the early 1990s women constituted about one-third of the graduates in computing but about 8 per cent of university computer academic staff (Shade, 1993). Women's use of computer networks is difficult to determine and may be subject to considerable current change. A low figure has been put as 10–15 per cent. In CompuServe, Genie and Prodigy 60–90 per cent of customers are male. In 'women's' (feminist) newsgroups some estimate use as about from 50:50 to 75:25 women:men. In unmoderated feminist newsgroups some estimates suggest 80 per cent of messages are posted by men. In Finland 'the numbers of women computer professionals have varied from nearly zero in the 1950s to one third in the early 1990s and further to twenty per cent in the late 1990s (Vehviläinen, 2000: 19). Meanwhile, women are using ICTs more and more and creating complex 'third wave feminisms'.

More broadly, there are a range of profoundly different, gendered understandings and conceptualizations of ICTs, the Internet and virtual reality. The Internet can be seen as patriarchical/hierarchical or feminist/non-hierarchical in form, and be subject to patriarchal welcome or critique, or feminist critique or welcome. This gives four possible broad (gendered) political positions:

1 patriarchal form/patriarchal welcome (progressive patriarchalism);
2 patriarchal form/feminist critique (second wave feminism?);
3 feminist form/patriarchal critique (antimodernist patriarchalism);
4 feminist form/feminist welcome (cyberfeminism, third wave feminism).[20]

Further gendered distinctions can be made in the more specific terms of whether the human 'interaction' with ICTs, the Internet and virtual reality is understood as primarily embodied or primarily disembodied, or whether this interaction constitutes some new transcendence of embodiment/disembodiment. These distinctions can be overlain on the four major patriarchal/feminist conceptualizations above.

ICTs are not only gendered; they are also sexualed and violenced. The Internet, initially developed as a network linking computers in the military, universities, hospitals, government and business, is now a major site for changing forms of sexuality, violence and sexual violence. ICTs provide major communication and organizational channels for sexuality and violence. They can be used to increase the formation of communities of users either for or against particular forms of sexuality and violence. The Internet and ICTs can be and are used for the delivery of sexuality, sexual performance, sexualized violence, violence and violation, as in the promotion of racist hatred and racial violence (Whine, 1997), or for opposition to them as in the formation of anti-bullying networks (see pp. 59–62).

Focus # 8: Globalization, ICTs and Sexualized Violence[21]

ICTs are part of the broader history of the publicization (Brown, 1981) of sexuality and the technologies of the senses. Increasingly complex technologies have developed from the peep show, photography and film, and the associated histories of 'the real', the glossy image, the pin-up, the star and the film icon. These constitute technologies of sexuality. The beginnings of film date from the late 1880s, with public film shows soon after in the mid-1890s. There was a quick realization of the sexual potential of films, as in the 1896 film, *The Kiss*, and the 1899 *The Kiss in the Tunnel*. The early 1900s saw a rapid expansion of film, along with a strong debate on censorship. In 1903 the first female pin-up company calendar was produced, and in 1913 the first female nude on a commercial calendar. 1911 saw the launch of *Photoplay*; by 1916 film magazines were shaping emotional lives; and by 1918 stars became objects of intense desire (Hearn, 1992b). Around the same time other technologies brought sexuality more into the public domains. Telephones were used for 'call girls'; specialist telephone sexual service, sex lines and telephone sex have followed. More recently, video and television technology has led to sex videos, sex channels and sex pay television. ICTs and other technologies have raised the possibilities of techno-sex, high-tech sex, non-connection sex, mobile phone sex, virtual sex, multimedia sex. New forms of sex, sexual storytelling, sexual genres, sex talk shows and sexual media have mushroomed (Plummer, 1995). Virtual, computer-generated celebrities, pin-ups and dates are no longer so novel (Waller, 2000).

There are almost daily reports of how the Internet and ICTs are changing the ways sexuality is done and experienced – in chat lines, sex lines, sexual identity group communities, Internet dating, email sex, cybersex, cyberaffairs, falling in love on the Net, virtual sex, and so on. In hotchatting, '... the chat mode is used to talk to each other about sexual fantasies in the past, present or future. The language is detailed, graphic and expressive, to try to transmit sexual activity over the computer' (Argyle and Shields, 1996: 64). Taking up cyber identities/cyber selves can involve gender-changing in various ways, such as gender swapping/bending/spoofing; its performance is dependent on others' continued participation. Denise Dalaimo (1997: 96) reports a case of a 'woman' forming a friendship, 'dating', having 'virtual sex' with her 'boyfriend' and then getting into financial troubles so that the 'boyfriend' sent 'her' 1000 dollars – a few weeks later he discovered his 'girlfriend' was a man. ICTs have multiple impacts on sexuality, and many of these changing forms are both local and global.[22]

There are many forms of sexualized violence on ICTs: in ICT communication itself, information-giving, building sexual communities, marketing, representation and doing sexual violence. There is growing evidence of email and Internet use for harassment, digi-bullying and shame flaming (Meikle, 1997; Hilpern, 1999), 'net sleazing' and 'trolling for babes'. Amy Bruckman (1993) reports how female MUDders may be besieged with attention. Pavel Curtis (1992) and Leslie Regan Shade (1993) noted that most promiscuous and sexually aggressive 'women' may often be men. Bruckman writes: 'If you meet a character named Fabulous HotBabe, she is almost certainly a he in real life.' Meanwhile research at Bryant College, Rhode Island, has found email flaming has led many women to adopt men's names to avoid harassment (Hilpern, 1999).

More broadly, Donna Hughes (1977) has summarized the global situation:

> The Internet has become the latest place for promoting the global trafficking and sexual exploitation of women. This global communication network is being used to promote and engage in the buying and selling of women and children. Agents offer catalogues of mail order brides, with girls as young as 13. Commercial sex tours are advertised. Men exchange information on where to find prostitutes and describe how they can be used. After their trips men write reports on how much they paid for women and children and write pornographic descriptions of what they did to those they bought. Videoconferencing is bringing live sex shows to the Internet. ... Global sexual exploitation is on the rise. The profits are high and there are few effective barriers at the moment. Because there is little regulation of the Internet, the traffickers and promoters of sexual exploitation have rapidly utilized the Internet for their purposes. ... The Internet is being used by men to promote and engage in the sexual exploitation of women and children.[23]

Men are the main producers and consumers of sexualized violence and sexual exploitation, on ICTs as elsewhere. ICTs need to be understood in terms of the collective and individual actions of particular groups of men, and the historically specific development of specific forms of masculinities, such as transnational business masculinities (Connell, 1998) or local pimping masculinities. Sexualized violence is a very important aspect of the development of ICTs and globalization. The types of sexual exploitation and modes of sexualized violence documented on the Internet include: prostitution, bride and sex trafficking, sex tours and tourism, pornography, information services and exchange of information on prostitution, and live sex shows through videoconferencing. All are very closely interconnected.

Newsgroups

The oldest Internet forum for the promotion of the sexual exploitation of women and children are specialist newsgroups and websites. One well known sex newsgroup announces its aim as 'to create market transparency for sex related services' (Atta and M., 1996). Postings from this newsgroup are archived into a World Wide Web site called *The World Sex Guide*, providing 'comprehensive, sex-related information about every country in the world'.

Hughes continues:

> The guide includes information and advice from men who have bought women and children. They tell others where and how to find and buy prostituted women and children in over ninety countries from seven world regions ... Details of the men's reports of their sex tours and buying experiences include: information on where to go to find prostitutes, hotel prices, telephone numbers, taxi fares, cost of alcohol, the sex acts that can be bought, the price for each act, and evaluations of the women's appearances and performances. ... The men ... describe, often in graphic detail, their experiences of using women and children. The scope and detail of this exchange is completely unprecedented. The women are completely objectified and evaluated on everything from skin color to presence of scars and firmness of their flesh. Women's receptiveness and compliance to men buyers is also rated. The men buying women and posting the information see and perceive the events only from their self interested perspective. Their awareness of racism, colonization, global economic inequalities, and of course, sexism, is limited to how these forces benefit them. A country's economic or political crisis and the accompanying poverty are advantages, which produce cheap readily available women for the men. Often men describe how desperate the women are and how little the men have to pay. The postings also reveal that men are using the Internet as a source of information in selecting where to go and how to find women and children to buy in prostitution. Men describe taking a computer print out of hotels, bar addresses and phone numbers with them on their trips, or describe how they used the Internet search engines to locate sex tours. ... The most voluminous coverage is on Bangkok, Thailand. ... names, addresses and phone numbers for 150 hotels where men will feel comfortable are listed.

> This rapid publishing electronic medium has enabled men to pimp individual women. Now, men can go out at night, buy a woman, go home, and post the details on the newsgroup. By morning anyone in the world with an Internet connection can read about it and often have enough information to find the same woman. ... in Nevada, one man bought a woman called "Honey" and named the brothel where she could be found. Within a couple of weeks other men went and bought "Honey"

themselves and posted their experiences to the newsgroup. Within a short period of time men were having an orgy of male bonding by describing what each of them did to "Honey." The men are keeping a special Web site on the Internet for men to post their experiences of buying this one woman.

Some men in newsgroups

... are quite straightforward about their misogyny and sadism. Other men reveal quite inadvertently their abuse of women. The reader can get a glimpse of the humiliation and physical pain most of the women endure at the hands of men who buy them by reading accounts of men's "bad experiences." To the men who buy women and children a "bad experience" means they didn't get their money's worth or that the woman didn't keep up the act of enjoying the men. It means she let her true feelings of pain, desperation, depression and hopelessness show. ... many of the girls and women in Bangkok's sex industry are virtual slaves. The men who buy them know that. ... On this newsgroup, the men tell each other that they can exploit the women and girls held against their will for sadistic practices.

Sex Tours and Sex Tourism

Sex tours, sex holidays and sex tourism, whose advertisements are posted on the Internet, are sometimes for individual men, more often organized tours. The main source countries are: China, Japan, Australia, New Zealand, Saudi Arabia, Qatar, Kuwait, USA, Canada, UK, Norway, Sweden, France, Germany, Switzerland, the Benelux countries and Singapore. The main destinations are: India, Indonesia, Thailand, Cambodia, Vietnam, Philippines, Morocco, Kenya, Hungary, Costa Rica, Cuba, Dominican Republic and Brazil. The Netherlands, Malaysia, Taiwan and South Korea are both source and destination countries. 'Sex tourism is big business and in most instances it has the implicit (or even direct) support of the host government. Sex tourism in many countries started with brothels established to service military bases' (Seager, 1997: 115). One agency, Pimps 'R' Us, runs sex tours to the Dominican Republic in the Caribbean from New York. Prices include computer lessons so the cost can be set against tax. Telephone sex lines are also located in Third World countries, such as Guyana and Pacific Islands (Tuvalu, Niue) (Brown, 1996).[24]

Hughes concludes:

Sex tours enable men to travel to 'exotic' places and step outside whatever community bounds may constrain them at home. In foreign cities they can abuse women and girls in ways that are more risky or difficult for them in their hometowns. As prostitution has become a form of tourism for men, it has become a form of economic development for poor countries. ... States set their own tourist policies and could, if they wanted, prevent or suppress the development of prostitution as a form of tourism. Instead, communities and countries have come to rely on the sale of women and children's bodies to be their cash crop. As the sex industry grows, more girls and women are turned into sexual commodities for sale to tourists. In the bars in Bangkok, women and girls don't have names – they have numbers pinned to their skimpy clothes. The men pick them by number. They are literally interchangeable sexual objects.

Prostitution and Trafficking in Women, Brides and Children

Sex tourism acts as sources of women trafficked for sexual exploitation to other countries. Women are imported legally and illegally from poor countries to centres of sex tourism in European countries to staff the brothels. The largest source of trafficked women is the countries of the former Soviet Union. ICTs also impact upon trafficking in women. This is of four main types: (i) women already prostitutes in one country 'exchanged' by their pimps in another; (ii) girls sold into prostitution by poor families, with or without the families' full knowledge of what is in store for them; (iii) women lured into the sex trade under false pretences, for example through work as waitresses, maids, domestic service; (iv) slave trade beginning with the kidnapping of women or girls from poor regions (Seager, 1997: 115). Trafficking easily blurs with prostitution and sex work, which are in turn often sustained by men's violence.

> (P)rostitution on a local scale can sometimes be a consensual business over which some women may exercise a degree of control. There are none of these mitigating circumstances in the global trafficking of women. The global sex trade is almost entirely coercive, sustained by high levels of violence and predicated on the thorough subordination of women. In the global sex network, women's bodies are commodities. Prostitutes are traded, girls are bought and exchanged among cartels, and international orders for fresh prostitute recruits are placed through brokers. The international trafficking of women and girls … thrives on economic disparities: between women and men at all scales, and between regions on a global scale. New regions and countries enter into the sex trade as their economic fortunes wax or wane. (Seager, 1997: 115)

An example of the last point is Eastern Europe providing more supply of women, China and Malaysia more demand from men.

The scale of trafficking in women and children and prostitution is difficult to appreciate. In Thailand estimates on the number of women in prostitution range from 300,000 to 2.8 million, of which a third are minors. Thai women are also in prostitution in many countries in Asia, Australia, Europe and the USA. The Centre for the Protection of Children's Rights, Bangkok estimates 200,000 masseuses in Bangkok, of which 100,000 are 20 or under, and 800,000 child prostitutes in Thailand (Bindel, 1996: 29). The following major routes of global sex trafficking are: Russia to Saudi Arabia; Russia/Ukraine to Germany; Romania to Turkey; Albania to Italy; Guatamala to Spain; Dominican Republic/Netherland Antilles to The Netherlands; Togo to Middle East/ Western Europe; Nigeria to Italy; Brazil/Colombia to Western Europe; Brazil/Mexico to Japan; Sri Lanka to Middle East/Pakistan; India to Pakistan/Middle East; Bangladesh to India/Pakistan; Nepal to India; Thailand to Japan/Western Europe/Australia/Malaysia/ Taiwan; China/Laos/Vietnam/Burma/Cambodia to Thailand; Vietnam to China/Cambodia; Cambodia to Malaysia; Philippines to Malaysia/Saudi Arabia/Japan/Taiwan/Hong Kong; long-distance internal trafficking in Brazil and China (Seager, 1997). The Netherlands is the strongest international proponent of legalized prostitution, Amsterdam being the main European city for sex tourism. Brothels were legalized in The Netherlands in 1997, with subsequent increased international trafficking to Amsterdam.

Hughes continues:

> Mail order bride agents have moved to the Internet as their preferred marketing location. The Internet reaches a prime group of potential buyers – men from Western countries with higher than average incomes. The new Internet technology enables Web pages to be quickly and easily updated; some services claim they are updating

their selection of women bi-weekly. The Internet reaches a global audience faster and less expensively than any other media. One mail order bride agent explained why he preferred operation on the Internet. 'So when the World-Wide Web came along, I saw that it was a perfect venue for this kind of business. ... on the Web you can publish high-resolution full-color photos which can be browsed by everyone in the WORLD ... .'

[Internet] agents offer men assistance in finding a 'loving and devoted' woman whose 'views of relationships have not been ruined by unreasonable expectations.' The agencies describe themselves as 'introduction services,' but a quick examination of many of the Web sites reveals their commercial interests in bride trafficking, sex tours and prostitution. ... Pictures of the women are shown with their names, height, weight, education and hobbies. Some catalogues include the women's bust, waist and hip measurements. The women's ages range from 13 to 50. One of the commonly promoted characteristics of women from Eastern Europe is that they 'traditionally expect to marry gentlemen that are 10 to 20 years older ...'.

International Agency Gimeney advertises: 'Here are Russian women in a hurry to leave, looking for willing, well-healed [sic] Western men to wed. Pick through them like peaches in the produce rack, neatly sorted by their age and hair colour. See something you like? Pay to get her address and write something nice – nearly all of them seem to know English' (Naughton, 1998). Men pay for these services on the Internet by credit card. Some sites list women with young children and ask if the men want women with or without children; some give pictures of naked children. Hughes suggests that children are being trafficked also in this way, with the men being subtly shown ways of acquiring women and children in one package.

Pornography

International respectable magazines, youth magazines and pornography magazine ownership, production and markets are becoming increasingly interlocked (Pinsent and Knight, 1998). Pornography is also being expanded through satellite television, pay television, video and the Internet. The USA is the biggest producer and consumer of pornography. Ninety per cent of all material downloaded from the Internet is pornography (Mackay, 2000: 64–5). Most violent and sadistic pornography, as well as much child pornography, is produced by Western men in the Third World (Bindel, 1996: 27). Bulletin Board Services are widely used for child and other forms of pornography (Karlén, 1996). There are increasing reports of high levels of access to pornography in corporate work time. Live videoconferencing is amongst the most advanced technology currently on the Web. This involves the buying of live sex shows, in which the man can direct the show in some cases.

PC *Computing* magazine urged entrepreneurs to visit pornography Web sites. 'It will show you the future of on-line commerce. Web pornographers are the most innovative entrepreneurs on the Internet' (Taylor & Jerome, 1997). The pornographers and other promoters of sexual exploitation are the Internet leaders in the developing privacy services and secure payment schemes. ... The most advanced technology on the Internet is live videoconferencing, in which live audio and video communication is transmitted over the Internet from video recorder to computer. ... used to sell live sex shows over the Internet. Real time communication is possible, so the man can personally direct the live sex show as he is viewing on his computer. ... The only limitation on this type of global sex show is the need for high-speed transmission, processing and multimedia capabilities. The software required is available free, but the most recent versions of Web browsers have these capabilities built into them. As more men have access to high-speed multimedia computer and transmission equipment, this type of private sex show will grow. There are no legal restrictions on this type of live sex show that can be transmitted over the Internet. ... as with all Internet transmissions, there are no nation-state border restrictions. With Internet technology a man maybe on one continent, while directing and watching a live strip show, a live sex show, or the sexual abuse of a child, on another.

Symbolic sex and image production is also subject to globalization. Laurel Davis (1997) has examined the annual 'Swimsuit issue' of *Sports Illustrated* and concluded that constructions of hegemonic masculinity are made on the backs of both people of colour and the symbolic dominance of the feminized (post)colonized other, often as the exotic backdrop to adventures, fantasies and a test of manhood (p. 105). Representation is thus pornographized globally. Pornography is also liable to virtualization, as the image once stored electronically can be reproduced and manipulated through techniques perfected in Hollywood: the woman is dispensable.

Sexual Exploitation and Organized Crime

Though transnational and national legal and policy frameworks distinguish between trafficking in women and children, prostitution, pornography and sex tourism, there are clear linkages between different types of sexploitation. This is obvious from Internet advertising. Agents use women in any way that is profitable. Most mail order bride agents on the Internet also offer tours. Men pay for the addresses of the women in the catalogues, and agents later organize group tours for men to meet the women with whom they have been corresponding.

'The Moscow trip is a logical conclusion to your correspondence efforts. The purpose of the tour is to meet as many lovely ladies as possible as soon as possible.' Men going to either Russia or the Philippines are assured of getting a wife to bring home, if that is their desire, or they are assured of the availability of many women. Men don't want to believe they are taking home a prostitute as a wife, so the men are assured that they will be introduced to marriageable women, as well as other 'available and willing' women. A man is usually offered the option of paying for an 'escort' for each day. 'Each and every day you will be escorted by your choice of lovely, elegant ladies.'

Advertisements from a US-based agency describe clearly what is offered and show the connections among the forms of sexual exploitation:

A picture of a Filipina tops the first page of *Travel Philippines*. She invites the reader ... to 'Come explore the Philippines with me!' The advertisement describes the Philippines as an 'exotic and interesting place to visit.' Information is given on tickets, lodging, food and water, money changing, night life and the tour schedule. Prostitution is briefly mentioned as being 'everywhere,' and a price range for prostitutes is listed. Men are told, 'You can partake or not, it's up to you. Most do partake.' Marriage is also briefly mentioned: 'As most of you know, the Philippines is the happy hunting ground for men seeking a wife. There are all kinds of women of every description. It's hard to go to the Philippines and not get caught up in the idea of marriage. The whole lifestyle seems to revolve around love, marriage and kids' ... On the next linked page the man is asked 'would you like to have a beautiful female companion as a private tour guide?' or 'would you like to have introductions to "decent" marriage minded ladies?' ... If he chooses the private tour guide he is directed to the X-Rated Escorted Tours. At the top of this page a picture of the same Filipina from the introductory page appears, this time with her breasts exposed. The woman invites the men to 'Come explore the Philippines and Me!' ...

The fee is paid to the travel agent-pimp, not the woman. ... If the man chooses the marriage option he is directed to the linked page on Over Seas Ladies. There he is asked if he is tired of watching TV and having women make him jump through hoops. He is told that the women for sale here 'respond to every gesture and kindness, no matter how small.' He is reassured that these women are not concerned about his age, appearance, or wealth. This is followed by thirteen pages of pictures of women from which he can choose ... . The agent-pimp sells the addresses of the women to the man. For an extra fee the buyer can have a life-time membership which entitles him to the addresses of all the women, those currently available and those in the future. ... The whole sexual exploitation racket comes full circle with the next linked page on Escorted Wife Seeking Tours. ... '... Your penpals that you have been writing to will be happy to see you. The new women you meet will be generally "good" girls, but there are plenty of bar girls there too and you will surely encounter some' ... . Bar girls, X-rated tours with 'private tour guides,' mail order brides – all are forms of sexual exploitation organized by the same agency for the profit of pimps, hotels and bars.

Such agents are very likely to be also involved in international trafficking of women. The CIA has identified trafficking in women as the third largest business of organized crime after weapons and drugs. It also estimates that about 50,000 women and children are being brought in to the USA every year to work as prostitutes or virtual slaves (Campbell, 2000a). The use of ICTs in trafficking, sexualized violence and organized crime more generally is likely to increase in the future.

Continuations ...

Globalization, TNCs and the new globalizing ICTs are matters of gender, sexuality, violence and violation. This is not to say they are necessarily violating – far from it. Rather that they cannot be understood without attention to their reformulation of gender, sexuality, violence and violation. TNCs and ICTs are both very large-scale and expanding social phenomena that transcend nations and are difficult to regulate and control. They break (organizational) boundaries, and in that partly lies their power and power for organization violations.

To understand these contemporary changes around sexualized violence demands attention to material, political and symbolic realms. In each case there are major contradictions. To paraphrase Waters (1995: 9), first, the production of 'exchangeable' (sexual) items involves local concentrations of (sexual) labour, (sexual) capital and (sexual) raw materials. Sexual contact is a local, immediate bodily matter. Global movement of people and goods accompanies local material 'exchanges', as in trafficking in women and children.

Second, political regulation of sexuality is constructed primarily through the nation, even with its simultaneous problematization, yet politics also proceeds through internationalization. ICTs transcend national boundaries. Debates on technological monitoring of ICTs, for example through screening devices, inter-mingle with political and legal opposition from libertarian, 'free speech' and anti-censorship lobbies, especially in the USA. The Philippines has banned sex tour and mail order bride agencies. The countries from which men come on tours and order brides could equally ban such agencies and prohibit their advertising from computers in their country. Many police investigations of child pornography on the Internet have been successful. Similar investigations of Internet advertising of sex tours, mail order brides and prostitution are needed, along with international judicial and police cooperation. The EU defines trafficking as a form of organized crime; its Internet advertising should be treated similarly. National regulation of sexuality accompanies gradual political internationalization.

Third, symbolic sexual 'exchanges' are seen by some as 'liberating' relation-ships from spatial referents: they can be produced anywhere, anytime, with few resource constraints on their production and reproduction; they are easily trans-portable. They often seek to appeal to what are seen as 'human sexual funda-mentals' and often claim universal significance. But people's symbolic meanings are not so easily liberated from power and violation. Symbolic sexuality globali-zes along with local meanings.

The relationship of sexuality, violence and sexualized violence with these changing technologies is thus complex. There appears to be a growing disjunc-tion between the scale of international and global material sex economies (pros-titution, trafficking in women, transport of people by unlawful force, deceit and coercion, bride purchase, pornography, sex shows, and so on) and the represen-tation and reproduction of the sexual through new technologies (in computer sex, cybersex, virtual sex, computer-aided imaging, and so on). This is both a social and an academic disjunction, as different scholars tend to focus on one or the other. Of special concern are both the social connections between the material and the representational, and the possibility that these two aspects may lead prac-tice and policy in quite contradictory directions.

ICTs embody features characteristic of late modernity and late modern organizational environments: 'action at a distance (distanciation)'; 'mediated com-munication' (instanciation); 'the economy of signs, especially risks' (demateriali-zation); and 'social reflexivity' (detraditionalization) (Tsoukas, 1999).[25] ICTs can be used and understood in all these ways, as well as their overlaps and inter-connections. ICTs offer complex potentials for gendered action at a distance, gen-dered mediated yet instant communication (as through visual monitors), gendered dematerialization of economies and gendered reflexivity in meaning. Sexualized violence is bodily, of the body, the possibility of face-to-face interaction, arousal, imaging, fantasy, intensity, attraction, touch, engulfment, violence, violation. One (usually male) person's 'sexuality' is another's (usually female's) violation. Though technology exists for ever-more virtualization of sex, sexuality, violence and sexualized violence, the material represented on ICTs is usually done some-where: '... sexual exploitation starts with real people and the harm is to real people.'[26]

7

Politics and Policy

Violations in and around organizations, as elsewhere, are personally and socially damaging. Their recognition, their analysis and action against them constitute a politics of organization violations. Problematizing violence and violation is likely to lead to this becoming a more significant political and policy focus in the future. Analysing social processes around violation may contribute to the creation of violation-free organizations and working environments. The political problem of how to effect the reduction and stopping of violation in and around organizations is a matter of political change. We have thus examined the processes by which violations become named, recognized and problematized within organizational settings, drawing on historical, documentary, experiential and other evidence. Not only have we analysed the ways in which violations come to be voiced and sometimes dealt with but also the ways in which they reconstitute organizational subtexts and so continue as grievances and violations for those suffering or witnessing violations. In addition to those organization violations that are problematized, there are many more that are not, even when they are resisted to some extent. These include all manner of everyday ignorings, demeanings, insults, put-downs, shoutings, and persistent and excessive negativities towards others in and outside the organization, that make some people's lives miserable or worse. While these are used overwhelmingly by those in relative power, they can be employed by those oppressed as resistances and even against those less powerful still.

In this final chapter the implications of organization violations for politics and policy are explored. This includes attention to the politics of recognition, of speaking the unspoken, and the politics of theory and knowledge. The generally low extent of explicit gendering of debates on organization violations, despite the empirical evidence to the contrary of the significance of gendered violation, is a concern and challenge for organization studies and the social sciences. It also involves discussion of the politics of organizing, of mundane violations and organizational culture, and of oppressions. More specific policy interventions include management, equal opportunities, legislation, cyberpolicy, as well as those around whistleblowing and professional misconduct. We conclude with a discussion of the need to open up debate on the creation and maintenance of violation-free organizations. We intend that by spelling out some of these debates, a political and policy analysis of organization violations can be furthered. This chapter, like the book as a whole, constitutes part of a politics of organization violations.

The Politics of Recognition: Speaking the Unspoken of Organization Violations

The 'discovery' of gender at work in organizations assisted the recognition of 'sex' at 'work' (Hearn and Parkin, 1987, 1995). Opening up the myth of the agendered, asexual organization has meant that longstanding silences have been broken. Sexuality and gender have been acknowledged as inextricable parts of both organizational structures and processes, and men's power and privilege. This has contributed to the recognition of new dimensions of organizational analysis such as those around violences and violations and their links with sexuality and gender – what were in effect previously unspoken forces. Now we 'speak' organization violations – the simultaneous production and reproduction of organizations and violations – seeking to bring them to the 'hearing' of organizational members, managers and theorists. This 'speaking' is, however, only part of a process whereby those with power and privilege seek to silence others. This is not a neat progression but a bumpy ride for those involved, as when harassed and bullied women have spoken out and sought redress from organizations, only to encounter a process of further intimidation.

Attention to 'violence in the workplace' has focused mainly on physical violence. A narrow focus on physical violence might draw attention to certain acts perpetrated apparently randomly by those 'outside' the organization (such as customers or those seeking to commit robbery), and thus could distract from the prime focus of violation being the organizational worlds themselves. Many subjected to regular bullying or racist or sexist taunts and harassment, yet unable to speak them, recognize them as violences. The more we explore the practices of harassment, bullying, intimidation and physical violence, the less we are inclined to see them as 'essentially' different or on a simple continuum or hierarchy which privileges one over another in terms of damage to the person. They are all organization violations but may be difficult to conceptualize as such with the equating of violence with certain physical assaults.

The secrecy and unspokenness of the range of violations and the need for them to be made open requires a conceptual framework which is meaningful in terms of what is happening to both the person and in the organization. The concept of 'organization violations' brings together what is happening to the violated person and in the organization in which it occurs, including attempts to keep them unspoken. 'Organization violations' is a way of analysing a range of organizational structures and processes and how they further or decrease violations and abusive practices. Even if the term violence is broadened to take account of the whole field we have covered, it would not be meaningful when perceived within the paradigm of physical assault and so would distract attention from the majority of issues we have raised. Furthermore, although 'organization violation' does not directly correlate with 'organization sexuality' (Hearn and Parkin, 1987, 1995), there are some similarities. Sexuality, like violence, can refer to a specific event but this does not cover the range of ways in which sexuality is perceived and defined. Sexuality and violation are both process and event: one a process of desiring and the other a process of damaging, both of which may provoke responses. However, a complication is that sexuality, inextricably linked with gender and power, can also be a means for damage. Organization violation is dynamic and ongoing; it intersects with and encompasses processes of sexuality, gender and power.

Organization violation refers to organizational violations of the person ranging from mundane, apparently innocuous experiences, through the somewhat more obvious physical and sexual violations of sexual harassment, bullying and some physical violence, to more structural oppressions. Organization violation is a framework for understanding a range of organizational processes, such as physical violence, emotional violence, harassment, bullying and intimidation, as well as exploitation, oppression, conflict, and so on. We conceptualize all the experiences discussed, from seemingly 'harmless' sexual/sexist banter, through to physical violence, rape and killing, as violations. In addition to the more obvious forms of violation, it is important to consider violation within routine organizational processes – in managerial and work cultures, in the ordinary enactment of authority, in normalized harassment, in dealing with the violation from others, in talking about violations, as well as the process of keeping records around violations.

Organization violations do not 'just happen'. They occur within complex organizational processes of recognition and response, and form part of the wider politics of and struggles for recognition in political movements. In some cases struggles for recognition have been characterized by the formation of collective groupings of those in similar social situations; with the recognition of organization violations, this has often been more difficult. Speaking the unspoken of organization violations is part of and contributes to their recognition; it constitutes a politics of recognition.

The Politics of Theory and Research

Social theory and social research are not just matters of intellect; they are also matters of politics. There has often been a general neglect of questions of violence and violation in social theory, and when they have been introduced they have usually been located either at a very broad societal level or an immediate interpersonal level, rather than the organizational level. The empirical evidence on the scope and frequency of violations in and around organizations represents a challenge to the social sciences as a central contemporary concern. Much existing research on organizations, violence and violations has been strongly influenced by psychological rather than sociological thinking. However, the sociology of violence is an elusive sociological field.

The development of the sociology of violence in the sociological canon lies in macro-historical social forces: conflicts between societies, cultures, nations, communities, ethnic groups and classes, in struggle, war, insurrection and sometimes revolutions. It is an ever-present of social and political thought, whether in the Hobbesian problem of social order in the face of 'the life of man, solitary, poor, nasty, brutish and short' (Hobbes, 1962: 143), Marxian class struggle, or functionalist control of 'the war of all against all' (Aberle et al., 1950). This is violence with a capital 'V', both in its incipient 'lust and rage' (1950) and its control. It is seen as 'Historical', in defiance of supposedly less dramatic forms. Interpersonal violence has often been seen as less substantially and structurally historical within mainstream history and sociology; it happens between neighbours, strangers and known others. It has been the concern of a number of extremely important sociological schools: first, the sociologists of 'subclass' and subculture; second, criminology, with its own long-established anxiety around gender; and then, third, feminist and gender-aware studies of violence in family and other personal relationships, characteristically of men to women and children. It has often been feminist work that has rectified some of these shortcomings of previous work, and placed the matter as firmly historical and sociological. Furthermore, the sociological 'specialisms' of the sociology of violence and organizational sociology have generally proceeded independently of each other, so that the insights from each have not been transferred to the other. This relative separation is partly a consequence of the gendering of sociology itself. The sociology of violence has been strongly affected by feminist studies on men's violence to women and children, whilst organizational sociology has, despite the growth of feminist and profeminist work, been much more impermeable to the recognition of gendered studies: it continues to be more fundamentally constructed through men's dominant definitions.

There are many social scientific problems in how to develop research on violation and organizations. These include how to further the explanation of violations and organizations in relation to each other. This applies within and between the various sociological sub-disciplines, especially organization studies and studies on violence but also the social sciences more generally. The interface of violations and organizations – hence organization violations – has not been an explicit central concern of contemporary social theory. Indeed where violations and organizations have been put together, they have often been conceptualized in other ways, including capitalist exploitation, managerial control, resistance, surveillance, institutionalization and power. Such conceptualizations keep organizations and violations safely apart, and the more explicit investigation of violation safely alone. There are thus a number of implications for social theory, organization theory and social research:

1   the *definitional* problem, particularly how the relationship of physical violence and non-physical violence is understood;
2   the *cultural and historical* problem of the recognition of violation and organizations – what counts as violation in organizations and how violation appears differently in different societies;
3   the *methodological* problem of how to study violation and organizations – it is difficult to study such violations by interviews alone or even by observations, especially when they take place secretly, behind closed doors and over a long period;
4   the *discursive* problem of the representation of violation, and the interrelations of the doing of violation, the experience of violation and discourses on violation;

5 the *scientific* problem of how to further the understanding of violation and organizations in relation to each other – within organization studies, studies on violence and sociology more generally;

6 the *policy and political* problems of how to effect the reduction and stopping of violation in and around organizations.

For all these reasons, organization violations need to occupy a central place within social theory, organization theory and social research.

The Politics of Knowledge

The place of violation within development of theory and social theory is part of the way in which knowledges are produced and reproduced. Definitions, analyses, explanations and so on all construct violations, and what are seen as and count as violations (Hearn, 1998). This theoretical point applies as much in specific organizations as it does in the field of (social) science. In both cases, management, that is particular organizational managements and the management of academic knowledge, are immensely important. In the latter case this includes both the management of disciplinary and research knowledge, and the management of universities and other institutions of higher education. This points to the crucial importance of critical gendered analysis of academia and academics. A recent and particularly oppressive case of 'academic harassment' (*Akahara*) has been successfully brought to the courts by Kumiko Ogoshi, a research associate at Nara Medical University, Japan, exposing the near-absolute patriarchal power of some male professors in the system (Normile, 2001; http://www.kcn.ne.jp/~jjj/akahara/acahara.htm). The enactment of violations in academic organizations and managements, such as the exclusion of women from senior management and 'academic harassments' more generally, itself constructs dominant understandings of violations, such as the lack of analysis of the interrelations of men, masculinities and organization violations. In short, violations not only damage and oppress certain people; they also exclude them and their voices from the speaking of violations and the making of knowledge about them. This is sometimes through mundane silencings, sometimes through harassment and bullying, sometimes through physical violence and even killing, perhaps the ultimate absence. Furthermore, increasingly, what counts as knowledge, as evidenced in the size and composition of the R&D sector, is being directed to and governed by capitalist organizations. This means that knowledge and the politics of knowledge around organization violations are themselves increasingly subject to those social and economic forces.

The Politics of Organizing and Organization

Organizations, and the organizational knowledges formed within them, are themselves formed in the context of historical structural relations of domination, control and violence, including those of public patriarchies. The basic activities of organizing, of forming and maintaining organizations often involve violation, depending as they do for their continuation upon obedience to authority that is to some degree unaccountable and unjustified. Thus a useful avenue of theoretical development in organizational analysis is the examination of the extent to which particular organizations, and examples of organizing, make explicit the forms and sources of authority in use, and how these authorities are gendered. In most cases, the unaccountable and unjustifiable authority of organizations is men's and it is that which is violating. In addition, organizational processes such as hierarchical exercise of power could mean that the very processes of organizations are processes of potential or actual violations. In terms of organization studies, the obvious point is that there has been little attention to the dialectics of bureaucracy and other modern organizations that may both produce/facilitate violations and constrain/control violations, and to the exercise of managerial and similar powers (such as by the police) in organizations as violent and violating or potentially so. Many concepts in organizational analysis such as 'power' and 'control' can be used as euphemisms for violation.

Mundane Violations and Organizational Culture

As has been stressed, organization violations recur in the everyday fabric of organizations. They include both obvious and dramatic violences; harassments, bullying and those physical violences that are becoming more fully recognized; structural oppression that may often be taken for granted; and mundane violations in organizations. This contradicts a 'commonsense' view of organizational worlds. An important, but as yet undeveloped, area of politics and policy is the embeddedness of violation in the mundane practices of organization and organizations, of doing organization(s) and (re)producing organizations. What is often called organizational culture is often itself a site of and shorthand for mundane organization violations. Furthermore, in one sense, 'violation' is like any other work object – to be worked on and made 'social'. Violation can be 'reduced' to the material task and the culture of the organization – it can be processed, reconstructed, ignored or joked about, like any other cultural organizational currency. However, for there to be a work process around violation may well bring extra complications for those concerned. For those responding to violation there are likely to be not just pain and distress but also strategies of avoidance.

The Politics of Policy

Management

Management and managerialism are often crucial in violating and abusive regimes and are one of the areas of organizations to which especial attention needs to be paid. There is overwhelming evidence of the explicit and complicit role of management in violations, particularly around sexual harassment and bullying, but also the ordinary enactment of managerial 'policy'. Managerial responses and representations are particularly important since they may help to resolve but can also exacerbate the incidence and impact of workplace violation. Management is fundamentally part of the structures and cultures to which it contributes. Managerial actions and controls, individual and collective, can also be crucial in the (re)production of violations and when planning for change in organizational responses to violence and violation. Managements can:

- be actively involved in harassment, bullying and other violations;
- ignore such violations and/or complaints about them;
- impose policies workloads and targets which lead to cultures of intimidation;
- attempt to implement policy and practical changes;
- develop understandings of 'positive' work environments where the importance of removing violation is recognized;
- explicitly create and maintain violation-free organizational environments.

Whatever legislation or equal opportunities policies, whatever encouragement is given to employees to 'blow the whistle', whatever policies are in place to empower staff and users, implementation is difficult without the wholehearted commitment of management (Cockburn, 1991; Itzin and Newman, 1995). The gendering and sexualing of management is also crucial. In the context of bureaucratic patriarchy, male managers, and a few female managers, may be constructed as and expected to be unemotional, objective, impartial, efficient and closely bound by rules. Women are defined as antithetical to this culture and as emotional, irrational, particularistic, subjective and focused on family rather than work. Similarly the professional project is also deeply gendered. It is difficult to move forward until these issues are addressed in organizations. Men's practices need to be a focus of change in organizational culture and the creation of violation-free organizations. For example, attention needs to be paid to the transformation of men who are workers and managers in agencies when exploring the gendering of violence to older people and children (Hearn, 1999a).

Equal Opportunities, Complaints and Procedures
Equal opportunities policies and practices would seem an obvious way forward in the protection of people at work. Particular organizations have their own policies and regulations on harassment, discrimination, bullying, health and safety, codes of conduct, equal opportunities, as well as physical violence. Most policies have a legal base but individual organizations can develop them to a greater or lesser extent beyond the legal framework. Such policies do 'speak' of a range of organizational discriminations but usually fall short of describing them as abuses of the person or violation. Key messages of equal opportunities research are the monitoring of policies and what, if any, sanctions are in place if they are contravened. Cockburn (1991) conceptualizes equal opportunities in terms of shorter and longer agendas. The 'short agenda' is the minimum position supported by top management without which no equality policy would get started, while the 'long agenda' involves more substantial kinds of change. 'The long agenda of equality policy is, then, combating sexism, racism, heterosexism and discrimination against people with disabilities, acknowledging and according high value to different kinds of bodies and different kinds of cultures – all perceived as equivalent, all afforded parity' (p. 219).

There is a need for strong procedures for dealing with sexual harassment, other harassments, bullying and physical violence in organizations. These should include formal complaints procedures as well as a variety of other ways of resolving and stopping such violations. Guidance should be as clear and simple as possible. Part of this is the clarification of responsibilities for handling procedures, and their interface with criminal law. Some harassment procedures have oddly not included bullying and physical violence as harassment, which therefore are outside their policy remit. This is not viable policy. In discussing bullying, Randall (1997) writes of a 'healthy organization' as one which 'will have in place anti-harassment policies and procedures which are fully integrated within the overall philosophy of the organization and are regarded as highly as its working techniques and practices. Such commitment will help employees feel the organization they work in is as secure as their own home and that they are valued, respected and cared about as people, not just staff members with specific functions' (p. 106). He points to the importance of managerial commitment to procedures to minimize harassment and deal with those intent on bullying.

Legislation and Regulation

Legislation does force employers to pay attention to questions of violation, but change is slow, as evidenced by the Equal Pay Act whereby the gap between men's and women's pay still exists and has recently widened. Not only is legislation fragmented and weak but individuals have great difficulty in using it. Only a tiny proportion of those violated successfully obtain redress through the law, often doing so at great personal cost and further damage to health. Specific legal measures to address particular issues have been cited earlier (see pp. 62–3). In the UK legal interventions in the prevention of, and redress against, various violations include the Race Relations Act 1976 (victimization), Sex Discrimination Act 1975 (victimization), Disability Discrimination Act 1995, Protection of Harassment Act 1997 (stalking), Public Interest Disclosure Act 1999, ('whistle-blowing') Criminal Justice and Public Order Act 1995, Trade Union Reform and Employment Rights Act 1993, Rehabilitation of Offenders Act 1974, Health and Safety at Work Act 1974, EC Code on the Protection of the Dignity of Women and Men at Work (90/C 157/02), Management of Health and Safety at Work Regulations 1992, EC Directives 1993, EU Ruling (4/96), changing Health and Safety Executive and RIDDOR guidelines following EU ruling (4/96). There are also those parts of the criminal law that relate to sexual violation, physical assaults, homicide, theft and damage to property.

Not all violences or violations fit into the above categories. Therefore there may not always be a suitable route for redress. Strengthening existing legislation and making it easier for people to have access to the law and bring cases to court and tribunals would be helpful but limited. The creation of new legislation to fill the gaps might be a step forward but would continue the fragmentation and create a more confused and cumbersome picture. This would also perpetuate the different categories under which violation can be dealt with and possibly continue the greater attention given to incidents of physical violence. Conceptualizing violation as we do would necessitate new legislative frameworks whereby the various categories of violation can be addressed and not seen as separate or placed on a continuum or hierarchy of violations. This is highly unlikely in the short term. However, many issues around equality and human rights no longer take place within the confines of the national legislative systems but are located and controlled within wider legislation, such as that of the EU,[1] and this may present more open-ended possibilities than some national systems.

Cyberpolicy, International Policy

The increasing impact of email, the Internet and cyberworlds has raised complex legal and policy issues for organizations and managements. In 1997 Morgan Stanley and Citibank were both sued by employees for allegedly allowing racist email messages to be distributed on corporate networks. In the latter case, the bank is alleged to have subjected black employees to 'a pervasively abusive, racially hostile working environment' through emails between white colleagues. The oil company Chevron paid out £1.3 million after being sued for sexual harassment by a woman because of the existence of sexist jokes on the company's email system, under the headline 'Why beer is better than women' (Hilpern, 1999). Kwikfit fired employees for exchanging obscene emails (Boughton, 2000). The Scottish housing association, Cairn, sacked two employees for exchanging sexually explicit emails and then had to pay compensation for unfair dismissal. The second-biggest USA chemical company fired 50 workers and suspended 200 for sending pornographic and violent email. Twenty employees of an international newspaper were fired for sending 'inappropriate and offensive' email. The USA navy disciplined more than 500 shore employees for sending sexually explicit electronic messages (Boughton, 2000).

Many companies (for example, Cadbury, Schweppes, Guinness, Lloyds TSB and Price Waterhouse Coopers) have formalized working practices regarding email (Ryle, 1999). The Merican Management Association found in their survey of 32,000 companies that one in seven reviewed email messages. Peapod software company in London has found 38 per cent do so (Boughton, 2000). In Finland, the IDC Research Institute forecast that 80 per cent of companies will supervise employees' Internet use by 2001 (Lähteenmäki, 2000). There is now an extensive counter-business in the monitoring of emails and websites. SRA markets the Assentor package which alerts employers to certain expressions deemed unsuitable in emails (Hilpern, 1999). Content Technologies has distributed similar Minesweeper surveillance software to 5,000 users worldwide (Boughton, 2000). JSB Software company has a subunit SurfControl Program which can offer packages that monitor about 3.5 million (and growing) 'negative' email addresses (pornography, gambling, racist and some games and shopping addresses), and blocks users' access to them if logging is attempted. They also have a 'positive' list of addresses of preferred sites. The package also provides systems controllers and managers with a picture of what is happening in employees' use of the Internet. Elron Software have their Internet Manager package in use in 3,000 companies. This prevents access if there are sufficient 'forbidden' keywords (which can be changed or re-weighted) on the webpages. The program also adds those negatively vetted pages on to the list of forbidden pages. This also gives the possibility of monitoring individual employees' use of the Internet, for example access to sports or financial transactions pages. This kind of surveillance is also justified by companies in terms of reducing the security risks of employees downloading viruses from unsafe sites. In the Nordic sister company of Coca-Cola everyone has to apply for Internet use, personal use is forbidden and random tests of use are made (Lähteenmäki, 2000).

The legal situation on these matters varies throughout the world. In the USA the employee's right to privacy is secondary to the employer's business interests. Employers are also concerned to demonstrate that they have taken reasonable precautions against, say, an employee accessing child pornography, in case another employee sues the company. In Europe the European Court of Human Rights ruled in 1998 that workers have a 'reasonable expectation' of privacy in electronic communication: ownership does not permit surveillance. The 2000 Human Rights Act made it compulsory for UK employers to tell their employees if they are monitoring their emails.[2] Legislative issues are generally becoming much more complex beyond the realm of the nation-state, in particular through the activities of multinational and transnational organizations, the use of ICTs and the development of transnational legal entities, such as the EU, that transcend national borders.[3]

These issues are crucial not only in general global commerce and state governance, but more specifically in the fields of pornography, prostitution, trafficking in women and children, and sex tourism (see Chapter 6). There are strong contradictions between national attempts to control what are clearly transnational activities and special difficulties in controlling ICTs across borders. In 1990 the Philippines banned sex tours and mail order brides, but these both continue. In 1995 Sweden was the first country to jail a citizen for sexual offences abroad. The 1996 Sex Offences (Conspiracy and Incitement) Act makes it an offence to incite someone to commit certain sexual offences against children abroad. Incitement can include telephone calls, faxes, and similar messages via the Internet received in the UK. In July 2000 the Regulation of Investigatory Powers Act was passed. This allows state surveillance of Internet traffic, including child pornography. There have been other legal and regulatory initiatives and debates in the EU, the USA and elsewhere. These have been both contested within the legal process itself and subverted through technological and other means. For example, the USA Communications Decency Act that would have limited some pornography on the Internet was declared unconstitutional by the Supreme Court. Malaysia, Russia and Singapore have laws on state interception of Internet material, though Internet crime and trafficking in women is well developed in Russia and elsewhere; the situation in France, Germany, Ireland, the USA and most other countries is much more laissez-faire (Greenslade, 2000). There is a host of international activity here, including the 1979 UN Convention on Discrimination Against Women (CEDAW), the 1993 UN Declaration on the Elimination of Violence against Women, the UN Convention on the Rights of the Child and legal and political initiatives on trafficking of women, sex tourism, Internet use, and so on. Their implementation is countered and severely contradicted by other laws, powerful opposed organized political forces, corruption, lack of enforcement and legal complexity. The EU is an important site of political struggle in these respects. There are marked differences of opinion on the status of prostitution in relation to violence against women and trafficking in women and children. The exclusion of prostitution and pimping from violence against women by the EC in 1998 points to the contradictions of such debates.

Whistleblowing

An aspect of legal and policy intervention that has attracted considerable debate in recent years is that of whistleblowing (Rothschild and Miethe, 1994). In Martin's (1984) book on hospital scandals, *Hospitals in Trouble*, one of the key themes was the treatment of those who tried to speak out in that they were subjected to abuse, intimidation and threats of dismissal. Scandals in children's homes, surveys on bullying, harassment in the police force, and so on suggest little has changed and how people speaking out may do so at considerable harm to themselves and their careers. The doctor who blew the whistle on the Bristol heart surgeons was not listened to, was frozen out of work in the UK and emigrated.[4] In the police force there is still an enormous amount of resentment if an officer 'breaks ranks' and tells tales on her or his colleagues (Gregory and Lees, 1999). Alison Taylor, former Director of Social Services in Gwynedd, who 'blew the whistle' on abuses in children's homes, identifies this as 'professional suicide' (Manthorpe and Stanley, 1999). Because of such scandals, Government suggested that more attention should be paid to protecting those who whistleblow particularly where bad professional practice is to be exposed. This is incorporated into the Public Interest Disclosure Act 1998 (Bully Online, 1999), made necessary because time and time again official inquiries have revealed that workers have been aware of real dangers to people in a variety of situations and have been too scared to sound the alarm. Under this Act a worker may take their employer to tribunal for any detriment (dismissal, redundancy, etc.) after a worker makes a disclosure ('blows the whistle') relating to:

- a criminal offence;
- a breach of legal obligation (e.g. duty of care);
- health and safety of an employee is likely to be endangered (e.g. by bullying);
- a miscarriage of justice;
- environmental damage;
- concealing information about any of the above;

provided the worker:

- reasonably believes it to be true;
- does not make the disclosure for personal gain;
- does not commit an offence by making the disclosure (e.g. breaking the Official Secrets Act).

Procedures should indicate to whom the whistleblower can take their complaint, and should ensure that these processes do not involve the complainant having of necessity to approach their line manager or any individual implicated.

It remains to be seen whether the Act will work in practice as concerns have been raised on the need to prove disclosure is in the 'public interest' rather than an onus on employers to justify why unacceptable victimization and harassment is taking place. One of the first people to use the Public Interest Disclosure Act 1998 was a school finance officer who was forced to resign after she blew the whistle about financial irregularities at the school as the stress she had been subjected to made her position untenable. She received compensation but is now in a lower paid job; however, she feels that her professional integrity has been valued and respected (Vasey, 2000).

This legislation is a step forward but much will depend on the interpretation of 'public interest'. From this early case it would seem that the costs are high. It may advance monitoring of professional malpractice or limitations in public services but falls short of giving serious attention to complaints and disclosures of harassment, intimidation and bullying as routine working practices. Manthorpe and Stanley (1999) cite Hunt and Campbell's study of social workers in 1998 which found that abuses may have to be 'stark and sizeable' before being reported. 'Serious' incidents such as physical, sexual or financial abuse were clearly identified as matters which had to be reported. 'Other areas of *misconduct* such as verbal abuse were not so clear and a more "*flexible*" interpretation placed on them' (p. 228; our emphases). This notion of 'misconduct' as a lesser offence than abuse illustrates the difficulty of whistleblowing as a means for creating violation-free organizations. Manthorpe and Stanley suggest 'it is only worth the risk if the abuse or neglect is judged so blatant that an individual feels it is worth paying the price (however calculated)' (p. 227). Until the reality of violation at work in its widest sense is recognized and its prevention seen as both in the 'public interest' and in the interests of employers, it is difficult to envisage a time when whistleblowing will not be punished. Whistleblowing should be important for day-to-day insidious damaging forms of abuse which should not be disregarded or only labelled as 'misconduct'. Until whistleblowing is seen as contributing to a violation-free environment, violations will continue to be denied, silenced and confined to the subtext of worker grievances.

Professional Misconduct and Abuse

There has been extensive debate, especially in the USA but also elsewhere, around the possible misconduct and abuse of professionals such as doctors, therapists and counsellors. Networks and organizations of survivors of professional abuse are well established. Legal powers are increasingly being used in the USA to control and curb professionals and courts are also being used to extend professionals' duties, such as that of psychiatrists to protect people from patients' violence. In the UK courts have traditionally deferred to professional expertise and 'mechanisms of legal regulation are heterogeneous and fragmented' (Rose, 1999: 155). Recent publicity in the UK has focused on professional misconduct and abuse in the medical profession, with the Harold Shipman case[5] and the Bristol heart surgery scandal as particularly shocking examples. In both situations attention had earlier been drawn to possible misconduct but had not been acted on. One element in such exercise of power is the nature of the professional project itself.[6] Leonard (1997) suggests one form of professional power is in the creation of subject positions such as patient, client and claimant by experts. Through 'disciplines' such as medicine or psychology, the bodies of subjects are disciplined thus 'the professions of welfare exercise disciplinary power' (p. 55). The 'lay person's' knowledge is discounted unless it confirms the expert's knowledge. Those subjected to such knowledge/power are effectively silenced in the constitution of expert knowledge as the 'truth'. This makes it much more difficult for violation to be not only 'spoken' but also heard if it is spoken. The ideology of the professional project is that professionals serve the public good which, combined with the notion of expert power as the truth and trust in self-regulation effectively silences those who see it as violating. The high publicity cases focus on death and physical harm whilst the day-to-day violations of being cast into a subject position are not perceived as such.

The Politics of Risk

Contemporary society has been characterized as a 'risk society' (Beck, 1992). According to Parton (1996: 109), this means that 'the normative basis is safety and the Utopia is particularly negative and defensive – preventing the worst and protection from harm'. Post-war confidence in experts and the notion that scientific insight meant that causes of danger could be identified and blame accorded accurately have contributed to this: 'Notions of reason and rationality informed the development of a blaming system that was increasingly positivistic, and believed that not only could causes be objectively identified but that they could be subject to improvement and change' (p. 107). With its origins in gambling and insurance, Rose (1999: 160) has examined the proliferation of risk management from simply contracting for insurance to daily lifestyle management such as choices of where to shop, diet, exercise, stress management, and so on:

> These new logics of risk management fragment the space of social welfare into a multitude of diverse pockets, zones, folds of riskiness each comprising a linking of specific current activities and conducts and general probabilities of their consequences. This inaugurates a virtually endless spiral of amplification of risk – as risk is managed in certain zones and forms of conduct (e.g. shopping in malls scanned by security cameras: foetal monitoring; low-fat diets to combat the risk of heart disease), the perceived riskiness of other unprotected zones is exacerbated (high streets; unsupervised pregnancies; the uneducated dietary habits of children and the poor). The culture of risk is characterized by uncertainty, plurality and anxiety, and is thus continually open to the construction of new problems and the marketing of new solutions.

This puts risk at the centre of the political agenda and even more so when, according to Rose (1999), it becomes a mechanism whereby professionals and managers are increasingly focused on the risks a particular group might pose to the health and safety of others. He argues that while the social notions of risk were universalizing, risk agencies such as police, social work, doctors, psychiatrists 'focus upon the "usual suspects" – the poor, the welfare recipients, the petty criminals, discharged psychiatric patients, street people. The logics of risk inescapably locate the careers and identities of such tainted citizens within a regime of surveillance which constitutes them all as actually or potentially "risky" individuals' (p. 260). In this sense, 'high risk' when applied to individuals or groups is a form of exclusion marginalizing people at the edge of society. Reconstructing this process as violation through the mechanisms of various organizations of control and surveillance is implicit but not part of a political agenda focused on the protection of members of the public not deemed to be deviant. Though not explicit, this can be seen primarily in terms of *physical* safety, within the predominant paradigm of physical danger and harm, so inhibiting developing wider understandings of violence and violation.

The concept of a risk society is very influential in contributing to notions of risk inside organizations. It makes it difficult to move outside the paradigm of physical harm or to relate violation to the day-to-day experiences of organizational members. It affects professional self-regulation as the political agenda of risk focuses on risk assessment as central in assessment and diagnosis (Rose, 1999). It influences attempts to widen the concept of violence within this political agenda. 'Risk' to workers would be seen primarily as those workers likely to be subjected to physical violence as part of their job by those deemed 'risky' such as mental health patients. It would not be seen in terms of wider harassment, bullying, intimidation and psychological harm. Stress at work may be seen as a hazard but would not be framed as 'risk' in the current understandings of the term. The implications of a risk society have been on the identification of users of organizations who constitute a risk and ways in which they are dealt with rather than an emphasis on the risk of organizational worlds for those working there. Rather than assessment of users as 'risky', organizations could be categorized according to the risks they pose to workers, members and those outside, in terms of the violations outlined. For example, it would appear that previously all-male environments seem to pose an extra threat to women who enter them.

Oppression, Exploitation, Discrimination and Exclusion

These discourses on risk and risk management, both those in policy-making and academia, have their own grave political limitations, especially in obscuring material inequalities and oppressions between social classes, groups, categories and individuals. Political struggles around these matters have also led to political consideration of complex micro-processes, including subjectivity and language.[7] Challenging negative language contributes to the 'institutionalization of sensitivity' within organizations and thus violation-free environments. In recent years debates on oppression have been re-formed under the political umbrella of 'social exclusion' in both national and transnational contexts. The move from a focus on oppression and discrimination to the notion of social exclusion could be seen as a further structural form of violation (Beresford and Wilson, 1998). While social exclusion was originally developed to describe the consequences of poverty and inequality, it now 'reflects a concern with deviance and non-fulfilment of perceived obligations, both moral and economic, and sees the solution to the problems of social, family and personal breakdown and disruption in terms of assimilation into the labour market and social control. It serves to maintain and reinforce social divisions and inequalities rather than challenge them' (p. 86). Beresford and Wilson argue that social exclusion is used to both categorize some as dangerous and deviant and others as unintentionally dependent who will continue to have support. This latter group includes disabled people, old people and chronically sick people with different responses to each category reflecting the categories of 'undeserving' and 'deserving' (Levitas, 1996). This conceptualization of social exclusion leaves large numbers of people without a voice in debates around the violations imposed by structural disadvantage.

Organizations, and thus organization violations, are set within a yet wider context of structural oppression, exploitation, discrimination and structural disadvantage. Indeed, as discussed, organization violations include such broader oppressions, exploitations and inequalities. These represent very large political questions around the huge disparities in power and resources, particularly when viewed in a global perspective. Oppressions have been increasingly and historically recognized through and in the context of political action by oppressed groups, such as women, black people, disabled people, older people and those discriminated on grounds of sexuality. They point to the importance of taking a very broad and historical view of damage and harm, rather than one that works from immediate behavioural observation. In the worst cases, oppressions lead to the direct killing of people, sometimes in very large numbers, the destruction of their ability to provide testimony to those violences and violations, and the destruction of witnesses to those violences and violations and thus their testimonies to those actions.

Towards Violation-Free Organizations and Workplaces

The concept of a violation-free organization or workplace may seem idealistic and utopian in the light of the material we have presented. Nevertheless, we see this as a necessary organizational state to work towards. Ishmael (1999: 147) suggests the creation of 'positive work environments' and believes it is possible to have a 'harassment free' work environment. This is achieved, she argues, by auditing the organization's culture and then managing the audit outcomes in a range of ways, key to which are the role of leadership and the importance of management styles. One way to start this is through conducting a comprehensive survey of the entire workforce to establish the extent of discrimination as well as asking questions of employees about the effectiveness of the organization in combating it. If implemented, she suggests this would lead to the development of a new culture and more appropriate policies and practices to achieve equality, value difference and create a positive environment for all workers. She is not presenting this as an easy option as she outlines the difficulties in operationalizing such changes, particularly the importance of management styles and cultures. The concept of a 'violation-free organization' allows violation to be voiced and dealt with explicitly. If this were an accepted aim then procedures to combat violations would reflect the 'long agenda' of change and pay attention to the prevention of violations, as well as the way complaints are managed. Independent social auditors or agencies outside the organizational hierarchy could deal with contentious situations and prevent people having to complain through the very structures which harass them in the first place (Collier, 1995). This is especially important in closed or enclosed organizations (see Chapter 5).

Movements towards violation-free organizations also have to be understood in the context of globalizing and glocalizing changes and processes. Recent debates on postmodernity and globalization raise some contradictory possibilities for the movement towards violation-free organizations. The idea of postmodern organizations as leaner, less hierarchical and more decentralized might offer a way forward in focusing on the structures of power maintaining abusive relationships. However, Thompson (1993) suggests that such organizational forms do not fundamentally break with centralized bureaucracy but 'that what we are seeing is a duality in which the decentralization of the labour process and production decisions ... is combined with increased centralization of power and control over spatially dispersed, but interdependent units. ... advances in computerization and telecommunications facilitate the concentration of "conception" (research, planning, directive and strategic management) at corporate headquarters, while "execution" is dispersed round the globe' (p. 190). He argues that 'information thus wraps itself around existing power structures unless a political struggle in the organization dictates otherwise' (p. 191). This would not suggest fundamental restructuring to reduce inequalities and produce violation-free environments. Leonard (1997) notes organizational change towards increased flexibility, decentralizing and informality may be experienced as hierarchical and bureaucratic with their short-term strategies for maintaining power and counteracting resistance and disorganization. Organizational change in capitalist enterprises is 'to increase the rate of profit and maintain labour regulation under global market conditions. The *purpose* of organizational change in "postmodern directions" should not ... be confused with some radical, emancipatory intention: such changes reflect the need to adapt to a changing environment while maintaining the maximum level of control' (pp. 104–5; emphasis in original). He recognizes that within postmodernity, expertise and deference to authority are increasingly challenged. He also sees new forms of expertise emerging which overtake overt social control by a 'profound internalization of expertise' (p. 99). Thus internalization is achieved without surveillance and control. Nevertheless he continues to seek for signs of an emancipatory project, particularly by drawing on the critical liberatory aspect of modernity as well as in identifying sites of resistance and struggle available. This could resonate with the possibility of violation-free workplaces through less hierarchical organizational forms.

The rapidly transnationalizing and glocalizing world also provides different understandings of and possibilities for organizing and organizations. When firms move worldwide to find markets and have products made up cheaply, this is not only the exploitation of local labour that is at issue but the ability to move beyond local, national restraints such as around equal opportunities or minimum wage policies. This fluid, mobile world makes it harder for abuses to be recognized let alone spoken. Cross-cultural studies explore differences in different national organizations but with glocalization there is debate as to what constitutes an organization in a rapidly changing global world. There needs to be a similar strong focus on how equality and fairness practices can protect workers from violations and create and maintain violation-free organizations and workplaces in the context of the glocalizing processes. This suggests the need for debates on global governance to take these questions on board, and for global laws and enforcements that facilitate and maintain violation-free organizations.

Organization violation concerns both the excessive controls that are possible, and increasingly possible, in and around organizations, and the responses to and indeed control of those controls. Changing, and possibly new, forms of organizing and organizations are developing that make for greater possibilities for organization violation, organizational and managerial controls thereof, responses to and indeed control of violations, and furthermore avoidance of and resistance to such control. Much of these changes involve the impact of ICTs, mobile phones, CCTV, mobility and access controls, monitoring of email, Internet and bank card use, and other electronic mechanisms in and around organizations. It is now possible to have not just one's clothing 'wired', as in a 'technojacket', but also one's own body, with all the possible uses and abuses that could entail. Electronic surveillance is now technologically possible for more and more intimate controls of persons, and thus violations, and indeed for the control of those controls. This represents part of the dialectics of contemporary organizations and is in contrast to the historic dialectics of bureaucracy. The separation of the public and the private are being gradually and remorselessly transformed and historically obliterated.[8] Most likely, organizations will, as now, involve multiple layers of modes of power, authority, decision-making and indeed violations, sometimes operating in contradiction with each other.

It may seem as if there is little to be done to counter or escape these trends (unless one is very rich indeed). There is now a major and growing industrial sector devoted to 'violence and safety' at work, such as security agencies, design consultancies and technological advisers. Their main focus is physical violence, and prevention of violence, sometimes through surveillance, sometimes through separation of possible 'antagonists', and sometimes through the creation of 'peaceful' environments. The unintended consequences of such approaches themselves need critical analysis. These include the development of self-surveillance and technologies of the self, the creation of increasingly separated social and spatial environments, and the embedded societal pervasiveness of concerns with risk, safety and violation.

While it is not inconceivable that this technology could also be developed to address the prevention and control of violation more broadly, it needs to be stressed that this is not simply a technological and technologically determined matter. Rather it is a question of politics, of how violation is to be understood, defined, recognized, problematized, responded to, acted against, studied, theorized and become part of knowledges, both 'lay' and 'expert'. This demands debate, action and consciousness-raising on organization violations both within individual organizations and more generally in civil society. There is also a need for greater expertise in the field of organization violations. This may be partly accomplished by broad education in schooling, organizations, management, professions, and so on, though independent 'auditing' specialists, both internal and external, are also needed, as with any complex field. This wider societal perspective is especially important with the increasing interlocking of organizations in networks or sets of inter-organizational relations.

Thus organizations and organization violations are increasingly characterized by contradictory combinations of increasing possibilities for violation and controls, increasing organizational control thereof, increasing self-surveillance by organizational members, managers and users, and increasing resistance to both organizational control and controls of violation. The social trajectory of organization violation is slowly becoming a more explicit part of organizational worlds and contemporary organizational life. The developing politics of organization violations are necessary and urgent.

Notes

Introduction

1. By 'sexualed' we mean how a particular interpretation is given sexual meaning or meaning in terms of sexuality. This might even include the apparent absence of sexual meaning, just as 'gendered' also might refer to the apparent absence of gendered meaning. We use this as distinct from 'sexual' which means pertaining to sexuality, or 'sexualized' which carries the connotation of having been given heightened sexual meaning, that is becoming sexual 'in' meaning.

Chapter 1

1. For example, Eichler, 1980; Carrigan et al., 1985; Connell, 1987.

2. The expansion of this area of study has been marked by the foundation of the journal *Gender, Work and Organization* in 1994. Since then a number of other journals have been established, including *Gender, Technology and Development* and the *International Review of Women and Leadership*. The considerable growth of research and published material over the last twenty years is such that, if we were to re-read all the material in our collection, we would never start to write. So now when we write on this subject, we have to be very selective.

3. See Marx and Engels, 1970. The theme of the social context of organizations recurs not only in modernist, critical and feminist traditions, but also in poststructuralist and postmodernist approaches to organizations.

4. 'Both sexes actually receive very similar genetic instructions ... even for the features that tell them apart. ... both sexes receive sets of instructions dealing with breast development, but in only one sex are the instructions acted upon. The same applies for all the other physical characteristics, which obviously distinguish men from women: genitals, shape, muscle growth, voice-box development, body hair and so on' (Nicholson, 1993: 12). For up to 6–7 weeks' gestation female and male embryos have externally identical genitalia – after that specific sexed development occurs. At every stage for the human the basic pattern is female away from which development proceeds to produce the male. The embryo will be female unless it has a Y chromosome. (In birds the opposite is true – the basic pattern is male and females are the departure from this.) While (social) sex is usually assigned by external examination, it is the analysis of chromosomal structure that provides the primary sex, in cases of doubt. However, these issues are complicated by a host of bio-cultural complications around the notion of 'sex' itself. These are both individual (for example, Eva Klobukowski, a 'woman' at the 1964 Olympics failed chromosomal tests in 1967) and societal (in some small societies 'girls' may turn to become 'boys' at puberty). It is worth noting that at the 1992 Winter Olympics women were tested for the presence of Y chromosome, and this was opposed by 22 French biologists and geneticists on the grounds that it was discriminatory to women (Nicholson, 1993: 16).

5. See, for example, Maccoby and Jacklin, 1974; Jacklin and Maccoby, 1975; Durkin, 1978.

6. There are a number of distinct problems with 'Masculinity–Femininity Scales' (see Eichler, 1980). These include: the general relationship between M–F Scales and Sex Role

Stereotypes; the use of narrowly culturally specific statements in their construction (for example, 'In American society, how desirable is it for a man to be ...'); the obscuring of the relation between cultural ideals and actual practices; the neglect of differences depending on which gender is assessing which gender; the bias of using college students; the selectivity of items used (40 out of 400). Additionally, these kinds of approaches to 'gender' represent in effect self-ratings of subjects measured against stereotypes of the judges, ossified into scales, so that concepts predefine and reify gendered reality.

7. Primary sex characteristics generally refer to chromosomal structure. Secondary sex characteristics include: gonadal structure (ovaries/testes); internal genital ducts (fallopian tubes and uterus/vas deferens and prostate); external genital development (vagina, vulva, clitoris/penis); hormonal structure (preponderance of oestrogen and progesterone, or androgens, including testosterone); presence/absence of breasts; and presence/absence of certain body hair. There are also major chromosomal variations beyond the main XX and XY types, with 15 additional types of intersexuality. Intersexual people were sometimes in the past told that they had been assigned to the 'wrong' sex/gender. Not surprisingly such news sometimes brought major psychological reactions, distress, mental illness, even suicide. For the last twenty-five years or more it has been recognized in medical cytogenetics that gender/social sex and psychological sex/gender identity are matters of upbringing. Furthermore, the differential hormonal levels of females/males are in fact 'average' levels, with both 'sexes' having 'female' and 'male' hormones. Oestrogen and testosterone levels are only slightly higher in females than males, outside of ovulation. It is not uncommon for females to have higher androgens than the average male, and, of course, hormonal levels can be changed by intervention. Henriques et al. (1984: 21–2) note the example of Puerto Rican girls sexually maturing from 6 months, with full breast development at 4 years because of excess of oestrogen through chicken diet (cited in Edley and Wetherell, 1995: 36).

8. Categoricalism refers here to the use of fixed categories of gender in theorizing and analysing gender and gender relations (Connell, 1985, 1987).

9. For example, Walby, 1986, 1990; Hearn, 1987, 1992b.

10. For example, Ekins and King, 1996; Kulick, 1998.

11. Citing Edwards, 1989.

12. Citing Evans, 1994.

13. Citing Jay, 1981; Lloyd, 1989; Butler, 1990; Grosz, 1994; Moore, 1994.

14. Citing Harding, 1986; Fitzsimmons, 1989; Haraway, 1990; Soper, 1995.

15. For example, there has been the establishment of the journal *Body and Society*.

16. See Kakar, 1970; Morgan, 1986: 204–8; Hearn, 1992b: 246.

17. This gendered/sexualed reinterpretation of Human Relations Theory is presented in more detail in *'Sex' at 'Work'* (Hearn and Parkin, 1987: 21–9).

18. For example, Adler and Izraeli, 1988, 1994; Walby, 1990; Cockburn, 1991; Witz, 1992; Savage and Witz, 1992; Mills and Tancred, 1992; Davidson and Burke, 1994, 2000; Reskin and Padavic, 1994; MacEwen Scott, 1994; Due Billing and Alvesson, 1994; Wilson, 1995; Collinson and Hearn, 1996; Oerton, 1996a, 1996b; Rantalaiho and Heiskanen, 1997; Alvesson and Due Billing, 1997; Wilson, 2001.

19. Ferguson's (1984) *The Feminist Case Against Bureaucracy*, a classic text in this debate, has been subject to further feminist critique by Due Billing (1994).

20. See Ferguson 1984; Bologh 1990, Morgan, 1996.

21. These features are discussed in a broader context in Harlow et al., 1995.

22. For example, Quinn, 1977; Horn and Horn, 1982; Gray, 1984; Schneider, 1984.

23. For example, Saghir and Robins, 1973; Chafetz et al., 1974; Bell and Weinberg, 1978; Brooks, 1981; Schneider, 1981, 1984; Levine and Leonard, 1984.

24. For example, Campaign for Homosexual Equality, 1981; Beer et al., 1983; GLC, 1985; Taylor, 1986.

25. For example, Hearn and Parkin, 1987, 1995; Hearn et al., 1989; Pringle, 1989.

26. While the legal definition of 'sex' has a very long history (for example, Temkin, 1987), the question of what constitutes 'sex' and 'sexual relations' has taken on even

greater precision and obscurity with the legal and journalistic investigations of the Clinton–Lewinsky saga (see *Symposium*, 1999).

27. See, for example, Hearn and Parkin, 1983, 1986–7; Green et al., 2000.

28. Hearn and Parkin, 1987: 61, 98, 102–3, 148–9, and elsewhere.

29. This is distinct from 'organizational sexuality' – which is a term we have specifically criticized as unsatisfactory, as it privileges one term over the other.

30. For example, Hearn and Parkin, 1987, 1995; Hearn, 1992b.

31. In addition, these critiques of heterosexuality lead to the consideration of questions of the relation of surface/appearance and reality/knowledge – whether this is in terms of the specifics of the sexuality of dress (Hearn and Parkin, 1987: 149–50; Sheppard, 1989) or the general epistemological significance of looks and appearance for the analysis of gender (Hearn, 1987: 11–15).

32. See, for example, Hanmer et al., 1994; Hearn, 1994; Itzin, 1995; Collinson and Collinson, 1996.

33. See Litewka, 1977; Coveney et al., 1984; Buchbinder, 1987; Kelly, 1988.

34. Harassment can be seen as 'repeated and persistent attempts by one person to torment, wear down, frustrate or get a reaction from another' (Bast-Petterson, 1995: 50).

35. For example, Iris Marion Young (1990) has explicated a plural categorization of oppression: exploitation, marginalization, powerlessness, cultural imperialism and violence. In contrast, Nancy Fraser (1997: 44–9) has outlined a concept of gender equity that encompasses a plurality of seven distinct normative principles: antipoverty, antiexploitation, income equality, leisure-time equality, equality of respect, antimarginalization, and antiandrocentrism.

36. The negative health effects of violations, oppressions and discriminations are being increasingly recognized, though still relatively unexplored. Landrine and Klonoff (1997) suggest that it is the presence and exposure to sexist acts rather than women's subjective appraisals of those acts which is the best predictor of women's negative symptoms. Krieger and Sidney (1996), from a survey of 4,000 black and white young adults in the USA, report that blood pressure was highest for working-class black adults who accepted discrimination as 'a fact of life' or who denied they experienced discrimination. It was lower for people who challenged unfair treatment. Feagin and Sikes (1994) in *Living with Racism* report relatively high levels of hypertension, angina and gastrointestinal ailments for black workers.

Chapter 2

1. See Hearn, 1992b; Itzin, 1995; Rantalaiho, 1997.

2. See O'Brien, 1981, 1986; Hearn, 1987, 1992b; Ferguson, 1989.

3. For example, Beechey, 1979; Rowbotham, 1979; Barrett, 1980; also see Atkinson, 1979.

4. These various critiques can also be understood in relation to the academic and political attacks on structuralist, especially Althusserian, Marxism, in the late 1970s and early 1980s, which itself can be seen as part of the reformulation of the European Left and the development then of Eurocommunism, in partial autonomy from Soviet and Chinese communism. They can also be seen as prefiguring the breakdown of the Soviet bloc in the late 1980s.

5. Similar contrasts have been made between family and social patriarchy (Eisenstein, 1981), private appropriation and collective appropriation (Stacey and Davies, 1983), personal and 'structural' forms of dominance, patriarchy and reorganized patriarchy (Holter, 1984) and private dependence and public dependence (Hernes, 1987).

6. Cited in Duncan, 1994, 1995; Rantalaiho, 1997.

7. This kind of complex analysis of differentiated patriarchies and the organizations within them is similar to earlier distinctions that have been made between gendered structures, cultures, social action, and identities in organizations (see Acker, 1992).

8. The journal, *Feminist Economics*, has also now been established. There are also clear signs of this development in the UN's recent gendered evaluations of work and time-use worldwide (*Human Development Report*, 1996, 2000). These insights have many significant implications for rethinking in gendered terms both societal economic systems and the organizations within them.

9. See O'Brien, 1981, 1986; Hearn, 1983, 1987.

10. For example, McKee and O'Brien, 1982; Gillis, 1985.

11. Such features of quarternary industry are discussed further in Chapter 6 in relation to new technology, the sex industries and globalization.

12. See Hearn and Parkin, 1987, 1995; Acker, 1990, 1992.

13. Cited in Walby, 1986: 116.

14. Cited in Fowler, 1985.

15. A number of rather similar incidents, including the prosecution and dismissal of a head carder for his sexual pressurizing and assault on young women under his authority in Oldham, Lancashire, in 1887, have been examined by Lambertz (1985).

16. For example, Hartmann, 1979; MacKinnon, 1982, 1983; Pateman, 1988; Lister, 1997.

17. See Hartmann, 1979; MacKinnon, 1983; Hearn, 1992b: 240–1.

18. This and the next two paragraphs draw on Hearn, 1992b, and Tilly, 1992.

19. A rather different approach to violence and death has been put forward by Amartya Sen in 'More than 100 million women are missing' (Sen, 1990) and elsewhere. Patterns of female mortality in many parts of the world suggest that pervasive discrimination against women (and especially girls) deprives them both of adequate food and basic health care (Nussbaum, 1992: 43). And nation-states are a fundamental part of both the cause and the possible amelioration of this dire situation.

20. Citing Herby, 1998.

21. Citing http://www.who.int/eha/emergenc/soe/sld003.htm.

Chapter 3

1. We are particularly grateful for discussions with David Collinson, Margaret Collinson and David Morgan on this section. Also see Hearn, 1998: 202–3.

2. See Honneth, 1992, 1995; Fraser, 1995, 1997.

3. Plummer (1995: 23–4) has recognized the accumulation of stories-telling by individuals, which then come together in interactive social worlds and public groupings, so providing possible 'negotiated networks of collective activity' for those of like mind or experience. Such social movements in effect provide new social infrastructures, and thus changing possibilities and categories of experience for those who follow historically.

4. The first study of sexual harassment at workplaces in Sweden was launched in 1987 by the Equality Ombudsman. The study, *FRID-A KvinnoFrid i Arbetslivet* (1987), conducted by Hagman (1988), brought to light the widespread harassment of women in Sweden. The most commonly used term in Swedish of 'sexual harassment' is 'sexuella trakasserier' (FRID-A, 1987; Adrianson, 1993), as in other Nordic languages. Norwegian researchers have used the definition "uonsket seksuell oppmerksomhet" (unwanted sexual attention), emphasizing the element of unwantedness, as in many UK definitions. Arguably, the Norwegian term, 'sexuella trakasserier', is such a strong expression that it easily labels the subject as a victim, and may even lead to a victim-identity (Sørensen, 1990: 19, cited in Varsa, 1993: 11–12).

In the working group of the Finnish Council for Equality there was considerable discussion of the Finnish translation of 'sexual harassment'. 'Harassment' was translated as 'häirintä ja ahdistelu'. 'Häirintä' comes from the verb 'häiritä', 'disturb, cause inconvenience', and 'ahdistelu' from 'ahdistella', molest, harass. In the USA the history of the word 'harassment' has connected with that of racial discrimination and discussion on human rights. In English, for example, one might say: 'Don't harass me!'. In the Finnish language there is no corresponding utterance. In the opinion of the working group of the Finnish Council for Equality, the terms 'häirintä' and 'ahdistelu' were the closest ones. Both terms were taken into use because the word 'häirintä' alone sounded too mild, while 'ahdistelu' alone was too strong.

There was also much discussion of whether it was better to talk about 'seksuaalinen' or 'sukupuolinen' harassment (seksuaalinen = sexual, sukupuoli = sex/gender, suku = kin/family, puoli = half). The phenomenon has usually to do with 'häirintä' and 'ahdistelu', the origin of which is sexual – that is, sexuality as a medium – but not necessarily so. The phenomenon does not necessarily have to be restricted to that. Talking about 'sexual' may produce an image that feeds the sexual desire of the harasser. However, this is not how it often is, for example when a group of heterosexual men tease a heterosexual man that he is gay. Sexuality is used as a medium, but it is not necessarily a question of anyone's sexuality. So that the phenomenon would be framed widely enough, the Finnish working group concluded with the term 'sukupuolinen'. There is also a theoretical reason for choosing the concept of 'sukupuolinen'. When the phenomenon has been highlighted in different parts of the world, it has at first been associated with sexuality. With more research, the more other related issues have come into the picture and become the subject of research, for example the control of women. Thus 'sukupuolinen' describes the phenomenon better, linking harassment to a much wider set of gender debates (Varsa, 1993: 11–12). These examples show the subtleties of linguistic difference: it is not possible to simply read off meanings from different languages directly; interpretation and cultural context are especially important.

5. For example, Farley, 1978: 54–60; Smith and Gray, 1985; Fielding, 1994.

6. Gregory and Lees (1999) also explore situations where trainee women train drivers were subjected to vicious forms of harassment when they moved from the female servicing jobs to enter the male preserve of driving.

7. As Coveney et al. (1984) note, hierarchy and dominance may be subject to eroticization for men.

8. Franks also makes the point that the dominant belief is of equality of opportunity rather than outcome. She goes on to say: 'So the credo goes that so long as the system makes sure there is fairness at the outset, it does not matter if the market allocates winners and losers.'

9. Similar issues have been explored by Cockburn (1991) on 'short agenda' and 'long agenda' changes, comparing organizational responses to equal opportunities policies from tokenistic responses to more significant policies for change.

10. Such policies stand in contrast to those attempts to recruit (usually senior and often male) staff through 'spousal' (usually heterosexual) hiring policies which are in use in the USA and elsewhere.

11. See, for example, Farley, 1978; MacKinnon, 1979; Hearn and Parkin, 1987, 1995; Collinson and Collinson, 1989.

12. This word is similar to the English 'mobbing', although in English it has rather different connotations: first, it is not generally used of human beings, but rather for animals, for example, birds; and second, it means to 'crowd round in order to attack or admire' (Schéele, 1993: 11). In Swedish the word means also bullying by one person. The Swedish 'mobbning' was mainly used initially in relation to bullying at schools, until it began to be used in relation to adults, 'vuxenmobbning' (Leymann, 1986). This is quite like the use of the word 'bullying' in English and 'kiusaaminen' in Finnish. The use of 'mobbing' in English might give one to understand that it is a question of many people attacking one person; this would be a misconception. The word 'mobbning' is best translated as bullying, rather than 'mobbing', except when the researcher her/himself uses the English word mobbing (see Leymann, 1990). The concept of 'psychological violence', 'psykiskt våld', is also used.

Schéele (1993) explains two other terms often used in Swedish literature: 'utstötning' and 'utfrysning'. The former, which means 'pushing out' or 'expulsion', consists of active, destructive, harmful treatment towards one person. The latter could be literally translated as 'freezing out'. It consists mostly of behaviour that demonstrates the supposed insignificance of the person. According to Schéele, these are the main types of 'kränkande särbehandling' (Schéele, 1993: 14). This term means 'hurtful, harmful, insulting or violating treatment' and is widely used in Sweden. In the literature (for example, Leymann, 1988, 1992a), the word 'utslagning' is also widely used as a synonym for the word 'utstötning'.

In Finnish, the word 'kiusaaminen' is used in the context of workplace violence in the literature (for example, Lindroos, 1996; Tasala, 1997), as is the term 'henkinen väkivalta' (see Vartia and Paananen, 1992; Vartia and Perkka-Jortikka, 1994), which means 'psychological violence'. As noted, 'kiusaaminen' is the equivalent of 'bullying'. 'Kiusaaminen' was previously used of children, usually in schools as 'koulukiusaaminen' – bullying at school – but nowadays the concept 'työpaikkakiusaaminen', which means 'bullying at work' or '(general) workplace harassment', is widely used.

13. In this book Field (1996) uses he/him to refer to men and women. He also considers bullies seem to prefer same-sex victims, speculating this is because one knows one's own gender best and bullies are keen to avoid the Sex Discrimination Act.

14. In a landmark case (Walker vs Northumberland County Council, 1995) a social services manager, who had two nervous breakdowns due to work intensification, was awarded considerable damages (£175,000) by an industrial tribunal after the council was found in breach of its duty of care (Carty, 1996).

15. Cited by Hickling, 1999.

16. Poyner and Warne, 1986, 1988; Joeman et al., 1989; Phillips et al., 1989; Hodgkinson and Stewart, 1991; HSE, 1992; Suzy Lamplugh Trust, 1994.

17. A summary of organizational policies on violence among trade unions, local authorities and other organizations is by NALGWC (n.d.).

18. General collections include the OECD Panel Group on Women, Work and Health (Kauppinen-Toropainen, 1993), and the Proceedings of the Nordic Workshop on Research on Violence, Threats and Bullying as Health Risks Among Health Care Personnel (Bast-Pettersen et al., 1995) which reviewed the detailed research in health and related organizations. Also see Appelberg (1996) on the impact of interpersonal conflicts on health, psychiatric morbidity and work disability; and Eklund (1996) on the health risks of conflict and harassment, specifically muscular-skeletal shoulder problems.

19. Research in central Scotland with over 3000 pupils aged between 11 and 16 from schools found that over one in three boys and one in 12 girls said that they had carried a weapon (McKeganey and Norrie, 2000).

20. Discussion of some of the recent cases involving famous sportsmen in the USA, as well as the more general issue, is included in Crosset, 2000; Steinberger, 2001. Also see DeKeseredy, 1990.

21. In April 2000 French driving-test examiners called a day of action against the growing number of assaults from failed customers (Henley, 2000).

22. While violation in travel, and indeed in stopping travelling, is clearly not new, the growth of more complex and more globalized travel, as in air travel, may be leading to changing forms of violation in and around transport organizations. This could be an important area for future research.

23. Citing 1993 information from Statistiska Centralbyrån, (Statistics Sweden).

24. The ILO estimates that 160 million people develop occupational diseases and 250 million suffer workplace injuries every year.

25. The UK legal framework of violence at work is surveyed in Leighton, 1999.

26. This echoes Gutek and Cohen's (1987) analysis of how working men are described having totally work-orientated descriptions and working women are described by personal and sexual attributions.

27. See, for example, French, 1995; Brooks-Gordon, 1995; Collinson and Hearn, 1996; Cheng, 1996.

28. See Hearn, 1994; this approach parallels that of 'organization sexuality'.

Chapter 4

1. See Bauman (1989) on the Holocaust, and the use of instrumental rationality (in preference to substantive rationality) to transform people into dehumanized objects; the creation of social distance between perpetrators and victims; and the allowing of victims to participate in the decisions that adversely affect them. Accordingly, Marsden and Townley (1999: 418) write: 'The Holocaust illuminates the rationality of all modern modes of organizing.' Also see Sievers (1995) on work and death, and Burrell (1997: chs. 4–5) on organizations, abattoirs, death, pain and disease.

2. Much of it, like the classic work of Gouldner, Merton and Selznick, is set within a distinctly non-gendered, neo-Weberian framework (see Morgan, 1996).

3. An invaluable summary of comparable economic, political and organizational changes is provided by David Harvey (1990).

4. This is a theme that has been debated from at least the 1960s.

5. There are many different possible starting points and many debates in analysing power. First, Clegg (1989) begins his critical survey of theories of power by identifying two crucial and distinct traditions: those of Hobbes and Machiavelli. Hobbes has personified that tradition that asks: what power is; Machiavelli the tradition that asks: what power does.

Second, in both of these perspectives on power, but especially the first, there is often an assumption of *the possession of power*. In the latter tradition, the question of possession of power is more problematized as power processes or political processes. Thus we can contrast the possession of power and the process(es) of power. The social bases approach to power relate to the social bases of the *possession* of power (French and Raven, 1959; also see Morgan, 1986). In contrast, a process approach is less concerned with who it is that possesses power, and more with the development and change in patterns of power over time, regardless of who might 'possess' that power.

Third, a number of writers have contrasted having (capacities) and doing power (exercising). Wrong (1979) identifies *dispositional* (having) and *episodic* (exercising) forms of power. Clegg also identifies: *dispositional* (based on capacities) and *episodic (agency)*, as well as *facilitative* forms of power. *Episodic Power* involves doing power, exercising power, power based on agency/intention and power based on the effective utilization of resource control or possession (Clegg, 1989: 84). It is closely equivalent to Lukes's one-dimensional approach to power, which itself draws on Dahl (1957). Such a view of power involves an ability to get another person to do something that he/she would not otherwise have done. *Dispositional power*, on the other hand, involves having power or the potential of power, but not necessarily using power, a set or sets of capacities/processes, recurrent tendencies of human beings to behave in certain ways (Clegg, 1989: 83). This raises the question of power *potential*. This fits closely with Weber's notion of domination, and has been elaborated further by Wrong. Weber defines power as 'the probability that an actor within a social relationship will be in a position to carry out his own will despite resistance, regardless of the basis on which this probability rests.' Weber distinguished power *(Macht)* from other forms of social control in which cooperation is present. Thus in the exercise of power, resistance and conflict are common or probable. This conception of power involves a process of overpowering. Weber illuminates aspects of power that would remain obscure in a strict Dahlian approach. We might also ask: does dispositional power underly episodic power? Or does it arise from episodic power, so producing non-decisions, hegemony, structures, even discourse? *Facilitative Power* is proposed in different ways by Parsons, Giddens and Foucault. This refers to the ability to achieve goals, to get things done. Although these are clearly very different kinds of theories, they all consider the productive aspect of power.

Fourth, we can contrast conscious intention and unconscious action or non-intentional action. Fifth, there is the recurring tension between agency and structure. Bachrach and Baratz (1962) attempt to link agency and structure. In non-decision-making, 'A devotes his energies to creating or reinforcing social and political values and institutional practices that limit the scope of the political process to public consideration of only those issues which are comparatively innocuous to A' (p. 948). This produces an organizing in and out of issues. And sixth, we may contrast causal and acausal accounts of power.

6. Authority is sometimes defined as socially legitimate power, with compliance based on the 'target's' perception of the legitimacy of the request.

7. Some place influence as the general category under which other power relations exist.

8. While in the 1974 book Lukes addressed 'objective interests', he later rejected this along with the idea of transcendental view interests that Habermas advocated.

9. It is not that there are different types of masculinities and femininities that are seen as 'natural' and appropriate in different contexts and cultures but that the dominant forms of masculinities associated predominately with male biological sex and hegemony (and construed in aversion to femininity) are those that dictate how organizations are run (Collinson and Hearn, 1996; Hamada, 1996).

10. This links with Wardhaugh and Wilding's (1993) propositions that management failure to act, despite numerous complaints from residents and staff, underlaid the corruption of care. They identify particular models of work and organization with professional and hierarchical factors which all form part of the corruption and thus perpetuation of the violences.

11. Drawing on the work of David Cooper and Franz Fanon.

12. At each level, and following the framework of Chapter 2, there are important considerations of patriarchy, capitalism and nationalism to be taken into account.

13. Previously, distinctions have been made between: (i) the place of violence in the context and formation of organizations; and (ii) variations in organizational orientations to violence (Hearn, 1994).

14. For example, retail (Health and Safety Executive, 1995); finance (Health and Safety Executive, 1993; Loss Prevention Council 1995); social work (Hester, 1994; Balloch, et al., 1995, Bibby, 1995); police (Uildriks and van Mastrigt, 1991).

15. They are as such not only 'enabling factors' for violence (cf. Salin, 1999).

16. Quoted in Reiman, 1984: 34, cited in Johnson, 1986: 182.

17. See Kimmel, 1990, for a comparison of boxing and pornography.

18. See, for example, The Stockholm International Forum on the Holocaust 2000, including the testimony of Arno Lustiger (2000), in which he criticizes Bettelheim, Arendt and others, and instead highlights the active resistance of Holocaust survivors.

19. For further discussion of these and related literatures, see Salin, 1999.

20. Of the 1045 callers to a trade union bullying hotline in Japan in October 1996, one in seven had attempted or contemplated suicide. One case of suicide followed excessive borrowing and stealing of money by bosses from an employee. Another employee was forced to write out the same report every fortnight, over and over again (Parry, 1997).

21. Another interesting example, analysed by Pierce (1995), is the construction of 'Rambo litigators' in US law firms.

Chapter 5

1. Having said that, care needs to be taken in assuming that there is an automatic correspondence or immediate cause and effect between institutionalization and the institutionalism of secondary adjustments. In some cases these latter actions may be linked to residents' previous institutional or other experiences, their psychological or medical condition, or even their choice of approach (Peele et al., 1977).

2. Bauman (1989) also speaks of the role of bureaucracy in seeking to silence moral considerations and adjust human actions to an ideal of rationality.

3. Cited in Wardhaugh and Wilding, 1993: 6–7.

4. Wardhaugh and Wilding also distinguish two different scandals in such settings, one in children's homes and one in long-stay hospitals. The 'Pindown' regimes were used to control difficult teenage behaviour and were seen as the acceptable policy goals of securing a desired change in behaviour but they led to violence judged to be 'intrinsically unethical, unprofessional and unacceptable' (Levy and Kahan, 1991: 167). This differs from violence in the long-stay hospitals which was unrelated to policy objectives and a clear betrayal of the ethic of care and respect for others within the institutions (Martin, 1984).

5. Cited in Aitkin and Griffin, 1996: 79.

6. Studies of the abuse of older people have often focused on violence in the home by relatives or strangers. Analyses of abuse of older people suggest that the majority is by men to women (Penhale, 1993; Aitkin and Griffin, 1996; Whittaker, 1996; Hearn, 1999).

7. This links with Wardhaugh and Wilding's (1993) propositions on the neutralization of moral concerns: ideological violence dehumanizes a group of people who can then be seen as less sentient and beyond the bounds of moral behaviour.

8. Some similarities can be noted with Menzies's (1960) study of routinization amongst nurses.

9. Catherine Bennett's study (1994) found that only 36 per cent of older people in residential homes claim to have made a choice themselves and 60 per cent had not visited any other home before admission. For nearly two-thirds, the choice of a home – 'the home that is no home' – had been taken from them (cited in Aitkin and Griffin, 1996: 88). This is also relevant when considering violations in children's homes.

10. This affirms Wardhaugh and Wilding's (1993) propositions, particularly on power and powerlessness.

11. Lee-Treweek's (1997) study of women care auxiliaries in a nursing home highlights the way in which paid carework has been marginalized within the sociology of work, though an increasingly important form of employment for women, with increasing private provision of care.

12. In the report allegations were made of abuse in six local authority community children's homes, an assessments centre, private residential establishments and five foster homes.

13. This echoes the suppression of student nurses' complaints about violence to patients at Whittington Hospital over a four-year period in the 1960s (Martin, 1984). The student nurses feared victimization when threatened with legal action if they continued. This affirms Wardhaugh and Wilding's (1993) observations that strong group loyalty can stifle criticism and complaints especially in inward-looking organizations.

14. The ideological division between public and private would relegate issues of gender and sexuality, along with caring and emotional expression, to the private domains of the family, leaving the public world as the domain of the masculine, rational and politics (Clark and Lange, 1979; Parkin, 1989; Hearn, 1992b; French, 1995).

15. Until the 1980s there was little recognition of issues around sexuality in children's homes and little training and research on them. Keith White (1987) raised the issue in respect of the care of adolescents: 'what is perhaps not realized by those who have not experienced the group care situation first hand is how much of daily living and planning revolves around the issue of sexual behaviour, taboos and fears. Any member of staff at any time is worried about being alone with a child' (p. 54).

16. *Managing Residential Care* (Burton, 1998) does not include 'gender' in the index, and there is only one page refering to sexuality, with one mention on that page (p. 39).

17. Stacey and Davies (1983) recognized this anomaly in health settings. They recognized that some settings were clearly neither public nor private forms because of their ambiguous location between the two, thus constituting an 'intermediate zone'. This reflects Goffman's observation that 'total institutions then are social hybrids, part residential community, part formal organization, and therein lies the sociological interest' (1969: 316).

18. This resembles statements from the inquiries into violence in long-stay hospitals where one inquiry report stated that 'in such conditions staff can become as institutionalized as patients' (Martin, 1984: 13).

19. On one occasion the researcher was locked in a room with a group of children and felt considerable frustration at not being heard by staff and released, thus causing her to be late for another appointment. She realized the negative ways in which she wanted to respond were not much different from some of the ways the children were behaving and reacting. These difficult behaviours were usually perceived by staff as 'being out of control', 'committing misdemeanours' or 'in the blood' rather than forms of revolt and resistances to institutionalized practices, particularly around divisive cultures between staff and residents (Parkin and Green, 1997a). Past abuse or rebellion against institutionalized regimes was rarely seen as a way of understanding behaviours which were more often interpreted as evidence of children's disturbance or inherent, individual deviance.

Chapter 6

1. Cited in Wright, 1998.

2. This use of 'culture' or 'cultural sensitivity' in organizations and management can be usefully reinterpreted within the context of more general political debates on the various forms of multiculturalism, less or more radical, and their critique (see, for example, McLaren, 1998).

3. Similar interpretations could be developed in relation to other social divisions, for example age or disability.

4. Similarly, while theories of globalization have become ever more popular as frames of reference for the contemporary social sciences, the theme of globalization is itself part of the dominant problematic of the modern social sciences from at least the works of Saint-Simon, Marx, Durkheim and Weber (Waters, 1995: 5–7).

5. There is a complex contradiction between the critique of grand narrative within postmodernism (following Lyotard) and the reassertion of the grand narrative as in the postmodern political economies of 'globalization'. This highlights the fundamental (one might say foundational) contradictions of postmodernism that are exposed by and within postcolonial theory and practice.

6. For example, one of the most comprehensive recent gendered syntheses of globalization is Peterson and Runyan's (1999) *Global Gender Issues*. Their perpsective is usefully supplemented by the more theoretical discussions of Gibson-Graham (1999) in *The End of Capitalism (as we knew it)* and the more practical reviews contained in Date-Bah's (1997) edited collection *Promoting Gender Equality at Work*. Other relevant texts that gender globalization in different ways include Mies, 1986, 1998; Grant and Newland, 1991; Fernandez Kelly, 1994; Waylen, 1996; Mir et al., 1998.

7. Combining the ratios between females:males for these four measures provides the GDI (Gender-related development index); this can then in turn be compared with the non-gendered HDI (Human development index). The figues for the top five, and lowest three on the Gender-related development index range from Canada with a GDI of .932, Norway .932, USA .927, Australia .927, and Iceland .925, to Niger with a GDI of .280, Burkino Faso .290, Ethiopia .297, Guinea–Bissau .298, and Mozambique .326 (*Human Development Report*, 2000).

8. The Gender Empowerment Measure (GEM) combines the proportions of women in these four political and occupational positions. Norway scores highest here with .825, followed by Iceland with .802, Sweden .794, Denmark .791 and Finland .757. At the lower end of the scale we find Niger with .119, Jordan .220, Egypt .274, Bangladesh .305, and Sri Lanka .309 (*Human Development Report*, 2000).

9. This GEM measure is far less comprehensive than the GDI, with data missing for 70 countries out of the 174 countries listed for the former, as opposed to 31 missing entries for the latter.

10. For a critique of globalization in terms of human rights and sexual exploitation, see Santos, 1999.

11. Cited in Tsoukas, 1999: 511.

12. 'In 1996, the total revenues of the 500 largest companies globally were $11.4 trillion, total profits were $404 billion, total assets were $33.3 trillion and the total number of employees was 35,517,692' (according to *Fortune Magazine*, cited in ILO, n.d.: 2).

13. Branko Milanovic, Principal Economist at the World Bank Research Department, has calculated that inequality, as measured by the Gini index using household survey data in over 100 countries, increased from 63 to 66 from 1988 to 1993. The comparable figures for the USA are an index of 35 and for Finland 25 (Milanovic, 2000). Additionally, these concentrations are also reflected in individual wealth accumulation. In the USA the top 1 per cent of earners have doubled their incomes in the last 20 years. The wealth of Bill Gates, the Walton family and the Sultan of Brunei is greater than the combined national income of Angola, Bangladesh, Nepal and 33 other countries. A yearly contribution of 1 per cent of the wealth of the 200 richest people would give free primary education to every child in the world (Elliott, 1999).

14. There is now an extensive global campaign against the corporate practices of Nike. These have been especially active on some US university campuses, so much so that the corporation has withdrawn its sponsorship of some college sports teams (Campbell, 2000b).

15. We are particularly grateful for work with Anne Kovalainen which has informed this section (see Hearn and Kovalainen, 2000).

16. Farrelly (1998) has reported on the targeting of multinational executives for kidnapping and ransom in parts of Asia, South America and Eastern Europe, and the associated insurance industry. Hiscox of Lloyds report 4,040 kidnappings in Colombia, 656 in Mexico and 523 in Brazil in 1991–8. 'Typical insurance cover might mean a premium of $12,000 for each $1million, the usual limit.'

17. The private sector global defence and security industry comprises about 300 companies, serving corporate and governmental clients. Prominent businesses include Military Professional Services (MPRI) of Alexandria, Virginia, which boasts 'more four-star generals than the Pentagon' and 'in 1995 managed a small war for the hitherto struggling forces of Croatia', and the UK-based Control Risks and Defence Systems (DSL) which draws on SAS and other elite veterans, and specializes in 'protection packages' (Fox, 1998).

18. Another rather different set of violations is reported in relation to the Gerber Corporation:

> … Gerber Products Company has been under fire from the [US] Center for Science in the Public Interest and others for diluting its baby foods with water, sugar and chemically modified starch. Buckling under mounting consumer and government pressure, Gerber now says it is reformulating its best-selling 2nd-Foods Bananas with Tapioca and a number of other products so as to eliminate those fillers. But Gerber, which controls 69 per cent of the USA market, and other non-organic baby foods still contain pesticides, according to a report from the Environmental Working Group. The report, 'Pesticides in Baby Food,' found 16 different pesticides in eight major foods, including three probable human carcinogens, five possible human carcinogens, five pesticides that disrupt the hormone system and eight nervous system toxins. (http://www.ratical.org/corporations/mm10worst96.html)

There are many other examples of corporate ignoring of health risks, ranging from tobacco companies to food and medicines. On the case of the Dow Corning Corporation's 'corporate crime against women', with their manufacture and promotion of silicone breast implants despite the known health risks, see Chapple, 1998. For examples of dangerous and degrading work practices in companies in China, Vietnam and Thailand producing toys for McDonald's and Disneyland, see Santos, 1999.

19. They draw their information from that on the list-serve for the European Network on Conflict, Gender and Violence on that day.

20. Similar differentiations can also be made in relation to other social divisions, including class, education and world region.

21. We are particularly grateful for work with Marjut Jyrkinen which has informed this section (see Hearn and Jyrkinen, 2000).

22. An especially interesting and destructive example of 'the power of love' was the worldwide spread of the ILOVEYOU computer virus in May 2000 which led to $1billion of damage. The fact that the virus spread so rapidly is testimony to the power and promise of those words rather than simple money.

23. This and the following extracts in this section are from Hughes (1997). A similar version of this paper is published in Hughes, 1999.

24. Similar uses have been made of Antigua's offshore banking regime for establishing Internet pornography business (Miller, 2000).

25. We are indebted to Pernilla Gripenberg for clarifying the application of Tsoukas's framework to ICTs.

26. Quotation from Donna Hughes; see note 23.

Chapter 7

1. Human rights legislation is part of UK law from October 2000. This adds to EU anti-discrimination laws in the Treaty of Amsterdam and other administrative measures.

2. This is in keeping with the European Convention on Human Rights. The UK legislation and the ECHR has multiple implications for gender, sexuality and violation, in providing for freedom of expression, privacy of home life and protection against discrimination in the enjoyment of those rights. For example, this facilitates less censorship of violent or pornographic videos under the rules of 'freedom of expression'. It also provides gays and lesbians with equal privacy rights to heterosexuals, so that it might be illegal to expel young people over 16 for having sex within an educational or similar residential institution.

3. For an invaluable resource on the legal and policy aspects of the Internet from a civil liberties perspective in the European context, see Liberty, 1999.

4. The Bristol case involved heart surgeons operating on children leading to an unusually high death rate. Attention was drawn to this by a whistleblowing colleague who was subsequently unable to obtain work in the UK, leading to his decision to move to Australia.

5. The Shipman case involved a Lancashire GP convicted of murdering older women in his practice.

6. The professional project is a gendered one with professionalism 'drawing on and affirming a particular nineteenth-century notion of bourgeois masculinity' (Davies, 1996; also see Witz, 1992).

7. The term 'political correctness', Hopton (1997) argues, has attracted negative comment from both sides of the political spectrum leading to a discourse of ridicule constructed via the tabloid newspapers, politicians, dramatists and authors which legitimates one point of view and distracts attention from alternative discourses. The alternative discourse would recognize that language which continually stigmatizes a person causing distress and low self-esteem is a form of structural discrimination or violation, and the way to alleviate such mental distress is to focus on social and political structures rather than presume individual pathology. He argues that political correctness should be part of looking ahead to a society where 'substantive equality is achieved through the institutionalization of sensitivity to the social, cultural and psychological needs of people whose culture and social and political experience is considerably different from one's own' (p. 55).

8. See Hearn, 1992b, 1999b.

Bibliography

Aberle, D.F., Cohen, A.K., Davis, A.K., Levy, Jr, M.J. and Sutton, F.X. (1950). The functional prerequisites of a society. *Ethics*, 60(2), 100–11.

Acker, J. (1990). Hierarchies, jobs, bodies: a theory of gendered organizations. *Gender and Society*, 4 (2), 139–58.

Acker, J. (1992). Gendering organizational theory. In A.J. Mills and P. Tancred (eds), *Gendering Organizational Analysis* (pp. 248–60). Newbury Park, CA: Sage.

Ackroyd, S. and Thompson, P. (1999). *Organizational Misbehaviour*. London: Sage.

Adams, A. (1992). *Bullying at Work: How to Confront and Overcome IT*. London: Virago.

Addelston, J. and Stiratt, M. (1996). The last bastion of masculinity: gender politics at The Citadel. In C. Cheng (ed.), *Masculinities in Organizations* (pp. 54–76). Thousand Oaks, CA: Sage.

Adkins, L. (1995). *Gendered Work*. Buckingham: Open University Press.

Adler, N. and Izraeli, D. (eds) (1988). *Women in Management Worldwide*, New York: M.E. Sharpe.

Adler, N. and Izraeli, D. (eds) (1994). *Competitive Frontiers: Women Managers in a Global Economy*. Cambridge, MA: Blackwell.

Adrianson, L. (1993). *Ett högt pris. Kartläggning av sexuella trakasserier vid Göteborgs universitet*. (High Price. Charting Sexual Harassment at Gothenburg University.) Jämställdhetskommittén vid Göteborgs universitet. (Committee for Equality at Gothenburg University.)

Airport controllers land punches (1997). *Evening Standard*, 28 August, 14.

Aitkin, L. and Griffin, G. (1996). *Gender Issues in Elder Abuse*. London and Thousand Oaks, CA: Sage.

Albrow, M. (1992). Do organizations have feelings? *Organization Studies*, 13(3), 313–29.

Alexander, S. and Taylor, B. (1980). In defence of 'patriarchy'. *New Statesman*, 99, 1 February, 161.

Allison, A. (1994). *Nightwork: Sexuality, Pleasure and Corporate Masculinity in a Tokyo Hostess Club*. Chicago: Chicago University Press.

Alvesson, M. and Due Billing, Y. (1997). *Understanding Gender and Organizations*, London: Sage.

Anderson, R., Brown, J. and Campbell, E.A. (1993). *Aspects of Sex Discrimination in Police Forces in England and Wales*. London: Home Office Police Research Group.

Andrea Adams Trust Factsheet (n.d.). *Workplace Bullying*. Brighton: Andrea Adams Trust.

Appelberg, K. (1996). *Interpersonal Conflicts at Work: Impact on Health Behavior, Psychiatric Morbidity and Work Disability*. Helsinki: Finnish Institute of Occupational Health.

Arendt, H. (1963). *Eichmann in Jerusalem*. (Repub. 1994.) Harmondsworth: Penguin.

Argyle, K. and Shields, R. (1996). Is there a body in the Net? In R. Shields (ed.), *Cultures of the Internet* (pp. 58–69). London: Sage.

Aromaa, K. (1993). Survey results on victimisation to violence at work. In K. Kauppinen-Toropainen (ed.), *OECD Panel Group on Women, Work and Health. National Report: Finland* (pp. 136–48). Helsinki: Publications of the Ministry of Social Affairs and Health 1993: 6.

Aromaa, K. and Heiskanen, M. (2000). Väkivalta. (Violence.) In M. Heiskanen, K. Aromaa, H. Niemi and R. Sirén, *Tapaturmat, väkivalta, rikollisuuden pelko* (Accidents,

Violence, Fear of Crime) (pp. 115–33). Helsinki: Tilastokeskus; Oikeuspoliittisen Tutkimuslaitokesen julkaisuja 171; Oikeus 2000: 1.

Aron, C.S. (1987). *Ladies and Gentlemen of the Civil Service: Middle Class Workers in Victorian America*. New York and Oxford: Oxford University Press.

Atkins, S. and Hoggett, B. (1984). *Women and the Law*. Oxford: Blackwell.

Atkinson, P. (1979). The problem with patriarchy. *Achilles Heel*, 2, 18–22.

Atta and M. (1996). Postings from this newsgroup are archived into a World Wide Web site called *The World Sex Guide*, Atta and M. (an48932@anon. penet.fi) *The World Sex Guide* (updated July 1996). Available at: http://www.paranoia.com/faq/prostitution

Aymer, C. (1992). Women in residential work: dilemmas and ambiguities. In M. Langan and L. Day (eds), *Women, Oppression and Social Work* (pp. 186–200). London: Routledge.

Bachrach, P. and Baratz, M.S. (1962). Two faces of power. *American Political Science Review*, 56(4), 947–52.

Bachrach, P. and Baratz, M. (1970). *Understanding Poverty: Theory and Practice*. New York/Oxford: Oxford University Press.

Balloch, S., Andrew, T., Ginn, J., McLean, J., Pahl, J. and Williams, J. (1995). *Working for the Social Services*. London: NISW.

Barbalet, J.M. (1987). Power, structural resources and agency. *Perspectives in Social Theory*, 8, 1–24.

Baron, C. (1987). *Asylum to Anarchy*. London: Free Association.

Barrett, M. (1980). *Women's Oppression Today*. London: Verso.

Bast-Pettersen, R., Bach, E., Lindström, K., Toomingas, A. and Kiviranta, J. (eds) (1995). *Research on Violence, Threats and Bullying as Health Risks among Health Care Personnel*. Copenhagen: TemaNord.

Bauman, Z. (1989). *Modernity and the Holocaust*. Cambridge/Oxford: Polity/Blackwell.

Bauman, Z. (1995). Searching for a centre that holds. In M. Featherstone, S. Lash and R. Robertson (eds), *Global Modernities* (pp. 140–54). London: Sage.

Bebbington, A. and Miles, J. (1989). The background of children who enter local authority care. *British Journal of Social Work*, 19, 349–68.

Beck, U. (1992). *Risk Society: Towards a New Modernity*. London: Sage.

Beechey, V. (1979). On patriarchy. *Feminist Review*, 3, 66–82.

Beer, C.R., Jeffrey, R. and Munyard, T. (1983). *Gay Workers: Trade Unions and the Law*. London: NCCL.

Bell, A.P. and Weinberg, M.S. (1978). *Homosexualities: a Study of Diversity Among Men and Women*. New York: Simon and Schuster.

Bellos, A. (1996). Judge throws out case of PC accused of groping. *Guardian*, 24 July, 3.

Bennett, C. (1994). Ending up. *Guardian Weekend*, 8 October, 12–14, 18, 20.

Beresford, P. and Wilson, A. (1998). Social exclusion and social work: challenging the contradictions of exclusive debate. In M. Barry and C. Hallett (eds), *Social Exclusion and Social Work: Issues of Theory, Policy and Practice* (pp. 85–96). Lyme Regis, Dorset: Russell House.

Bergström, A.-M. (1995). Threat and violence against health care personnel. In R. Bast-Pettersen, E. Bach, K. Lindström, A. Toomingas and J. Kiviranta (eds), *Research on Violence, Threats and Bullying as Health Risks Among Health Care Personnel* (pp. 17–20). Copenhagen: TemaNord.

Berridge, D. (1994). Foster and residential care reassessed: a research perspective. *Children and Society*, 8 (2), 132–50.

Bessant, J. (1998). Women in academia and opaque violence. Paper at Winds of Change and the Culture of Universities, International Conference, Sydney, University of Technology, July.

Bettelheim, B. (1960). *The Informed Heart*. Glencoe, ILL: Free Press.

Bettelheim, B. (1979). *Surviving the Holocaust*. New York: Knopf.

Bibby, P. (1995). *Personal Safety for Social Workers*. Aldershot: Ashgate.

Bindel, J. (ed.) (1996). *Women Overcoming Violence & Abuse*. Research Paper No. 15. Bradford: Reseach Unit on Violence, Abuse and Gender Relations, University of Bradford.

Binney, V., Harkell, G. and Nixon, J. (1981). *Leaving Violent Men*. London: Women's Aid Federation, England.

Bion (1948, 1949, 1950). Experiences in groups. *Human Relations*, 1, 2, 3.

Björkqvist, K., Österman, K. and Hjelt-Bäck, M. (1994). Aggression among university employees. *Aggressive Behavior*, 20: 173–84.

Blackstock, C. and Rees, P. (1998). Racism rife in force, say black police. *Independent on Sunday*, 26 April, 5.

Bland, L., Brunsdon, C., Hobson, D. and Winship, J. (1978). Women 'inside' and 'outside' the relations of production. In Women's Studies Group, Centre for Contemporary Cultural Studies, University of Birmingham (eds), *Women Take Issue* (pp. 35–78). London: Hutchinson.

Bologh, R.W. (1990). *Love or Greatness? Max Weber and Masculine Thinking – a Feminist Inquiry*. London and Boston: Unwin Hyman.

Bondi, L. (1998). Sexing the city. In R. Fincher and J.M. Jacobs (eds), *Cities of Difference* (pp. 177–200). New York: Guilford Press.

Bonnington Report (1984). *Residential Services, the Next Ten Years*. London: The Social Care Association Publications.

Borchorst, A. (1990). *The Scandanavian Welfare States: Patriarchal, Gender Neutral or Women-Friendly?* Aarhus: Institute for Political Science, University of Aarhus.

Borchorst, A. (1994). Scandanavian welfare states – patriarchal, gender neutral or women friendly? *International Journal of Contemporary Sociology*, 31 (1), 45–67.

Borchorst, A. and Siim, B. (1987). Women and the advanced welfare state – a new kind of patriarchal power? In A.S. Sassoon (ed.), *Women and the State: the Shifting Boundaries of Public and Private* (pp. 128–57). London: Hutchinson.

Boseley, S. (1997). Navy counts the cost of a culture of sexual abuse. *Guardian*, 8 February, 8.

Boughton, I. (2000). No such thing as a private email. *Guardian Office*, 4 September, 2.

Bourke, J. (1999). *An Intimate History of Killing*. London: Granta.

Bowcott, O. (1997). Paedophile inquiry at 33 homes for children. *Guardian*, 16 December, 6.

Bowker, L.H. (ed.) (1998). *Masculinities and Violence*. Thousand Oaks, CA: Sage.

Bowlby, J. (1953). *Childcare and the Growth of Love*. Harmondsworth: Penguin.

Bradford, D.L., Sargent, A.G. and Sprague, M.S. (1975). Executive man and woman: the issue of sexuality. In F.E. Gordon and M.H. Strober (eds), *Bringing Women into Management* (pp. 39–58). New York: McGraw-Hill.

Brewis, J. and Grey, C. (1994). Re-eroticizing the organization: an exigesis and critique. *Gender, Work and Organization*, 1 (2): 67–82.

Brewis, J. and Linstead, S. (2000). *Sex, Work and Sex Work: Eroticizing Organization*. London: Routledge.

Brindle, D. (1998a). Home truths. *Guardian*, 13 May, 2–3.

Brindle, D. (1998b). Stronger safeguards for children. *Guardian*, 6 November, 10.

Bristol Women's Studies Group (1979). *Half the Story: an Introduction to Women's Studies*. London: Virago.

British Crime Survey (1995). London: HMSO.

Brooks, V. (1981). *Minority Stress and Lesbian Women*. Lexington, MA: Lexington.

Brooks-Gordon, B. (1995). Struggling in the City: the subordination of women traders in the London oil broking market and their coping strategies. Paper at BPS Psychology of Women Section Conference, Leeds University, July 9th.

Brophy, J. and Smart, C. (1982). From disregard to disrepute: the position of women in family law. In E. Whitelegg, M. Arnott, E. Bartels, V. Beechey, L. Birke, S. Himmelweit, D. Leonard, S. Ruchl and M.A. Speakmann (eds), *The Changing Experience of Women* (pp. 207–25). Milton Keynes: Open University Press.

Brown, A. (1996). Call a porn line and help a Third World country. *Independent on Sunday*, 11 August, 12.

Brown, C. (1981). Mothers, fathers, and children: from private to public patriarchy. In L. Sargent (ed.), *Women and Revolution: the Unhappy Marriage of Marxism and Feminism* (pp. 239–67). New York: Maple; London: Pluto.

Bruckman, A. (1993). Gender swapping on the Internet. Available via anonymous FTP from media.mit.edu in pub/MediaMOO/Papers: gender swapping. Cited in Shade (1993).

Buchbinder, H. (1987). Male heterosexuality. The socialized penis revisited. In H. Buchdinder, V. Burstyn, D. Forbes and M. Steedman (eds), *Who's on Top? The Politics of Heterosexuality* (pp. 63–82). Toronto: Garamond.

Bully OnLine (1999). timfield@successunlimited.co.uk

Burke, M.E. (1993). *Coming Out of the Blue: British Police Officers Talk about their Lives in 'The Job' as Lesbians, Gays and Bisexuals*. London and New York: Cassell.

Burrell, G. (1997). *Pandemonium: Towards a Retro-Organization Theory*. London: Sage.

Burrell, G. (1999). Normal science, paradigms, metaphors, discourses and genealogies of analysis. In S.R. Clegg and C. Hardy (eds), *Studying Organizations: Theory and Method* (pp. 388–404). London: Sage.

Burris, B.H. (1996). Technocracy, patriarchy and management. In D.L. Collinson and J. Hearn (eds), *Men as Managers, Managers as Men: Critical Perspectives on Men, Masculinities and Managements* (pp. 61–77). London: Sage.

Burstyn, V. (1983). Masculine dominance and the state. In R. Miliband and J. Saville (eds), *The Socialist Register 1983* (pp. 45–89). London: Merlin.

Burton, J. (1998). *Managing Residential Care*. London and New York: Routledge.

Butler, J. (1990). *Gender Trouble: Feminism and the Subversion of Identity*. New York/London: Routledge.

Calás, M. (1992). An/other silent voice? Representing 'Hispanic women' in organizational texts. In A. Mills and P. Tancred (eds), *Gendering Organizational Analysis* (pp. 201–21). Newbury Park, CA: Sage.

Calás, M.B. and Smircich, L. (1991). Voicing seduction to silence leadership. *Organization Studies*, 12 (4), 567–601.

Calás, M.B. and Smircich, L. (1993). Dangerous liaisons: the 'feminine-in-management' meets 'globalization'. *Business Horizons*, March/April, 71–81.

Cammermeyer, M. (1995). *Serving in Silence*. Harmondsworth: Penguin.

Campaign for Homosexual Equality (1981). *What About the Gay Workers?* London: CHE.

Campbell, D. (2000a). Girls sold as sex slaves in the US, CIA report finds. *Guardian*, 3 April, 11.

Campbell, D. (2000b). Nike gives US universities the boot as student anti-sweatshop demands rise. *Guardian*, 6 May, 7.

Cardy, C. (1992). *Training for Personal Safety at Work*. Aldershot: Gower.

Carrigan, T., Connell, R.W. and Lee, J. (1985). Towards a new sociology of masculinity. *Theory and Society*, 14(5): 551–604.

Carty, E. (1996). £175,000 for workload stress. *Guardian*, 27 April, 6.

Carty, V. (1997). Ideologies and forms of domination in the organization of the global production and consumption of goods in the emerging postmodern era: a case study of Nike Corporation and the implications for gender. *Gender, Work and Organization*, 4(4), 189–201.

Chafetz, J., Sampson, P., Beck, P. and West, J. (1974). A study of homosexual women. *Social Work* 19(6): 714–23.

Chapple, C.L. (1998). Dow Corning and the silicone breast implant debacle: a case of corporate crime against women. L.H. Bowker (ed.), *Masculinities and Violence* (pp. 179–96). Thousand Oaks, CA: Sage.

Cheng, C. (ed.) (1996). *Masculinities in Organizations*. Thousand Oaks, CA: Sage.

Clark, L.M.G. and Lange, L. (eds) (1979). *The Sexism of Social and Political Theory*. Toronto: University of Toronto Press.

Clegg, S. (1989). *Frameworks of Power*. London: Sage.

Cline, H.F. (1968). *The Determinants of Normative Patterns in Correctional Institutions*. Scandinavian Studies in Criminology 2. London: Tavistock.

Cobbe, F.P. (1878). Wife Torture in England. *The Contemporary Review*, April, 55–87.

Cobbe, F.P. (1894). *Life of Frances Power Cobbe by Herself. Volume 2*. London: Bentley.

Cockburn, C.K. (1983). *Brothers: Male Dominance and Technological Change*. London: Pluto.

Cockburn, C.K. (1990). 'Equal opportunities' intervene. In J. Hearn and D. Morgan (eds), *Men, Masculinities and Social Theory* (pp. 72–89). London and Boston: Unwin Hyman.

Cockburn, C.K. (1991). *In the Way of Women: Men's Resistance to Sex Equality in Organizations*. Basingstoke: Macmillan.

Coles, J. (1998). Rough traders. *Guardian*, 20 April, 2–3.

Collier, R. (1995). *Combating Sexual Harassment in the Workplace*. Buckingham and Philadelphia, NJ: Open University Press.

Collins, E.G.C. (1983). Managers and lovers. *Harvard Business Review*, 61(5), 141–53.

Collinson, D.L (1992). *Managing the Shopfloor. Subjectivity, Masculinity and Workplace Culture*. Berlin: de Gruyter.

Collinson, D.L. and Collinson, M. (1989). Sexuality in the workplace: the domination of men's sexuality. In J. Hearn, D. Sheppard, P. Tancred-Sheriff and G. Burrell (eds), *The Sexuality of Organization* (pp. 91–109). London: Sage.

Collinson, D.L. and Collinson, M. (1997). 'Delayering management': time–space surveillance and its gendered effects. *Organization*, 4(3), 375–407.

Collinson, D.L. and Hearn, J. (1994). Naming men as men: implications for work, organizations and management. *Gender, Work and Organization*, 1(1), 2–22.

Collinson, D.L. and Hearn, J. (eds) (1996). *Men as Managers, Managers as Men. Critical Perspectives on Men, Masculinities and Managements*. London: Sage.

Collinson, M. and Collinson, D.L. (1996). 'It's only Dick ...': the sexual harassment of women managers in insurance sales. *Work, Employment and Society*, 10(1), 29–56.

Connell, R.W. (1985). Theorising gender. *Sociology*, 19(2), 260–72.

Connell, R.W. (1987). *Gender and Power*. Cambridge: Polity.

Connell, R.W. (1990). The state, gender and sexual politics: theory and appraisal. *Theory and Society*, 19(5), 507–44.

Connell, R.W. (1993). The big picture: masculinities in recent world history. *Theory and Society*, 22(5), 597–623.

Connell, R.W. (1998). Men in the world: masculinities and globalization. *Men and Masculinities*, 1(1), 3–23.

Coote, A. and Campbell, B. (1982). *Sweet Freedom: The Struggle for Women's Liberation*. London: Picador.

Coveney, L., Jackson, M., Jeffreys, S., Kaye, L. and Mahoney, P. (1984). *The Sexuality Papers: Male Sexuality and the Social Control of Women*. London: Hutchinson.

Crosset, T. (2000). Athletic affiliation and violence against women: a structural prevention project. In J. McKay, M.A. Messner and D. Sabo (eds), *Masculinities, Gender Relations and Sport* (pp. 147–61). Thousand Oaks, CA: Sage.

Cunningham, M. (1984). *Powerplay: What Really Happened at Bendix*. New York: Ballantine.

Curry, T.J. (1991). Fraternal bonding in the locker room: a pro-feminist analysis of talk about competition and women. *Sociology of Sport Journal*, 8, 119–35.

Curtis, P. (1992). MUDding: social phenomena in text-based virtual realities. Proceedings of DIAC 92. Available via anonymous FTP from parcftp.xerox.com in pub/MOO/papers/ DIAC92. Cited in Shade (1993).

Dahl, R.A. (1957). The concept of power. *Behavioral Science*, 2, 201–5.

Dalaimo, D.M. (1997). Electronic sexual harassment. In B.R. Sandler and R.J. Shoop (eds), *Sexual Harassment on Campus: a Guide for Administrators, Faculty and Students* (pp. 85–103). Boston: Allyn & Bacon.

Dallalfar, A. and Movahedi, S. (1996). Women in multinational corporations: old myths, new constructions and some deconstruction. *Organization*, 3(4), 546–59.

Date-Bah, E. (ed.) (1997). *Promoting Gender Equality at Work*. London: Zed.

Davidson, M. and Burke, R. (eds) (1994). *Women in Management: Current Research Issues*. London: Paul Chapman.

Davidson, M. and Burke, R. (eds) (2000). *Women in Management: Current Research Issues II*. London: Sage.

Davies, C. (1996). The sociology of the professions and the profession of gender. *Sociology*, 30(4), 661–7.

Davis, L. (1997). *The Swimsuit Issue and Sport: Hegemonic Masculinity in Sports Illustrated*. Albany, NY: State University of New York Press.

Davies, N. (1997). Horror upon horror. *Guardian*, 24 September, 2–3, 7.

Dawson, S. (1996). *Analysing Organisations* (3rd edn). London: Macmillan.

De Maria, W. (1996). Open spaces, secret places: workplace violence towards whistle-blowers. In P. McCarthy, M. Sheehan and W. Wilkie (eds), *Bullying: From Backyard to Boardroom* (pp. 33–46). Alexandria, Australia: Millennium Books.

DeKeseredy, W.S. (1990). Male peer support and woman abuse: the current state of knowledge. *Sociological Focus*, 23(2), 129–39.

Delacoste, F. and Alexander, P. (eds) (1988). *Sex Work: Writings by Women in the Sex Industry*. London: Virago.

Delgado, A. (1979). *The Enormous File: a Social History of the Office*. London: John Murray.

Delphy, C. (1977). *The Main Enemy*. London: Women's Research and Resources Centre.

Delphy, C. (1984). *Close to Home*. London: Hutchinson.

D'Emilio, J. (1983). Capitalism and gay identity. In A. Snitow, C. Stansell and S. Thompson (eds), *Desire: the Politics of Sexuality* (pp. 140–52). New York: Monthly Review; London: Virago.

D'Emilio, J. and Freedman, E. (1988). *Intimate Matters: a History of Sexuality in America*. New York: Harper & Row.

den Ouden, M., Bos, H. and Sandfort, T. (1999). Mobbing: victims and health consequence. Paper presented at the Ninth European Congress on Work and Organizational Psychology: Innovations for Work, Organization and Well-Being, Espoo-Helsinki, Finland, 12–15 May.

Dixon, N. (1976). *On the Psychology of Military Incompetence*. London: Jonathan Cape.

Dobash, R.E. and Dobash, R.P. (1979). *Violence Against Wives: A Case Against Patriarchy*. London: Open Books.

Due Billing, Y. (1994). Gender and bureaucracies: a critique of Ferguson's 'The Feminist Case Against Bureaucracy'. *Gender, Work and Organization*, 1(4), 179–93.

Due Billing, Y. and Alvesson, M. (1994). *Gender, Management and Organizations*. Berlin: de Gruyter.

Duncan, S. (1994). Theorizing differences in patriarchy. *Environment and Planning A*, 26, 1177–94.

Duncan, S. (1995). Theorizing European gender systems. *Journal of European Social Policy*, 5(4), 263–84.

Durkin, J.J. (1978). The potential of women. In B.A. Stead (ed.), *Women in Management* (pp. 42–6). Englewood Cliffs, NJ: Prentice-Hall.

Dworkin, A. (1979). *Pornography: Men Possessing Women*. London: Women's Press.

Dyer, C. (1994). Sex is a law letter word. *Guardian*, 18 October, 18.

Dyer, C. (1997a). Damages for Wren made ill by sex harassment. *Guardian*, 24 June, 4.

Dyer, C. (1997b). Woman 'raped and bullied in Territorial Army job'. *Guardian*, 7 July, 6.

Dyer, R. (1985). Male sexuality in the media. In A. Metcalf and M. Humphries (eds), *The Sexuality of Men* (pp. 28–43). London: Pluto.

Edley, N. and Wetherell, M. (1995). *Men in Perspective: Practice, Power and Identity*. Hemel Hempstead: Prentice Hall, Harvester Wheatsheaf.

Edwards, A. (1989). The sex–gender distinction: has it outlived its usefulness? *Australian Feminist Studies*, 10, 1–12.

Eekelaar, J. (1978). *Family Law and Social Policy*. London: Weidenfeld & Nicolson.

Eichler, M. (1980). *The Double Standard: A Feminist Critique of Feminist Social Science*. London: Croom Helm.

Einarsen, S. and Raknes, B.I. (1991). *Mobbing i arbeidslivet. En undersøkelse av forekomst og helsemessige konsekvenser av mobbing på norske arbeidsplasser* (Bullying in Working Life: A Study of the Prevalence and Health-Related Consequences in Norwegian Workplaces). Bergen: University of Bergen.

Einarsen, S. and Raknes, B.I. (1997). Harassment in the workplace and the victimization of men. *Violence and Victims*, 12, 247–63.

Einarsen, S. and Skogstad, A. (1996). Bullying at work: epidemiological findings in public and private organizations. *European Journal of Work and Organizational Psychology*, 5(2), 185–201.

Einarsen, S., Matthiesen S. and Skogstad, A. (1998). Bullying, burnout and well-being among assistant nurses. *Journal of Occupational Health and Safety: Australia and New Zealand*, 14(6), 563–8.

Einarsen, S., Raknes, B.I. and Mathieson, S.B. (1994). Bullying and harassment at work and their relationships to work environment quality: an exploratory study. *European Work and Organizational Psychologist*, 4(4), 381–401.

Eisenstein, Z. (1981). *The Radical Future of Liberal Feminism*. New York: Longman.

Ekins, R. and King, D. (eds) (1996). *Blending Genders: Social Aspects of Cross-dressing and Sex-changing*. London: Routledge.

Eklund, J. (1996). Conflicts and harassment as risk factor for musculoskeletal shoulder problems. In S.A. Robertson (ed.), *Contemporary Ergonomics* (227–32). London: Taylor & Francis.

Elliot, G. (1972). *The 20th Century Book of the Dead*. New York: Charles Schribner's & Sons.

Elliott, L. (1999). Rise and rise of the super-rich. *Guardian G2*, 14 July, 2–3.

Ellis, J.B. (1869). *The Sights and Secrets of the National Capital: A Work Descriptive of Washington City in its Various Phases*. Chicago: Jones, Junkin and Co.

Elshtain, J.B. (1981). *Public Man, Private Woman*. Oxford: Martin Robertson.

Enloe, C. (1983). *Does Khaki Become You? The Militarization of Women's Lives*. Boston: South End Press; London: Pluto.

Epstein, D. (1994). Keeping them in their place: (hetero)sexist harassment, gender and the enforcement of heterosexuality. Paper at British Sociological Association annual conference 'Sexualities in Social Context', University of Central Lancashire, March.

Eriksen, T.H. (1997). Our creative diversity. Paper to conference on Culture and Rights, Sussex University, 15–16 July.

Etzioni, A. (1961). *A Comparative Analysis of Complex Organizations*. Glencoe, IL: Free Press.

European Commission (1991). Code of practice on sexual harassment. Reproduced in *Equal Opportunities Review*, 41, 9–42.

European Commision (1999). *Sexual Harassment at the Workplace in the European Union*. Luxembourg: European Commission.

Evans, J. (1994). *Feminist Theory Today: An Introduction to Second-Wave Feminism*. London: Sage.

Farley, L. (1978). *Sexual Shakedown: the Sexual Harassment of Women on the Job*. London: Melbourn House.

Farquarson, A. (1999). I'll make your life a misery. *Guardian*, 17 April, 32–3.

Farrelly, P. (1998). Danger zones. *Observer Business*, 11 October, 5.

Feagin, J.R. and Sikes, M.P. (1994). *Living with Racism: the Black Middle Class Experience*. Boston: Beacon.

Ferguson, A. (1989). *Blood at the Root*. London: Pandora.

Ferguson, H. (1990). Rethinking child protection practices: a case for history. In Violence Against Children Study Group, *Taking Child Abuse Seriously* (pp. 121–42). London: Unwin Hyman/Routledge.

Ferguson, K. (1984). *The Feminist Case Against Bureaucracy*. Philadelphia, NJ: Temple University Press.

Fernandez Kelly, M.P. (1994). Making sense of gender in the world economy: focus on Latin America. *Organization*, 1(2), 249–75.

Field, T. (1996). *Bully in Sight: How to Predict, Resist, Challenge and Combat Workplace Bullying*. Wantage: Wessex Press.

Field, T. (1999a). Workplace Bullying Press Releases: http://www.successunlimited. co.uk/press.htm

Field, T. (1999b). *Those Who Can, Do. Those Who Can't, Bully*. Bully OnLine: http://www.successunlimited.co.uk/worbal.htm

Fielding, N. (1994). Cop canteen culture. In T. Newburn and E.A. Stanko (eds), *Just Boys Doing Business? Men, Masculinities and Crime* (pp. 46–63). London: Routledge.

Fineman, S. (ed.) (1993). *Emotion in Organizations*. London/Newbury Park, CA: Sage.

Firestone, S. (1970). *The Dialectic of Sex*. London: Jonathan Cape.

Fitzgerald, L. and Shullman, S.L. (1993). Sexual harassment: a research analysis and agenda for the 1990s. *Journal of Vocational Behavior*, 42, 5–27.

Fitzsimmons, M. (1989). The matter of nature. *Antipode*, 21, 106–20.

Foucault, M. (1977). *Discipline and Punish: the Birth of the Prison* (1st pub. 1975). Harmondsworth: Allen Lane.

Foucault, M. (1980). *Power/Knowledge: Selected Interviews and Other Writings 1972–1977* (ed. C. Gordon). Brighton: Harvester.

Foucault, M. (1981). Questions of method: an interview with Michel Foucault. *Ideology and Consciousness*, 8, 1–14.

Fowler, L. (1985). Women and work – sexual harassment, patriarchy and the labour process. Unpub. MS, MSc Industrial Sociology, Bradford: University of Bradford.

Fox, R. (1998). Private armies make a killing. *The European*, 25–31 May, 26–7.

Frank, B. (1987). Hegemonic heterosexual masculinity. *Studies in Political Economy*, 24: 159–70.

Franks, S. (1999). *Having None of It: Women, Men and the future of Work*. London: Granta Books.

Fraser, N. (1995). From redistribution to recognition? Dilemmas of justice in a 'post-socialist' age. *New Left Review*, 212, 68–93.

Fraser, N. (1997). *Justice Interruptus: Critical Reflections on the 'Postsocialist' Condition*. New York and London: Routledge.

Freeman, M.D.A. (1987). *Dealing with Domestic Violence*. Bicester, Oxon.: CCH Editions.

French, J.R.P., Jr. and Raven, B. (1959). The bases for social power. In D. Cartwright (ed.), *Studies in Social Power* (pp. 150–67). Ann Arbor, MI: University of Michigan Press.

French, K. (1995). Men and locations of power: why move over? In C. Itzin and J. Newman (eds), *Gender, Culture and Organizational Change: Putting Theory into Practice* (pp. 54–67). London and New York: Routledge.

FRID-A (1987). *Sexuella trakasserier i arbetslivet* (Sexual Harassment in Working Life). Stockholm: JämO.

Gabriel, Y. (1998). An introduction to the social psychology of insults. *Human Relations*, 51(11), 1329–54.

George, P. (1998). County cricket clubs plagued by racism. *Independent on Sunday*, 5 April, 8.

Gherardi, S. (1995). *Gender, Symbolism and Organizational Cultures*. London: Sage.

Gibson-Graham, J.K. (1999). *The End of Capitalism (as we knew it)*. Cambridge, MA: Blackwell.

Giddens, A. (1990). *The Consequences of Modernity*. Cambridge: Polity.

Gillis, J. (1985). *For Better, For Worse: British Marriage 1600 to the Present*. New York and Oxford: Oxford University Press.

GLC (1985). *Danger! ... Heterosexism at Work*. London: GLC.

Goffman, E. (1961). *Asylums*. Harmondsworth: Penguin.

Goffman, E. (1969). The characteristics of total institutions. In A. Etzioni (ed.), *A Sociological Reader on Complex Organizations* (2nd edn) (pp. 312–38). New York and London: Holt, Rinehart and Winston.

Grant, R. and Newland, K. (eds) (1991). *Gender and International Relations*. Milton Keynes: Open University Press.

Gray, S. (1984). Romance in the workplace: corporate rules for the game of love. *Business Week*, 2847, 70–1.

Green, L. (1998). *Caged by Force, Entrapped by Discourse: a Study of the Construction and Control of Children and their Sexualities within Residential Children's Homes*. PhD thesis, Huddersfield: University of Huddersfield.

Green, L. and Parkin, W. (1999). Sexuality, sexual abuse and children's homes – oppression or protection? In The Violence Against Children Study Group (eds), *Children, Child Abuse and Child Protection: Placing Children Centrally* (pp. 176–92). Chichester and New York: John Wiley.

Green, L. Parkin, W. and Hearn, J. (2001). Power. In E. Wilson (ed.), *Organizational Behaviour Reassessed: the Impact of Gender* (pp. 188–214). London: Sage.

Greenslade, R. (2000). I arrest you for emailing. *Guardian Media*, 31 July, 6–7.

Gregory, J. and Lees, S. (1999). *Policing Sexual Assault*. London and New York: Routledge.

Grosz, E. (1987). Feminist theory and the challenge to knowledges. *Women's Studies International Forum*, 10(5), 475–80.

Grosz, E. (1994). *Volatile Bodies:Towards a Corporeal Feminism, Theories of Representation and Difference*. Bloomington, IN: Indiana University Press.

Gutek, B.A. (1985). *Sex and the Workplace: Impact of Sexual Behaviour and Harassment on Women, Men and Organizations*. San Francisco, CA: Jossey-Bass.

Gutek, B.A. (1989). Sexuality in the workplace: key issues in social research and organizational practice. In J. Hearn, D. Sheppard, P. Tancred-Sherriff and G. Burrell (eds), *The Sexuality of Organization* (pp. 56–70). London/Beverly Hills, CA: Sage.

Gutek, B.A. and Cohen, A. (1987). Sex ratios, sex-role spillover, and sex at work: a comparison of men's and women's experiences. *Human Relations*, 40(2), 97–115.

Gutek, B.A. and Morasch, B. (1982). Sex ratios, sex-role spillover and sexual harassment of women at work. *Journal of Social Issues*, 38(4), 55–74.

Gwartney-Gibbs, P.A. and Lach, D.H. (1994). Gender and workplace dispute resolution: a conceptual and theoretical model. *Law and Society Review*, 23(1), 265–96.

Haapaniemi, M. and Kinnunen, A. (1997). Muuttunut työtilanteiden väkivalta 1980–1993. (Changes in violence at work 1980–1993.) *Työ ja ihminen*, 1, 14–23.

Haavio-Mannila, E. (1994). Erotic relations at work. In M. Alestalo, E. Allardt, A. Rychard and W. Wesolowski (eds), *The Transformation of Europe* (pp. 293–315). Warsaw: IFIS Publishers.

Haavio-Mannila, E. (1998). Attraction and love at work. In D. van der Fehr, A. Jónasdóttir and B. Rosenbeck (eds), *Is there a Nordic Feminism?* (pp. 198–216). London: Taylor & Francis.

Hagman, N. (1988). *Sextrakasserier på jobbet. Myter. Fakta. Råd*. (Sexual Harassment at Work. Myths. Facts. Advice.) Stockholm: Wahlström & Widstrand.

Hall, A. (2000). Pilot calms 'kamikaze' passenger. *Daily Mail*, 30 March, 5.

Hall, E. (1995). *We Can't Even March Straight*. London: Vintage.

Hamada, T. (1996). Unwrapping Euro-American masculinity in a Japanese multinational corporation. In C. Cheng (ed.), *Masculinities in Organizations* (pp. 160–76). Thousand Oaks, CA: Sage.

Hanmer, J. and Hearn, J. (1999). Gender and welfare research. In F. Williams, J. Popay and A. Oakley (eds), *Welfare Research: A Critical Review* (pp. 106–30). London: UCL Press.

Hanmer, J., Hearn, J., Maynard, M. and Morgan, D. (1994). Violence by organisations, violence in organisations, and organisational responses to violence. In J. Hanmer and J. Hearn (eds) (compiled with 16 others), *Violence, Abuse and Gender Relations Research Strategy Report to the ESRC* (pp. 76–84). Violence, Abuse and Gender Relations Unit, Research Paper No. 11, Bradford: University of Bradford.

Hansard Society (1990). *Women at the Top*. London: Hansard Society.

Haraway, D. (1990). *Primate Visions – Gender, Races and Nature in the World of Modern Science*. New York and London: Routledge.

Harding, S. (1986). *The Science Question in Feminism*. Milton Keynes: Routledge.

Harlow, E. and Hearn, J. (1995). Cultural constructions: contrasting theories of organizational culture and gender construction. *Gender, Work and Organization*, 2(4), 180–91.

Harlow, E., Hearn, J. and Parkin, W. (1995). Gendered noise: organizations and the silence and din of domination. In C. Itzin and J. Newman (eds), *Gender, Culture and Organizational Change* (pp. 89–105). London: Routledge.

Harper, K. (1996). High flyer jailed for violence on plane. *Guardian*, 15 November, 8.

Harper, K. (1999). BA won't snitch on violent passengers. *Guardian*, 4 May, 12.

Harries-Jenkins, G. and Van Doorn, J. (eds) (1976). *The Military and the Problem of Legitimacy*. London/Beverly Hills, CA: Sage.

Hartmann, H. (1979). The unhappy marriage of Marxism and feminism. *Capital and Class*, 8(2), 1–33.

Harvey, D. (1990). *The Condition of Postmodernity*. Oxford: Blackwell.

Hauserman, N. (1999). Comparing conversations about sexual harassment in the United States and Sweden: print media coverage of the case against Astra USA. *Wisconsin Women's Law Journal*, 14, 45–68.

Health and Safety Executive (1993). *Prevention of Violence to Staff in Banks and Building Societies*. London: HSE Books.

Health and Safety Executive (1995). *Preventing Violence to Retail Staff*. London: HSE Books.

Hearn, J. (1983). *Birth and Afterbirth: a Materialist Account*. London: Achilles Heel.

Hearn, J. (1987). *The Gender of Oppression: Men, Masculinity and the Critique of Marxism*. Brighton: Wheatsheaf; New York: St. Martin's.

Hearn, J. (1992a). *Health, Bodies and Men's Violences: Making Connections*, Violence, Abuse and Gender Relations Research Unit, Research Paper No. 2. Bradford: University of Bradford.

Hearn, J. (1992b). *Men in the Public Eye. The Construction and Deconstruction of Public Men and Public Patriarchies*. London and New York: Routledge.

Hearn, J. (1993). Emotive subjects: organizational men, organizational masculinities and the deconstruction of 'emotions. In S. Fineman (ed.), *Emotion in Organizations* (pp. 148–66). London and Newbury Park, CA: Sage.

Hearn, J. (1994). The organisation(s) of violence: men, gender relations, organisations and violences. *Human Relations*, 47(6), 707–30.

Hearn, J. (1996a). Deconstructing the dominant: making the one(s) the other(s). *Organization*, 3(4), 611–26.

Hearn, J. (1996b). Men's violence to known women: historical, everyday and theoretical constructions by men. In B. Fawcett, B. Featherstone, J. Hearn and C. Toft (eds), *Violence and Gender Relations* (pp. 22–37). London: Sage.

Hearn, J. (1998). *The Violences of Men: How Men Talk About and How Agencies Respond to Men's Violence to Women*. London: Sage.

Hearn, J. (1999a). Ageism, violence and abuse: theoretical and practical perspectives on the links between child abuse and elder abuse. In The Violence Against Children Study Group (eds), *Children, Child Abuse and Child Protection: Placing Children Centrally* (pp. 81–96). London: John Wiley.

Hearn, J. (1999b). Sex, lies and videotape: the Clinton–Lewinsky saga as a world historical footnote. *Sexualities*, 2(2), 263–8.

Hearn, J. and Collinson, D.L. (1994). Theorizing unities and differences between men and between masculinities. In H. Brod and M. Kaufman (eds), *Theorizing Masculinities* (pp. 148–62). Newbury Park, CA: Sage.

Hearn, J. and Jynkinen, M. (2000). Uuclet teknologiat, globalisaatio ja seksiteollisuus (New technologies, globalization and the sex industry). *Naistutkimus. Kvinnoforskning*, 4/2000: 67–71.

Hearn, J. and Kovalainen, A. (2000). *Gender Relations in Transnational organizations: A Theoretical, Conceptual and Methodological Overview.* Meddelanden working papers. Helsinki: Swedish School of Economics and Business Administration, Finland.

Hearn, J. and Parkin, P.W. (1983). Gender and organizations: a selective review and a critique of a neglected area. *Organization Studies*, 4(3): 219–42.

Hearn, J. and Parkin, P.W. (1986–87). Women, men and leadership: a critical review of assumptions, practices and change in the industrialized nations. *International Studies of Management and Organizations*, 16(3–4), 33–60.

Hearn, J. and Parkin, W. (1987). *'Sex' at 'Work': the Power and Paradox of Organization Sexuality.* Brighton: Wheatsheaf; New York: St. Martin's.

Hearn, J. and Parkin, W. (1992). Gender and organizations: a selective review and a critique of a neglected area. In A. Mills and P. Tancred (eds), *Gendering Organizational Analysis* (pp. 48–66). Newbury Park, CA: Sage.

Hearn, J. and Parkin, W. (1993). Organizations, multiple oppressions and postmodernism. In J. Hassard and M. Parker (eds), *Postmodernism and Organizations* (pp. 148–62). London: Sage.

Hearn, J. and Parkin, W. (1995). *'Sex' at 'Work': the Power and Paradox of Organization Sexuality* (rev. edn). Hemel Hempstead: Prentice Hall/Harvester Wheatsheaf.

Hearn, J., Sheppard, D., Tancred-Sheriff, P. and Burrell, G. (eds) (1989). *The Sexuality of Organization.* London and Newbury Park, CA: Sage.

Henley, J. (2000). Test examiners driven to protest. *Guardian*, 14 April, 6.

Henriques, J., Hollway, W., Urwin, C., Venn, C. and Walkerdine, V. (1984). *Changing the Subject.* London: Methuen.

Herby, P. (1998). Arms transfers, humanitarian assistance and international humanitarian law. *International Review of the Red Cross*, 325. Cited in: Nanthikesan, 1999.

Hernes, H. (1987). *Welfare State and Woman Power.* Oslo: Norwegian University Press.

Hernes, H. (1988a). Scandinavian citizenship. *Acta Sociologica*, 31(3), 199–215.

Hernes, H. (1988b). The welfare state citizenship of Scandinavian women. In K.B. Jones and A.G. Jonasdottir (eds), *The Political Interests of Gender* (pp. 183–217). London: Sage.

Hester, M. (1994). Violence against social services staff: a gendered issue. In C. Lupton and T. Gillespie (eds), *Working with Violence.* Basingstoke: Macmillan.

Hickling, K. (1999). *Harassment at Work: A General Population Study.* Masters thesis, Huddersfield: University of Huddersfield.

Hilpern, K. (1999). Heat of the moment. *Independent on Sunday, Real Life Section*, 14 March, 11.

Hirdman, Y. (1988). Genussystemet – reflexioner kring kvinnors sociala underordning (The gender system-reflections on women's social subordination). *Kvinnovetenskaplig Tidskrift*, 3, 49–63.

Hirdman, Y. (1990). Genussystemet (The gender system). In *Demokrati och Makt i Sverige* (Democracy and Power in Sweden). Stockholm: Statens Offentliga Utredningar.

HMSO (2000). *Lost in Care*, The Waterhouse Report. London: HMSO.

Hobbes (1962). *Leviathan.* London: Collier–Macmillan.

Hodgkinson, P. and Stewart, M. (1991). *Coping with Catastrophe.* London: Routledge.

Hofstede, G. (1980). *Culture's Consequences: International Differences in Work-Related Values.* London: Sage.

Hofstede, G. (1991). *Cultures and Organizations: Software of the Mind*. London: McGraw-Hill.

Hofstede, G. (1993). Cultural constraints in management theories. *Academy of Management Executive*, 7(1), 81–93.

Hofstede, G. (ed.) (1998). *Masculinity and Femininity: The Taboo Dimension of National Cultures*. London: Sage.

Högbacka, R., Kandolin, I., Haavio-Mannila, E. and Kauppinen-Toropainen, K. (1987). *Sexual Harassment*, Equality Publications, Series E. Abstracts 2/1987. Helsinki: Ministry of Social Affairs, Finland.

Holter, H. (ed.) (1984). *Patriarchy in a Welfare Society*. Oslo: Universitetsforlaget.

Honneth, A. (1992). Integrity and disrespect: principles of a conception of morality based on a theory of recognition. *Political Theory*, 20(2), 187–201.

Honneth, A. (1995). *The Struggle for Recognition: the Moral Grammar of Social Conflicts*. Cambridge, MA: MIT Press.

Hopton, J. (1997). Anti-discriminatory and anti-oppressive practice: a radical humanist perspective. *Critical Social Policy*, 17(3), 47–61.

Horn, P.D. and Horn, J.C. (1982). *Sex in the Office. Power and Passion in the Workplace*. Reading, MA: Addison-Wesley.

HSE (1992). *Violence to Staff*. London: HSE Books.

http://www.heed.net/charter/doc2.html (Press release: Feminist Majority Foundation and Alliance for Democracy: Environmental, Human Rights, Women's and Pro-Democracy Groups Petition Attorney-General of California to Revoke Unocal's Charter, 10 September, 1998.)

http://www.kcn.ne.jp/~jjj/akahara/acahara.htm (Workplace bullying in universities in Japan: Japanese named it 'academic harassment').

http://www.ratical.org/corporations/CmurderProf.html (Corpse Murder Profile – Two Dictatorships: Shell and the Present Nigerian Military Government.)

http://www.ratical.org/corporations/mm10worst96.html (Mokhiber, Russell. The Ten Worst Corporations. *Multinational Monitor* (founder Ralph Nader) Internet Corporate Rap Sheet, December 1996.)

http://www.who.int/eha/emergenc/soe/sld003.htm (World Health Organization: State of the World's Emergencies). Cited in Nanthikesan, 1999.

Huggins, M.K. and Haritos-Fatouros, M. (1998). Bureaucratizing masculinities among Brazilian torturers and murderers. In L.H. Bowker (ed.), *Masculinities and Violence* (pp. 29–54). Thousand Oaks, CA: Sage.

Hughes, D.M. (1997). 'Trafficking and sexual exploitation on the Internet', *Feminista! The Online Journal of Feminist Construction*. Vol. 1, No. 8. Available at http://www.feminista.com/v1n8/hughes.html

Hughes, D.M. (1999). The Internet and the global prostitution industry. In D.M. Hughes and C. Roche (eds), *Making the Harm Visible: Global Sexual Exploitation of Women and Girls. Speaking Out and Providing Services* (pp. 64–86). Kingston, RI: Coalition Against Trafficking in Women.

Human Development Report (1996). New York/Oxford: Oxford University Press for the United Nations Development Programme.

Human Development Report (2000). New York/Oxford: Oxford University Press for the United Nations Development Programme. Available at: http://www.undp.org/hdro/

Humphrey, J. (2000). Organizing sexualities, organization inequalities: lesbians and gay men in public service occupations. *Gender, Work and Organization*, 6(3), 134–51.

ILO (n.d.). Multinational corporations. At: http://www.itcilo.english/actrav/telearn/global/ilo/multinat/multinat.htm

Institute of Management (1995). *National Management Salary Survey*, Kingston-on-Thames: Institute of Management.

Institute of Management/Remuneration Economics (1998). *UK National Management Survey*. London: Institute of Management.

Institute of Personnel and Development (1998). *Harassment at Work*. Key Facts. London: IPD.

Ishmael, A. (with Alemoru, B.) (1999). *Harassment, Bullying and Violence at Work*. London: The Industrial Society.

Isotalus, N. and Saarela, K.J. (1999). Väkivaltatyötapaturmat Suomessa. (Violence-related occupational accidents in Finland.) *Työ ja ihminen*, 13(2), 137–49.

Itzin, C. (1995). Gender, culture, power and change: a materialist analysis. In C. Itzin and J. Newman (eds), *Gender, Culture and Organizational Change* (pp. 246–72). London: Routledge.

Itzin, C. and Newman, J. (eds) (1995). *Gender, Culture and Organizational Change*. London: Routledge.

Jacklin, C.N. and Maccoby, E.E. (1975). Sex differences and their implications for management. In E. Gordon and M.H. Strober (eds), *Bringing Women into Management* (pp. 23–38). New York: McGraw-Hill.

Jackson, N. and Carter, P. (1995). Efficiency as violence. Paper at the International Workshop on Organization and Violence, Drogheda, Ireland, April. Mimeo, University of Newcastle.

Jackson, S. (1987). Residential care and education. *Children and Society* 12, 335–50.

Jaques, E. (1955). Social systems as a defence against persecutory and depressive anxiety. In M. Klein, P. Heimann and R. Money-Kyrle (eds), *New Directions in Psychoanalysis* (pp. 3–23). London: Tavistock.

Jaques, E. (1976). *A General Theory of Bureaucracy*. London: Heinemann.

Jay, N. (1981). Gender and dichotomy. *Feminist Studies*, 7, 38–56.

Jermier, J.M., Gaines, J. and McIntosh, N.J. (1989). Reactions to physically dangerous work: a conceptual and empirical analysis. *Journal of Organizational Behavior*, 10, 15–33.

Jermier, J.M., Knights, D. and Nord, W.R. (eds) (1994). *Resistance and Power in Organizations*. London: Routledge.

Joeman, L.M., Phillips, C.M. and Stockdale, J.E. (1989). *The Risks in Going to Work*. London: Suzy Lamplugh Trust.

Johnson, R. (1986). Institutions and the promotion of violence. In A. Campbell and J.J. Gibbs (eds), *Violent Transactions* (pp. 181–205). Oxford: Blackwell.

Johnson, T. (1909). *Our Noble Families*. Glasgow: 'Forward' Publishing Co.

Jones, J. (1993). Child abuse: developing a framework for understanding power relationships in practice. In H. Ferguson, R. Gilligan and R. Torode (eds), *Surviving Childhood Adversity. Issues for Policy and Practice* (pp. 76–89). Trinity College, Dublin: Social Studies Press.

Jukes, A. (1993). *Why Men Hate Women*. London: Free Association Books.

Kahan, B. (1994). *Growing up in Groups*. London: HMSO.

Kakar, S. (1970). *Frederick Taylor: a Study in Personality and Innovation*. Cambridge, MA: MIT Press.

Kappeler, S. (1995). *The Will to Violence: The Politics of Personal Behavior*. Cambridge: Polity.

Karlén, H. (1996). Child pornography and paedophiles in Sweden. In M. Jyrkinen (ed.), *Changing Faces of Prostitution* (pp. 91–6). Helsinki: Unioni – the League of Finnish Feminists.

Karner, T.X. (1998). Engendering violent men: oral histories of military masculinity. In L.H. Bowker (ed.), *Masculinities and Violence* (pp. 197–232). Thousand Oaks, CA: Sage.

Kauppinen, K. and Gruber, J. (1993a). *Sexual Harassment of Women in Nontraditional Jobs: Results from Five Countries*. CEW Research Reports. Ann Arbor, MI: Center for the Education of Women, University of Michigan.

Kauppinen, K. and Gruber, J. (1993b). Antecedents and outcomes of woman-unfriendly behavior: a study of Scandinavian, former Soviet, and American women. *Psychology of Women Quarterly*, 17, 431–56.

Kauppinen-Toropainen, K. (ed.) (1993). *OECD Panel Group on Women, Work and Health*. Helsinki: Ministry of Social Affairs.

Kehoe, L. (1998). Think before you send that e-mail. *Financial Times*, Weekend, 30/31 May, 7.

Kelly, L. (1987). The continuum of sexual violence. In J. Hanmer and M. Maynard (eds), *Women, Violence and Social Control*, London: Macmillan.

Kelly, L. (1988). *Surviving Sexual Violence*. Cambridge: Polity.

Kelman, H. (1973). Violence without moral restraint: reflections on the dehumanisation of victims and victimisers. *Journal of Social Issues*, 29, 25–61.

Kimmel, M.S. (1990). Insult or injury: sex, pornography and sexism. In M.S. Kimmel (ed.), *Men Confront Pornography* (pp. 305–19). New York: Crown.

Kivimäki, M., Vahtera, J., Pentti, J. and Ferrie, J.E. (2000). Factors underlying the effect of organizational downsizing on health of employees: Longitudinal cohort study. *British Medical Journal*, 320, 971–5.

Klein, S. (1996). A longitudinal study of the impact of work pressures on group cohesive behaviors. *International Journal of Management*, 13(1), 68–75.

Knauss, P.R. (1987). *The Persistence of Patriarchy: Class, Gender, and Ideology in Twentieth Century Algeria*. New York: Praeger.

Kondo, D. (1990). *Crafting Selves: Power, Gender, and Discourses of Identity in a Japanese Workplace*. Chicago: University of Chicago Press.

Korten, D. (1998). Taming the giants. Available at: wysiwyg://191/http://www.geocities.com/RainForest/3621/KORTEN.HTM

Krieger, N. and Sidney, S. (1996). Racial discrimination and blood pressure: the CARDIA study of young black and white adults. *American Journal of Public Health*, 86(10), 1370–8.

Kulick, D. (ed.) (1998). Special issue on transgenderism in Latin America. *Sexualities*, 1(3), 259–359.

Lacey, H. (1999). 'I feel like the most hated woman in the Met'. *Independent on Sunday*, 21 March, 5.

Lambertz, J. (1985). Sexual harassment in the nineteenth century English cotton industry. *History Workshop Journal*, 19 (Spring), 29–61.

Landrine, H. and Klonoff, E.A. (1997). *Discrimination Against Women: Prevalence, Consequences, Remedies*. Thousand Oaks, CA: Sage.

Lash, S. and Urry, J. (1994). *Economies of Signs and Space*. London: Sage.

Lähteenmäki, P. (2000). Ohjelmisto vahtii pomon puolesta. (Program supervises on behalf of the boss.) *Helsingin Sanomat*, 27 August, E3.

Ledwith, S. and Colgan, F. (eds) (1996). *Women in Organisations: Challenging Gender Politics*. Basingstoke: Macmillan.

Leeds TUCRIC (1983). *Sexual Harassment of Women at Work*. Leeds: Leeds TUCRIC.

Lee-Treweek, G. (1997). Women, resistance and care: an ethnographic study of nursing auxiliary work. *Work, Employment and Society*, 11(1), 47–63.

Lehtiniemi, A. and Palmu, T. (1995). Health. In E.-S. Veikkola and T. Palmu (eds), *Women and Men in Finland* (pp. 19–30). Helsinki: Statistics Finland.

Leidner, R. (1993). *Fast Food, Fast Talk: Service Work and the Routinization of Everyday Life*. Berkeley, CA: University of California Press.

Leighton, (1999). Violence at work. the legal framework. In P. Leather, C. Brady, C. Lawrence, D. Beale and T. Cox (eds), *Work-related Violence* (pp. 19–33). London: Routledge.

Leonard, P. (1997). *Postmodern Welfare: Reconstructing an Emancipatory Project*. London and Thousand Oaks, CA: Sage.

Lessnoff, M. (1986). *Social Contract*. London: Macmillan.

Levine, M. and Leonard, R. (1984). Discrimination against lesbians in the workforce. *Signs*, 9(4), 700–9.

Levitas, R. (1996). The concept of social exclusion and the new Durkheimian hegemony. *Critical Social Policy*, 16(1), 5–20.

Levy, A. and Kahan, B. (1991). *The Pindown Experience and the Protection of Children: The Report of the Staffordshire Child Care Inquiry 1990.* Stafford: Staffordshire County Council.

Leymann, H. (1986). *Vuxenmobbning. Om psykiskt våld i arbetslivet.* (Bullying of Adults. On Psychological Violence in Working Life.) Lund: Studentlitteratur.

Leymann, H. (1988). *Ingen annan utväg. Om utslagning och självmord som följd av mobbning i arbetslivet.* (No other way. Expulsion and Suicide as Consequences of Bullying at Work.) Stockholm: Wahlström & Widstrand.

Leymann, H. (1990). Mobbing and psychological terror at workplaces. *Violence and Victims,* 5, 119–26.

Leymann, H. (1992a). *Från mobbning till utslagning i arbetslivet.* (From Bullying to Expulsion from Work Life.) Stockholm: Publica.

Leymann, H. (1992b). *Lönebidrag och mobbad. En svag grupps psykosociala arbetsvillkor i Sverige.* (State Subsidies and the Bullied. The psycho-social Working Conditions of a Vulnerable Group.) Stockholm: Arbetarskyddsstyrelsen.

Leymann, H. (1992c). *Oetisk kommunikation i partiarbetet.* (Unethical Communication in Political Parties.) Stockholm: Arbetarskyddsstyrelsen.

Leymann, H. (1992d). *Vuxenmobbning på svenska arbetsplatser. En rikstäckande undersökning med 2.428 intervjuer.* (Adult Bullying in Swedish Workplaces. A Nationwide study with 2,428 Interviews.) Stockholm: Arbetarskyddsstyrelsen.

Leymann, H. and Tallgren, U. (1989). Undersökning av frekvensen av vuxenmobbning inom SSAB med ett nytt frågeformulär. (A study of the frequency of adult bullying in SSAB with a new questionnaire.) *Arbete, människa, miljö,* 1, 3–12.

Leymann, H. and Tallgren, U. (1990). Mobbing. Men and women do it in different ways. *Working Environment,* 18–19.

Liberty (ed.) (1999). *Liberating Cyberspace: Civil Liberties, Human Rights and the Internet.* London: Pluto/Liberty.

Lindroos, R. (1996). *Kiusaamisen kurjuus yhteisöissä ja työyhteisöissä.* (The Misery of Bullying in Communities and Workgroups.) Työpoliittinen tutkimus nro 164. Helsinki: Ministry of Labour.

Lindroth, S. and Leymann, H. (1993). *Vuxenmobbning mot en minoritetsgrupp av män inom barnomsorgen. Om mäns jämställdhet i ett kvinnodominerat yrke.* (Adult Bullying of a Minority Group of Men within Childcare. On the Equality of Men in a Woman–dominated Occupation). Stockholm: Arbetarskyddsstyrelsen.

Lister, R. (1997). *Citizenship: Feminist Perspectives.* London: Macmillan.

Litewka, J. (1977). The socialized penis. In J. Snodgrass (ed.), *A Book of Readings for Men Against Sexism* (pp. 16–35). Albion, CA: Times Change Press.

Little, M. (1999). New research on residential care. *Children and Society,* 13(1), 61–6.

Lloyd, G. (1989). Woman as other: sex, gender and subjectivity. *Australian Feminist Studies,* 10, 13–22.

Loader, B.D. (ed.) (1997). *The Governance of Cyberspace.* London: Routledge.

Loss Prevention Council (1995). *Technical Briefing Note for Insurers.* London: Loss Prevention Council.

Lukes, S. (1974). *Power: a Radical View.* London: Macmillan.

Lustiger, A. (2000). Testimony in remembrance: http://www.holocaustforum.gov.se/conference/official_documents/abstracts/lustiger.htm

Maccoby, E.E. and Jacklin, C.N. (1974). *The Psychology of Sex Differences.* Stanford, CA: Stanford University Press.

MacDougall, A. (1999). *The Homophobia Continuum and Male Heterosexual Culture.* Doctoral thesis. Colchester: Essex University.

MacEwen Scott, A. (ed.) (1994). *Gender Segregation and Social Change: Men and Women in Changing Labour Markets.* Oxford: Oxford University Press.

Mackay, J. (2000). *The Penguin Atlas of Human Sexual Behavior.* New York: Penguin.

MacKinnon, C.A. (1979). *The Sexual Harassment of Working Women.* New Haven, CT: Yale University Press.

MacKinnon, C.A. (1982). Feminism, Marxism, method and the state: an agenda for theory. *Signs*, 7(3), 515–44.

MacKinnon, C.A. (1983). Feminism, marxism, method and the state: toward feminist jurisprudence. *Signs*, 8 (4), 635–58.

MacKinnon, C.A. (1989). *Toward a Feminist Theory of the State*. Boston, MA and London: Harvard University Press.

Madge, N. (1994). *Children in Residential Care in Europe*. London: National Children's Bureau.

Manthorpe, J. and Stanley, N. (1999). Shifting the focus from bad apples to users' rights. In N. Stanley, J. Manthorpe and B. Penhale (eds), *Institutional Abuse: Perspectives across the Life Course* (pp. 223–40). London and New York: Routledge.

Marsden, R. and Townley, B. (1999). The owl of Minerva: reflections on theory in practice. In S.R. Clegg and C. Hardy (eds), *Studying Organizations: Theory and Method* (pp. 405–21). London: Sage.

Martin, J. (1992). *Cultures in Organizations*. New York: Oxford University Press.

Martin, J.P. (1984). *Hospitals in Trouble*. Oxford: Basil Blackwell.

Marx, K. and Engels, F. (1970). *The German Ideology*. London: Lawrence & Wishart.

Mathews, J. (1997). Power shift. *Foreign Affairs*, 76, 50–66. Cited in Tsoukas (1999).

Mayo, E. (1960). *The Human Problems of an Industrial Civilization* (1st pub. 1933). New York: Viking.

McGhie, T. (1999). Firms begin to take bullying seriously. *Guardian*, 5 April, 16.

McKee, L. and O'Brien, M. (eds) (1982). *The Father Figure*. London: Tavistock.

McKeganey, N. and Norrie, J. (2000). Association between illegal drugs and weapon carrying in young people in Scotland: schools' survey. *British Medical Journal*, 320, 8 April, 982–4.

McKendrick, N., Brewer, J. and Plumb, J.H. (1983). *The Birth of a Consumer Society: the Commercialization of Eighteenth Century England*. London: Hutchinson.

McLaren, P. (1998). White terror and oppositional agency: towards a critical multiculturalism. In D.T. Goldberg (ed.), *Multiculturalism: a Critical Reader* (pp. 46–74). Malden, MA: Blackwell.

McLaughlin, M.L., Osborne, K.K. and Smith, C.B. (1995). Standards of conduct on Usenet. In S.G. Jones (ed.), *Cybersociety: Computer-mediated Communication and Community* (pp. 90–111). Thousand Oaks, CA: Sage.

McPherson Report (1999). London: HMSO.

Meikle, J. (1997). E-mail in the office fans flames of electronic rage. *Guardian*, 31 May, 9.

Menzies, I.E.P. (1960). A case study in the functioning of social systems as a defense against anxiety: a report of a study of the nursing service of a general hospital. *Human Relations*, 13 (2), 95–121.

Menzies, I.E.P. (1970). *The Functioning of Social Systems as a Defence Against Anxiety*. London: Centre for Applied Social Research, The Tavistock Institute of Human Relations.

Merton, R.K. (ed.) (1952). *Reader in Bureaucracy*. New York: Free Press; London: Collier Macmillan.

Mies, M. (1986). *Patriarchy and Accumulation on a World Scale: Women in the International Division of Labour*. London: Zed.

Mies, M. (1998). Globalization of the economy and woman's work in a sustainable society. *Gender, Technology and Development*, 2(1), 3–37.

Milanovic, B. (2000). Is world inequality increasing? Public lecture announcement, University of Helsinki, 18 May.

Miller, P. (1992). The Tavistock mission: a review essay. *Human Relations*, 45, 411–26.

Miller, P. and Rose, N. (1988). The Tavistock programme: the government of subjectivity and social life. *Sociology*, 22, 171–92.

Miller, S. (2000). Unmasked net porn gang face arrest in Britain. *Observer*, 30 July, 13.

Mills, A. and Tancred, P. (eds) (1992). *Gendering Organizational Analysis*. Newbury Park, CA: Sage.

Milne, S. (1998). Minorities face jobs bias from leading firms. *Guardian*, 8 January, 10.

Milne, S. (1999) More people killed at work than by war, Aids and accidents. *Guardian*, 28 April, 11.

Ministry of Foreign Affairs (1993). *CEDAW Convention. Second Periodic Report by Finland*. Helsinki: Tabloid.

Ministry of Social Affairs and Health (1995). *Violence Against Women in Finland*. Helsinki: MSAH.

Mir, R.A., Calás, M.B. and Smircich, L. (1998). Global technoscapes and silent voices: challenges to theorizing global cooperation. In D. Cooperrider and J. Dutton (eds), *The Organizational Dimensions of Global Change: No Limits to Cooperation*, Thousand Oaks, CA: Sage.

Moore, H. (1994). 'Divided we stand': sex, gender and sexual difference. *Feminist Review*, 47, 78–95.

Morgan, D.H.J. (1987). Masculinity and violence. In J. Hanmer and M. Maynard (eds), *Women, Violence and Social Control* (pp. 180–92). London: Macmillan.

Morgan, D. (1994). Theater of war: combat, the military and masculinities. In H. Brod and M. Kaufman (eds), *Theorizing Masculinities* (pp. 165–82). Thousand Oaks, CA: Sage.

Morgan, D. (1996). The gender of bureaucracy. In D.L. Collinson and J. Hearn (eds), *Men as Managers, Managers as Men* (pp. 46–60). London: Sage.

Morgan, G. (1986). *Images of Organization*, Newbury Park, CA: Sage.

Morrison, T. (ed.) (1992). *Racing Justice, Engendering Power: Essays on Anita Hill, Clarence Thomas and the Others on the Constructing of Social Reality*. London and New York: Chatto and Windus.

Mullender, A. and Perrott, S. (1998). Social work and organisations. In R. Adams, L. Dominelli and M. Payne (eds), *Social Work: Themes, Issues and Critical Debate* (pp. 67–77). London: Macmillan.

Nanthikesan, S. (1999). Arms trade: a global epidemic. *Development*, 42(4), 45–8.

NATFHE (1998). *Advice for NATFHE Branches: Whistleblowing*. London: NATFHE.

National Association of Local Government Women's Committees (1991). *Responding with Authority: Local Government Initiatives to Counter Violence Against Women*. Manchester: NALGWC.

Naughton, J. (1998). The women are laid out like peaches on a market stall .... *Observer Review*, 22 February, 9.

Nelson, J.A. (1996). *Feminism, Objectivity and Economics*. London: Routledge.

Nicholson, J. (1993). *Men and Women: How Different are They?* Oxford: Oxford University Press.

Niedl, K. (1995). *Mobbing/bullying am Arbeitsplatz. Eine empirische Analyse zum Phänomen sowie zu personalwirtschaftlich relevanten Effekten von systematischen Feindligkeiten*. (Mobbing/Bullying in the Workplace. An Empirical Analysis of a Phenomenon and Personal Economically Relevant Effects on Systematic Hostilities.) Doctoral dissertation. Munich: Rainer Hampp Verlag.

Nkomo, S. (1992). The emperor has no clothes: rewriting 'race in organizations'. *Academy of Management Review*, 17(3), 487–513.

Normile, D. (2001). Women faculty battle Japan's koza system. *Science*, 291(5505), 2 February, 817–18.

NOW Legal Defense and Education Fund (1996). *The Impact of Violence in the Lives of Working Women: Creating Solutions – Creating Change*. New York: NOW Legal Defense and Education Fund.

Nussbaum, M. (1992). Justice for women! *New York Review of Books*, 8 October, 43–8.

Oakley, A. (1972). *Sex, Gender and Society*. London: Temple Smith.

Oakley, A. (1985). *Sex, Gender and Society*. Aldershot: Gower.

O'Brien, M. (1981). *The Politics of Reproduction*. London: Routledge and Kegan Paul.

O'Brien, M. (1986). *Reproducing the World*. Boulder, CO: Westview.

Oerton, S. (1996a). *Beyond Hierarchy: Gender, Sexuality and the Social Economy*. London: Taylor & Francis.

Oerton, S. (1996b). Sexualizing the organization, lesbianizing the women: gender, sexuality and flat organizations. *Gender, Work and Organization*, 3(1), 289–97.

One in Eight (1997). UK workers are victims of bullying at work. *Management Services*, February, 7.

Paananen, T. and Vartia, M. (1991). *Henkinen väkivalta työpaikoilla: Kysely- ja haastattelututkimus valtion työterveyshuollossa ja työterveyshuollon auttamiskeinot*. (Mental Violence in Workplaces: A Questionnaire and Interview Study of State Occupational Health and its Means of Assistance.) Helsinki: Finnish Institute of Occupational Health.

Pankhurst, C. (1913). *The Hidden Scourge and How to End It*. London: E. Pankhurst.

Parkin, D. and Maddock, S. (1994). A gender typology of organizational culture. In C. Itzin and J. Newman (eds), *Gender and Organizational Change: Putting Theory into Practice* (pp. 89–105). London: Routledge.

Parkin, W. (1989). Private experiences in the public domain: sexuality and residential care organizations. In J. Hearn, D.L. Sheppard, P. Tancred-Sheriff and G. Burrell (eds), *The Sexuality of Organization* (pp. 110–24). London: Sage.

Parkin, W. and Green, L. (1997a). Kickboxing the system: divisive cultures and counterproductive resistances in residential child care. Paper at British Sociological Association Annual Conference, 'Power and Resistance', York, April.

Parkin, W. and Green, L. (1997b). Cultures of abuse within residential child care. *Early Child Development and Care*, 133, 73–86.

Parry, R.L. (1997). Japan's workers aren't sacked, they're driven to suicide. *Independent on Sunday*, 23 March, 17.

Parsons, T. and Bales, R. (eds) (1955). *Family, Socialization and Interaction Process*. New York: Free Press.

Parton, N. (1996). *Social Theory, Social Change and Social Work*. London and New York: Routledge.

Pateman, C. (1988). *The Sexual Contract*. Cambridge: Polity.

Peele, R., Luisada, P.V., Lucas, M.J., Rudisell and Taylor, D. (1977). 'Asylums revisited, *American Journal of Psychiatry*, 134(10), 1077–81.

Penhale, B. (1993). The abuse of elderly people: considerations for practice. *British Journal of Social Work*, 23(2), 95–112.

Peretti, J. (2000). Guns and poses. *Guardian G2*, 3 August, 4–5.

Peterson, V.S. and Runyan, A.S. (1999). *Global Gender Issues* (2nd edn). Boulder, CO: Westview.

Phillips, C.M., Stockdale, J.E. and Joeman, L.M. (1989). *The Risks in Going to Work. The Nature of People's Work, the Risks They Encounter and the Evidence of Sexual Harassment, Physical Attack and Threatening Behaviour*. London: Suzy Lamplugh Trust.

Pierce, J. (1995). *Gender Trials: Emotional Lives in Contemporary Law Firms*. Berkeley: University of California Press.

Pinsent, P. and Knight, B. (1998). *Teenage Girls and their Magazines*. London: NCRCL.

Plummer, K. (1995). *Telling Sexual Stories: Power, Change and Social Worlds*. London: Routledge.

Povinelli, E.A. and Chauncey, G. (1999). Thinking sexuality transnationally: an introduction. *GLQ: a Journal of Lesbian and Gay Studies*, 5(4), 439–49.

Poyner, B. and Warne, C. (1986). *Violence to Staff: A Basis for Assessment and Prevention*. London: Tavistock Institute of Human Relations/Health and Safety Executive.

Poyner, B. and Warne, C. (1988). *Preventing Violence to Staff*. London: Tavistock Institute of Human Relations/Health and Safety Executive.

Pringle, R. (1988). *Secretaries Talk. Sexuality, Power and Work*. London, Verso; Sydney: Allen and Unwin.

Pringle, R. (1989). Bureaucracy, rationality and sexuality: the case of secretaries. In J. Hearn, D.L. Sheppard, P. Tancred-Sheriff and G. Burrell (eds), *The Sexuality of Organization* (pp. 158–77). London: Sage.

Quine, L. (1999). Workplace bullying in NHS Community Trust: staff questionnaire survey. *British Medical Journal*, 3(18), 23 January, 228–32.

Quinn, R.E. (1977). Coping with Cupid: the formation, impact and management of romantic relationships in organizations. *Administrative Science Quarterly*, 22, 30–45.

Randall, P. (1997). *Adult Bullying: Perpetrators and Victims*. London and New York: Routledge.

Rantalaiho, L. (1997). Contextualizing gender. In L. Rantalaiho and T. Heiskanen (eds), *Gendered Practices in Working Life* (pp. 16–30). London: Macmillan.

Rantalaiho, L. and Heiskanen, T. (eds) (1997). *Gendered Practices in Working Life*. London: Macmillan.

Rasi, R.A. and Rodriguez-Nogues, L. (eds) (1995). *Out in the Workplace: the Pleasures and Perils of Coming Out on the Job*. New York: Alyson.

Rayner, C. (1997). The incidence of workplace bullying. *Journal of Community and Applied Social Psychology*, 7(3), 199–208.

Rayner, C. and Hoel, H. (1997). A summary of the review of literature relating to workplace bullying. *Journal of Community and Applied Social Psychology*, 7, 181–91.

Reed, E. (1975). *Women's Evolution: From Matriarchal Clan to Patriarchal Family*. New York: Pathfinder.

Reed, M.I. (1993). Organizations and modernity: continuity and discontinuity in organization theory. In J. Hassard and M. Parker (eds), *Postmodernism and Organizations* (pp. 163–82). London and Newbury Park, CA: Sage.

Reiman, J.H. (1984). *The Rich get Richer and the Poor get Prison: Ideology, Class and Criminal Justice*. New York: Wiley.

Remy, J. (1990). Patriarchy and fratriarchy as forms of androcracy. In J. Hearn and D. Morgan (eds), *Men, Masculinities and Social Theory* (pp. 43–54). London and Boston: Unwin Hyman.

Reskin, B. and Padavic, I. (1994). *Women and Men at Work*, Thousand Oaks, CA: Pine Forge Press.

Reynaud, E. (1983). *Holy Virility: the Social Construction of Masculinity*. London: Pluto.

Rich, A. (1980). Compulsory heterosexuality and lesbian existence. *Signs*, 5(4), 631–60.

Rich, A. (1983). *Compulsory Heterosexuality and Lesbian Existence*. London: Onlywomen.

Rimmerman, C.A. (ed.) (1996). *Gay Rights, Military Wrongs: Political Perspectives on Lesbians and Gays in the Military*. Garland Reference Library of Social Science, vol. 1049. New York: Garland.

Ritzer, G. (1993). *The McDonaldization of Society*. Newbury Park, CA: Pine Forge.

Robertson, R. (1995). Glocalization: time-space and homogeneity-heterogeneity. In M. Featherstone, S. Lash and R. Robertson (eds), *Global Modernities* (pp. 25–44). Sage, London.

Robertson, R. and Khondker, H.H. (1998). Discourses of globalization: preliminary considerations. *International Sociology*, 13(1), 25–40.

Roper, M. (1996). 'Seduction and succession': homosocial circuits of desire in management. In D.L. Collinson and J. Hearn (eds), *Men as Managers, Managers as Men. Critical Perspectives on Men, Masculinities and Managements* (pp. 210–26). London: Sage.

Rose, N. (1999). *Powers of Freedom*. Cambridge: Cambridge University Press.

Rothschild, J. and Miethe, T.D. (1994). Whistleblowing as resistance in modern work organizations: the politics of revealing organizational deception and abuse. In J.M. Jermier, D. Knights and W.R. Nord (eds). *Resistance and Power in Organizations* (pp. 252–73). London: Routledge.

Rowbotham, S. (1979). The trouble with 'patriarchy'. *New Statesman*, 98, 970.

Rubenstein, M. (1992). *Preventing and Remedying Sexual Harassment at Work: A Resource Manual* (2nd edn). London: Eclipse.

Rutherford, S. (1999). *Organisational Cultures, Patriarchal Closure and Women Managers*. Doctoral thesis. Bristol: University of Bristol.

Ryan, P.J. and Rush, G.E. (eds) (1997). *Understanding Organized Crime in Global Perspective*. Thousand Oaks, CA: Sage.

Ryle, S. (1999). Amorous and sexist office e-mails set for clampdown. *Observer*, 24 January, 7.

Saghir, M.T and Robins, E. (1973). *Male and Female Homosexualities: a Comprehensive Investigation*. Baltimore, MD: Williams and Wilkins.

✐Salin, D. (1999). *Explaining Workplace Bullying: a Review of Enabling, Motivating, and Triggering Factors in the Work Environment*. Helsinki: Meddelanden Working Papers, Svenska handelshögskolan.

Santos, A.F. (1999). Globalization, human rights and sexual exploitation. In D.M. Hughes and C. Roche (eds), *Making the Harm Visible: Global Sexual Exploitation of Women and Girls. Speaking Out and Providing Services* (pp. 64–86). Kingston, RI: Coalition Against Trafficking in Women.

Savage, M. and Witz, A. (eds) (1992). *Gender and Bureaucracy*. Oxford: Blackwell.

Schattschneider, E.E. (1960). *The Semi-Sovereign People: A Realist View of Democracy in America*. New York: Holt, Rinehart and Winston.

Schéele, A. von (1993). *Mobbning. En arbetsmiljöfråga.* (Bullying. A Question of Work Environment.) Stockholm: Arbetarskyddsnämnden.

Schneider, B.E. (1981). Coming out at work: detriments and consequences of lesbians' openness in their workplaces. Paper at the Annual Meeting of the Society for the Study of Social Problems, Toronto.

Schneider, B.E. (1984). The office affair: myth and reality for heterosexual and lesbian women workers. *Sociological Perspectives*, 27(4), 443–64.

Scott, J. (1986). Gender: a useful category of historical analysis. *American Historical Review*, 91(5), 1053–75.

Scraton, P., Sim, J. and Skidmore, P. (1981). *Prisons Under Protest*. Milton Keynes: Open University Press.

Seager, J. (1997). *The State of Women in the World Atlas*. New Edition, Penguin, Harmondsworth.

Sedgwick, E.K. (1991). *The Epistemology of the Closet*, Berkeley, CA: University of California Press.

Sedley, A. and Benn, M. (1982). *Sexual Harassment at Work*. London: NCCL Rights for Women Unit.

Select Committee on Violence in Marriage (1975). *Report, together with the Proceedings of the Committee Vol. 2: Report, Minutes of the Committee and Appendices*. London: HMSO.

Sen, A. (1990). More than 100 million women are missing. *New York Review of Books*, 29 December.

Shade, L.R. (1993). Available via FTP: pub/freenet/93conference/leslie_regan_shade.txt

Shapiro, M.J. (1997). *Violent Cartographies: Mapping Cultures of War*. Minneapolis, MN: University of Minnesota Press.

Sheffield, E. (1997). Children's home 'saw 10 years of abuse'. *Guardian*, 9 October, 11.

The Shell Report 1999. *People, Planet & Profits: An Act of Commitment* (1999). London: Royal Dutch/Shell Group of Companies.

The Shell Report 2000. *How do we stand? People, Planet & Profit* (2000). London: Royal Dutch/Shell Group of Companies.

Sheppard, D. (1989). Organizations, power and sexuality: the image and self-image of women managers. In J. Hearn, D. Sheppard, P. Tancred-Sherriff and G. Burrell (eds), *The Sexuality of Organization* (pp. 139–57). London/Beverly Hills, CA: Sage.

Shields, R. (ed.) (1996). *Cultures of the Internet: Virtual Spaces, Histories, Living Bodies.* London: Sage.

Sievers, B. (1995). *Work, Death and Life Itself.* Berlin: Walter de Gruyter.

Sievers, B. (2000). Competition as war: towards a socio-analysis of war in and among corporations. *Socio-Analysis,* 2(1), 1–27.

Signorile, M. (1994). *Queer in America: Sex, the Media and the Closets of Power.* New York: Anchor.

Sims, D., Fineman, S. and Gabriel, Y. (1993). *Organizing and Organizations: an* Introduction. London: Sage.

Sinclair, A. (1995). Sex and the MBA. *Organization,* 2(2), 295–319.

Sinclair, I. and Gibbs, I. (1996). *Quality of Care in Children's Homes.* Social Work Research and Development Unit Working Paper Series B, No. 3, York: University of York.

Skelton, A. (1999). The inclusive university? A case study of the experiences of gay and bisexual higher educators in the UK. In P. Fogelberg, J. Hearn, L. Husu and T. Mankkinen (eds), *Hard Work in the Academy* (pp. 190–209). Helsinki: Helsinki University Press.

Sklair, L. (2001). *The Transnational Capitalist Class.* Oxford: Blackwell.

Sluka, J.A. (ed) (2000). Death Squad. *The Anthropology of State Terror.* Philadelphia: University of Pennsylvania Press.

Smith, D. (1990). *The Conceptual Practices of Power: a Feminist Sociology of Knowledge.* Boston: Northwestern University Press.

Smith, D.J. and Gray, J. (1985). *The Police and the People in London: the PSI Report.* Aldershot: Gower.

Smith, J. (1993). *Misogynies.* London: Faber & Faber.

Smith, M.A. and Kollock, P. (eds) (1999). *Communities in Cyberspace.* London: Routledge.

Soper, K. (1995). *What is Nature? Culture, Politics and the Non-Human.* Oxford: Blackwell.

Stacey, M. (1986). Gender and stratification: one central issue or two? In R. Crompton and M. Mann (eds), *Gender and Stratification* (pp. 214–23). Cambridge: Polity.

Stacey, M. and Davies, C. (1983). *Division of Labour in Child Health Care: Final Report to the SSRC.* Coventry: University of Warwick.

Standing, H. and Nicolini, D. (1997). *Review of Workplace-related Violence.* Contract Research Report 143/1997. London: HSE.

Statistics Sweden (1995). *Living Conditions Report No 88. Victims of Violence and Property Crime 1978–1993.* Stockholm: Statistics Sweden (National Council for Crime Prevention – (Brå).

Steineberger, M. (2001). Lawlessness breaks out on and off court. *Financial Times Weekend,* 10–11 February, 22.

Steiner-Scott, E. (1997). 'To bounce a boot off her now and then ...': domestic violence in post-famine Ireland. In M.G. Valiulis and M. O'Dowd (eds), *Women and Irish History* (pp. 125–43). Dublin: Wolfhound.

Stone, L. (1977). *The Family, Sex and Marriage 1500–1800.* London: Weidenfeld & Nicolson.

Stress UK (1999). Got a *medical* concern?: http://www.stress.org.uk/tuc.htm

Suzy Lamplugh Trust (1994). *Violence and Aggression at Work: Reducing the Risks.* London: Suzy Lamplugh Trust.

Sydie, R.A. (1987). *Natural Woman, Cultured Man.* Milton Keynes: Open University Press.

Sylvester, R. (1998). Children in care homes to get abuse hotline. *Independent on Sunday,* 29 November, 4.

Symposium on the Clinton–Lewinsky affair (1999). *Sexualities,* 2(2), 247–66.

Sørensen, R. (1990). *Det går på verdigheten løs! Om seksuell trakassering på arbeidsplassen.* (It's about one's Dignity! On Sexual Harassment in the Workplace.) Oslo: Masters' Thesis, Department of Sociology, University of Oslo.

Tasala, M. (1997). *Työpaikkakiusaamisen noidankehät*. (The Vicious Circles of Bullying in the Workplace.) Helsinki: Suomen mielenterveysseura.

Tattum, D. and Lane, D. (1988). *Bullying in Schools*. Stoke-on-Trent: Trentham.

Taylor & Jerome (1997). Pornography as innovator. *PC Computing*, February, 65.

Taylor, F.W. (1947). *Scientific Management*. New York: Harper.

Taylor, N. (ed.) (1986). *All in a Day's Work. A Report on Anti-Lesbian Discrimination in Employment and Unemployment in London*. London: Lesbian Employment Rights.

Temkin, J. (1987). *Rape and Legal Process*. London: Sweet & Maxwell.

Thomas, A.M. and Kitzinger, C. (1994). 'It's just something that happens': the invisibility of sexual harassment in the workplace. *Gender, Work and Organization*, 1(3), 151–61.

Thompson, P. (1993). Postmodernism: fatal distraction. In J. Hassard and M. Parker (eds), *Postmodernism and Organizations* (pp. 183–203). London and Newbury Park, CA: Sage.

Thylefors, I. (1987). *Syndabockar. Om utstötning och mobbning i arbetslivetb*. (Scapegoats. On Expulsion and Bullying in Working Life.) Stockholm: Natur och Kultur.

Tilly, C. (1992). Where do rights come from? In L. Mjøset (ed.), *Contributions to the Comparative Study of Development: Proceedings for Vilhelm Aubert Memorial Symposium* (pp. 9–36). Oslo: Oslo University.

Timmerman, G. and Bajema, C. (1999). Sexual harassment in Northwest Europe. *European Journal of Women's Studies*, 6, 419–39.

Toomingas, A. and Henrik, N. (1995). Reports of violence and threats against Swedish health care personnel. In R. Bast-Pettersen, E. Bach, K. Lindström, A. Toomingas and J. Kiviranta (eds), *Research on Violence, Threats and Bullying as Health Risks Among Health Care Personnel* (pp. 11–13). Copenhagen: TemaNord.

Travis, A. (1998). Straw acts on racism in Home Office. *Guardian*, 24 August, 7.

Tsoukas, H. (1999). David and Goliath in the risk society: making sense of the conflict between Shell and Greenpeace in the North Sea. *Organization*, 6(3), 499–528.

TUC (1998a). *Beat Bullying at Work: a Guide for Trade Union Representatives and Personnel Managers*. London: TUC.

TUC (1998b). *Bullied at Work? Don't Suffer in Silence. Your Guide to Tackling Workplace Bullying*. London: TUC.

TUC (1999). *Violent Times: Preventing Violence at Work*. London: TUC.

Uildriks, N. and van Mastrigt, H. (1991). *Policing Police Violence*. Aberdeen: Aberdeen University Press.

Ursel, J. (1986). The state and the maintenance of patriarchy: a case study of family, labour and welfare legislation in Canada. In J. Dickinson and B. Russell (eds), *Family, Economy and the State* (pp. 150–91). London and Sydney: Croom Helm.

Utting, W. (1997). *People Like Us: the Report of the Review of the Safeguards for Children Living Away from Home*. London: HMSO.

VandenBois, G. and Bulutao, E.Q. (eds) (1996). *Violence on the Job: Identifying Risks and Developing Solutions*. New York: APA.

Varsa, H. (1993). *Sukupuolinen häirintä ja ahdistelu työelämässä. Näkymättömälle nimi*. (Sexual Harassment in Working Life. Naming the Invisible.) Sosiaali- ja terveysministeriö. Tasa-arvojulkaisuja. Sarja A: Tutkimuksia 1/1993. Helsinki.

Vartia, M. (1991). Bullying at workplaces. In S. Lehtonen, J. Rantanen, P. Juuti, A. Koskela, K. Lindström, P. Rehnström and J. Saari (eds), *Towards the 21st Century. Work in the 1990s. International Symposium on Future Trends in the Changing Working Life* (pp. 131–5). Helsinki: Institute of Occupational Health; Oitmäki: Finnish Employers' Development Institute.

Vartia, M. (1993). Psychological harassment (bullying, mobbing) at work. In K. Kauppinen (ed.), *OECD Panel Group on Women, Work and Health. National Report: Finland* (pp. 149–52). Helsinki: Publications of the Ministry of Social Affairs and Health 1993: 6.

Vartia, M. (1995). Bullying at workplaces. In R. Bast-Petterson, E. Bach, K. Lindström, A. Toomingas, and J. Kiviranta (eds), *Research on Violence, Threats and Bullying as Health Risks Among Health Care Personnel* (pp. 29–31). Copenhagen: TemaNord.

Vartia, M. (1996). The sources of bullying – psychological work environment and organizational climate. *European Journal of Work and Organizational Psychology*, 5(2): 203–14.

Vartia, M. and Hyyti, J. (1999). Workplace bullying experienced by male and female prison officers. Paper presented at the Ninth European Congress on Work and Organizational Psychology: Innovations for Work, Organization and Well-Being, Espoo-Helsinki, Finland, 12–15 May.

Vartia, M. and Paananen, T. (1992). *Henkinen väkivalta työssä.* (Psychological Violence at Work.) Helsinki: Finnish Institute of Occupational Health.

Vartia, M. and Perkka-Jortikka, K. (1994). *Henkinen väkivalta työpaikoilla. Työyhteisön hyvinvointi ja sen uhat.* (Psychological Violence in Workplaces. Well-being and Threats to it in Workplaces.) Helsinki: Gaudeamus.

Vasey, O. (2000). £10,000 for woman who blew the whistle. Payout for finance officer who spoke up. *Telegraph and Argus*, 28 March, 1, 3.

Vehviläinen, M. (2000). Gender and information technology. In C. Mörtberg (ed.), *Where Do We Go From Here? Feminist Challenges of Information Technology* (pp. 17–37). Luleå: Luleå University of Technology.

Veikkola, E.-S. and Palmu, T. (eds) (1995). *Women and Men in Finland.* Helsinki: Statistics Finland.

Veikkola, E.-S., Hänninen-Salmelin, E. and Sinkkonen, S. (1997). Is the forecast for wind or calm? In E.-S. Veikkola (ed.), *Women and Men at the Top: A Study of Women and Men at the Top* (pp. 82–7), Gender Statistics 1997: 1. Helsinki: Statistics Finland.

Vidal, J. (1997). The real politics of power. *Guardian Society*, 30 April, 4–5.

Vinnicombe, S. (2000). The position of women in Europe. In M.J. Davidson and R.J. Burke (eds), *Women in Management: Current Research Issues II* (pp. 9–25). London: Sage.

Wainwright, M. (1996). 'Culture of sex bias' in police. *Guardian*, 16 May, 7.

Wainwright, M. (1999). Doing the right thing. *Guardian*, 19 May, 6.

Walby, S. (1986). *Patriarchy at Work.* Cambridge: Polity.

Walby, S. (1990). *Theorising Patriarchy.* Cambridge: Polity.

Walby, S. (1997). *Gender Transformations.* London: Routledge.

Waller, E. (2000). The unreal deal. *Guardian G2*, 2 August, 17.

Wardhaugh, J. and Wilding, P. (1993). Towards an explanation of the corruption of care. *Critical Social Policy*, 37 (Summer), 4–31.

Waring, M. (1988). *Counting for Nothing.* Wellington, New Zealand: Allen and Unwin.

Waters, M. (1989). Patriarchy and viriarchy. *Sociology*, 23(2), 193–211.

Waters, M. (1995). *Globalization.* London: Routledge.

Waylen, G. (1996). *Gender in Third World Politics.* Buckingham: Open University Press.

Weber, M. (1958). *The Protestant Ethic and the Spirit of Capitalism.* New York: Charles Scribner and Sons.

Whine, M. (1997). The far right on the Internet. In B.D. Loader (ed.), *The Governance of Cyberspace* (pp. 209–27). London: Routledge.

White, K. (1987). Residential care of adolescents: residents, carers and sexual issues. In G. Horobin (ed.), *Sex, Gender and Carework: Research Highlights in Social Work* (pp. 52–65). London: Jessica Kingsley.

White, S.K. (1987). Justice and the postmodern problematic. *Praxis International*, 7(3/4), 306–19.

Whittaker, T. (1996). Violence, gender and elder abuse. In B. Fawcett, B. Featherstone, J. Hearn and C. Toft (eds), *Violence and Gender Relations: Theories and Interventions* (pp. 147–60). London: Sage.

Wilkinson, S. and Kitzinger, C. (eds) (1993). *Heterosexuality.* London: Sage.

Williams, R. (1976). *Keywords.* Glasgow: Fontana.

Wilson, E. (ed.) (2001). *Organizational Behaviour Reassessed: the Impact of Gender*. London: Sage.

Wilson, F. (1995). *Organizational Behaviour and Gender*. London: McGraw-Hill.

Wise, S. and Stanley, L. (1987). *Georgie Porgie: Sexual Harassment in Everyday Life*. London: Pandora.

Witz, A. (1992). *Professions and Patriarchy*. London and New York: Routledge.

Woods, J.D. and Lucas, J.H. (1993). *The Corporate Closet: the Professional Lives of Gay Men in America*. New York: Free Press.

Woods, M. and Whitehead, J. (with Lamplugh, D.) (1993). *Working Alone: Surviving and Thriving*. London: IPM/Pitman.

Woodward, A. (1996). Multinational masculinities and European bureaucracies. In D.L. Collinson and J. Hearn (eds), *Men as Managers, Managers as Men: Critical Perspectives on Men, Masculinities and Managements* (pp. 167–85). London: Sage.

Workplace Bullying News (updated May 1999): http://www.successunlimited.co.uk./news.htm

Workplace Bullying Press Releases (1999): http://www.successunlimited.co.uk./press.htm

Wright, L. and Smye, M. (1997). *Corporate Abuse*. New York: Simon and Schuster.

Wright, S. (ed.) (1994). *The Anthropology of Organizations*. London: Routledge.

Wright, S. (1998). The politicization of 'culture'. Presidential address, section H, British Association for the Advancement of Science, Royal Anthropological Institute, available at: http://lucy.ukc.ac.uk/rai/AnthToday/wright.htm

Wrong, D. (1979). *Power: Its Forms, Bases and Uses*. Oxford: Blackwell.

Yodanis, C. and Godenzi, A. (2000). Male violence: the economic costs. A methodological review. *In Men and Violence Against Women Seminar 7–8 October 1999 Proceedings* (pp. 117–28). EG/SEM/VIO (99) 21, Strasbourg: Council of Europe.

Young, I.M. (1990). *Justice and the Politics of Difference*. Princeton, NJ: Princeton University Press.

Yuval-Davis, N. (1997). *Gender and Nation*. London: Sage.

Zuboff, S. (1989). *In the Age of the Smart Machine*. New York: Basic Books.

Index

Page numbers in *italics* refer to tables.